HOW TO STUDY

How To Study

CLIFFORD T. MORGAN, University of Texas

JAMES DEESE, The Johns Hopkins University

SECOND EDITION

McGRAW-HILL BOOK COMPANY

NEW YORK ST. LOUIS SAN FRANCISCO
TORONTO LONDON SYDNEY MEXICO PANAMA

HOW TO STUDY

Library of Congress Catalog Card Number: 74-93452

43113

1234567890 BABA 74321069

TABLE OF CONTENTS

chapter 1 EFFICIENT LEARNING

chapter 2 ORGANIZING TIME

chapter 3 CLASSROOM LEARNING

chapter 4 READING BETTER AND FASTER

chapter 5 STUDYING TEXTBOOKS

chapter 6 TAKING EXAMINATIONS

chapter 7 WRITING PAPERS

chapter 8 STUDYING A FOREIGN LANGUAGE

chapter 9 STUDYING MATHEMATICS AND THE SCIENCES

chapter 10 GETTING HELP AND BEING HELPFUL

chapter 11 LIVING COLLEGE LIFE

PREFACE

This book has been written mainly for the ever-growing number of students who continue their studies beyond high school. It is for all who are studying or who plan to study, either full time or part time, in a college, university, engineering or technical school, or any other school of higher education. You can make use of this book in two ways: in a regular course on how to study, or to learn by yourself a good set of study habits.

The book is a practical guide in methods of studying. It presents specific instructions for planning and using time, getting the most out of a textbook, outlining and taking notes, and preparing for and taking examinations. It also gives directions for dealing with special problems such as studying foreign languages, the sciences, and mathematics, and for writing themes and reports. The program of study spelled out here is based on years of educational research and has been soundly tested on thousands of students. We know that it works.

Although it is never too late to improve your study skills (they are valuable in the workaday world as well as in school), it is hardly ever too early to begin. If you are a high-school student planning to continue your studies after high school, we urge you to read and master the techniques presented here. We think too that your parents should read the book so that they can give you a helping hand and understand better some of the academic problems you are up against.

Learning to study isn't easy. You must do more than read a book like this hurriedly. You'll have to work at it hard. You should do the exercises to be found in the book, and do the other things it specifically tells you to do. After that, you should keep the book handy and, as study problems arise, use it for a reference. Look up the section that bears on your problem, and try especially hard to carry out the remedy it prescribes. It may take a long time to put into practice all the techniques for improvement you'll find here. But if you work at it, you will be richly rewarded.

This edition, we believe, has been greatly improved over the first because of helpful comments received from people too numerous to mention individually. Students, teachers, librarians, and authors reading the first edition have brought shortcomings to our attention or have suggested topics for inclusion or expansion. To them we are grateful. They have helped us make this a more accurate, complete, and up-to-date version of the earlier book.

Special thanks are due Mrs. Ann L. Sanford who, besides typing the manuscript, helped us with library research and proofreading.

Clifford T. Morgan
James Deese

HOW TO STUDY

chapter 1

EFFICIENT LEARNING

If you are studying in college, planning to go to college, taking night courses, or in any way acquiring any sort of formal education above the high school level, this book is for you. As its title implies, it is about studying, but studying in the broad sense of all that students must do to be an academic success in college and to do these things efficiently.

Studying—learning, that is—is a set of skills that must be developed and practiced for different educational levels and for different kinds of material. Your skills must have been adequate or superior for the high school level or you would not now be going to college. But they are probably not efficient for the demands of college work. At least that is what educators concerned with study habits have concluded about the great majority of college students. If you take a good look at your study habits, you will undoubtedly find that there are some things—perhaps a lot of things—that you are doing very badly. The purpose of this book is to help you discover them and to show you how to improve. If it succeeds in doing that—and thousands of students have said that it has—it should prove more valuable than any other book you use in college.

Surveys of the problems of college students show that inefficient study is one of the biggest and most persistent problems students have. They also show that students who recognize poor study methods as one of their problems can be helped. And by making a systematic approach to the problem, you can find better ways of studying that are effective *for you*. That is what this book will try to do: It is meant to describe the modern methods of study that have evolved through survey and research and to present them in such a way that you can put them to use.

Who May Improve

This book is not just for the poor student. The good student as well as the poor one stands to benefit by becoming more efficient in his study habits. The poor student, that is, the student who is failing or barely passing, feels the need more because of his precarious state, but sometimes the good student can profit more by learning proper techniques than the poor one can. Many universities now offer courses in how to study, either as separate courses or as part of orientation courses. At first the courses were offered only to students in difficulty. In time, however, they found that the best students could also profit from the courses and were often the ones to benefit most.

So no matter how well you think you study, you ought to spend some time with this book. There should be something in it you do not know and that will pay important dividends. If you are already making top grades, you can hardly raise your average; but what is perhaps more important, you may be able to achieve your level with less effort and time and with more satisfaction and lasting value. If you have something less than top grades, you can obtain these benefits plus raising your grade average, especially in those subjects that give you the greatest trouble.

The Art of Studying

Now, what is studying? You may think it is what you do when you sit down with a textbook to prepare for the next class or examination. That, of course, is part of it, but only a small part of it. Studying is really an all-out effort at learning, and it is only practiced successfully when you learn, and learn well and efficiently. To get a specific idea of all the things involved in effective study and of the shortcomings you may have, read and answer the questions in the inventory of study skills (How good a student are you?). We'll run over the points in a general way in the paragraphs that follow.

How Efficient Are You?

The art of studying begins with the way you manage your life. A manufacturer would not last very long if he waited until his employees ran out of materials before he bought new stock. Neither does a student do very well by waiting to begin studying until just before an examination or the deadline for a paper.

Budgeting time. In order to keep up in studying, you must budget time. You must plan ahead for the day, the week, and even the term. When you start out in the morning, you should have a pretty good idea of what you are going to do that day and then stick to it reasonably well. You must do the same thing, looking further ahead, for the bigger items in the educational schedule, such as quizzes, examinations, and term papers. Without such a budget, you won't have the time you need to do the studying

HOW GOOD A STUDENT ARE YOU?

Read carefully each of the following questions, and answer it honestly by writing a "yes" or "no" in the margin to the left of the question. When you are finished, see the directions for scoring at the end of the test.

1. Can you think of anything that prevents you from doing your best work?
2. Do you usually study every day in the same place?
3. Do you usually know in the morning just how you are going to spend your day?
4. Does your desk have anything on it that might distract you from your work?
5. When studying, do you frequently skip the graphs or tables in your textbook?
6. Do you frequently make simple charts or diagrams to represent points in your reading?
7. When you find a word in your reading that you do not know, do you usually look it up in the dictionary?
8. Do you usually skim over a chapter before reading it in detail?
9. Do you usually glance through a chapter, looking at the paragraph headings, before reading it in detail?
10. Do you usually read the summary at the end of a chapter before reading the chapter?
11. Do you keep your notes for one subject all together?
12. Do you usually take your notes in lecture in outline form?
13. Do you usually take your notes on reading in outline form?
14. Do you usually try to summarize your readings in a sentence or short paragraph?
15. After you have read a chapter and taken notes on it, do you usually write a summary of the chapter as a whole?
16. Do you sit up studying late the night before an examination?
17. In preparing for an examination, do you try to memorize the text?
18. When you memorize something, do you usually do it all at one time?
19. Do you at times try to analyze your work to see just where you may be weak?
20. Do you often write an answer to a question and then realize that it seems to be the answer to some other question on the examination?
21. Do you consciously try to use facts you learn in one course to help you in your work on some other course?
22. Do you usually take notes in class just as rapidly as you can write?

Some years ago Luella Cole Pressey gave questions like these to fifty good students and fifty poor ones at Ohio State University. Good students more often than poor ones answered them as follows: (1) no, (2) yes, (3) yes, (4) no, (5) no, (6) yes, (7) yes, (8) yes, (9) yes, (10) yes, (11) yes, (12) yes, (13) yes, (14) yes, (15) yes, (16) no, (17) no, (18) no, (19) yes, (2) no, (21) yes, (22) no.

you should. Study skills won't do too much good if you haven't managed your affairs so that you can employ them.

How to budget time is not just a matter of putting in so many hours a week at study or even of making sure to have work done on time. There are definite reasons for doing things at particular times: for studying German or chemistry at one hour of the day rather than at another. We can't go into these reasons just now, but later we'll help you devise a schedule, a budget, for your particular case and show you how to revise it in the light of your experience with it.

Organizing work. Besides budgeting, the art of study also involves a number of things you may not have taken too seriously: getting to class on time so that you don't miss the instructor's directions for studying and examinations, not cutting any more classes than you can help, finding a good place to study free of distractions, making sure to have good lighting, equipment, and other physical facilities for work, knowing when and where to ask the teacher questions about the work, regulating intrusions on your time, and resisting temptations to postpone study, getting and following directions for the work entailed in each course, having the proper note-taking materials, and keeping them well arranged and accessible. Some of these points may be obvious, some not. Even when you recognize that they are important, you may not succeed in doing what you should about them. Hence you may need help in actually doing the most obvious things.

To indicate just what they are, we are going to ask a series of questions. Read each one carefully, ask it of yourself, and try to answer it. In this way you will be able to see what we are going to cover later and where you may be able to benefit from this book.

How Are Your Notes?

Take the problem of keeping notes on classwork and reading. Do you take notes? Some students don't. What kind of notes do you take? Do you think they are adequate?

Do you keep having the feeling that the instructor springs things on you in examinations that were not in the lectures or reading? If you do, it is probably because your notes are inadequate. Start out by thinking of all the things that are wrong with your notes and how you might improve them. You'll find some specific suggestions about this later on in Chapter Five.

Can You Read?

"That's a stupid question," you say; "of course I can read." Indeed you can. But have you ever thought about how well you read? Some people read so poorly that, by comparison with people who read well, they are practically illiterate. Have you ever thought about how fast you read? How much faster could you read? (Nearly everybody can read faster than he does without special training in reading fast.) How much of what you read do you remember? (Most students don't remember more than half of what they read, even right after they have read it.) Can you decide what is worth trying to remember? Do you read charts and tables in a book? The captions for them? What do you do when you first start to read an assignment? What do you do when you finish reading the assignment? (Some students close the book and turn to something else.) How many times do you read an assignment? When? Do you read a textbook the same way you read a novel? Do you read chemistry and anthropology in the same way? If not, what's the difference?

How Do You Prepare?

Now, finally, let's raise some questions about your preparation for classes and examinations. Do you do assigned readings *before* or *after* you go to class? If you do readings before in some courses and not in others, which courses and why? Do you go to class with questions you would like answered? How often do you review your reading and your notes? When do you review? Do you review the same way for all subjects, or do you review differently for each course? Why? What does an essay examination test? An objective examination? How should you review for these different types of test? Do you run short of time in taking examinations? Why? Do you ever make foolish mistakes on examinations that cost you a lower grade? What are they? Why did you make them? Do the early examinations and quizzes in a course help you to prepare for, and do better on, later examinations? If not, why not? (They should.)

These are enough questions for the time being. The best student doesn't know the answer to all these questions, and when he thinks he does, he is often wrong. We're going to answer them all in this book—and more too, for these don't cover by any means all the items important in effective study.

Basic Skills

There is one general problem in studying effectively that we have not yet mentioned. This is a deficiency in what we'll call *basic skills*. These are skills that students are supposed to have mastered when they come to college but often haven't.

Better reading. One was implied above in the question about how fast you read. By any standard of what they *could* do, most college students are miserable readers. Not only do they read too slowly, they don't read the right way. They move their lips, retrace their words, and do other things that impede their comprehension of what they read as well as slow them down. This is something that is hard for us to remedy with a book, and it may require special training, but we can help the person who is only moderately handicapped by poor reading skills.

Vocabulary. Another important skill has to do with vocabulary. Students are not expected to know all the words they encounter in college, for learning the meaning of more technical and abstract words is part of acquiring a college education. And some teachers and textbook writers are unnecessarily addicted to long,

complicated words and sentences. But some students, for one reason or another, have not learned the precise meaning of words that all college students are supposed to know. You would be surprised how often during an examination students come up to the instructor to ask the meaning of the most elementary (to the instructor) sort of word. Such students have not been paying attention to the ways words are used in everyday writing, and they have not been making the dictionary the bosom companion it ought to be. They are cripples hobbling through their classes and textbooks, missing the point of much of what they read and hear, merely because they do not really understand the words being used. You may be such a cripple, but fortunately something can be done to correct your verbal limp.

Mathematical skills. Simple arithmetic and elementary mathematics is a third skill in which all too many college students are deficient. The deficiency is especially serious for the student who undertakes a science curriculum, but it severely handicaps even the liberal-arts student. Many students can't solve correctly simple problems in multiplication and division, and an elementary algebraic equation like $y = a + bx$ freezes them in their tracks. This weakness is a serious handicap in college work. They may be able to get through history, French, or literature while being morons in mathematics, but they usually have at least one required course in the sciences. Moreover, many other subjects, such as psychology, political science, and economics, involve at least a little figuring with numbers and symbols. Even if they run the gantlet of college courses without being downed by their poor mathematical skills, they'll have their troubles when they go into business, or even when they try to manage their personal finances. This skill, then, is something students ought to assess and do something about if they are lacking in it.

We've tried to tell you in this section why nearly everybody who is now doing or planning to do college work needs to know more about how to study. We hope we have convinced you, because we have found out from experience and from surveys of students that they do need to learn more about how to study. We know, furthermore, that almost all who need to improve their study habits actually can. Each person has his own combination of deficiencies, in budget management, specific techniques of study, or in basic skills. In subsequent chapters, we'll try to show you what you can do about them. In the meantime, we'll give some background for college work and consider the motivation for doing it.

College is Different

In high school, your fellow students probably represented a fair cross section of American young people. In any case, it included many students not headed for college. For that reason, the pace and standards of education were geared to the average student, not to the superior one, and the work you had to do was based on what could be expected of the average student. Like many people, you may have discovered that you could get by with very little work. Or even if you did work reasonably hard, competition was not so stiff, and you did not have to be particularly efficient about studying.

Standards of Work

Now what is the situation in college? Although there are some exceptions, most college students stood in the upper half or even higher of their high school classes. In many colleges with high entrance requirements, they stood in the upper 10 or even 5 per cent. Certainly many more of the superior students than the poorer ones go on to college. Now you are in a faster league. All around you are students who were honor students, or at least very good students, in high school. You might have been the valedictorian of your high-school class, but there are usually dozens of valedictorians in a class of college freshmen. In college the pace and standards of education are geared to a superior group of students, not the average you knew in high school. The kind

of work you used to do to merit an A or B can now easily get marked C, D, or even F.

Most students who go to college don't realize how much will be expected of them. Because many students don't gird themselves for a much tougher job of studying, they are disappointed and discouraged with their poor showing. This is why we believe this book is especially useful for the high-school student and the student entering college. If such a student can get a real idea of what is ahead and how to prepare for it, his chances of staying in college, liking it, and doing well will be enormously increased. You would be surprised how many students drop out of college without graduating. Many of these people are as able as those who make the grade, and in very many cases a little knowledge of the proper approach to study would have kept them in college.

On Your Own Now

Aside from competition and standards of work, there's another big difference between high school and college. In high school the work was pretty well laid out for you. Most of it was covered in class, and homework, which was easy for the superior student, could be done mostly in the one or two periods set aside for study. You were graded to a large extent on what you did in class and on day-to-day homework. You might have had a few term papers and long-range assignments to do on your own, but for the most part you were paced by the daily round of classes.

All this is reversed in college. You spend relatively few hours in class, and except for laboratories and quiz sections, you are not graded very heavily on your participation in class. Instead of having an hour or two of homework for five or six hours of class, you now have two or three hours of outside work for every hour of class. There are no study periods in which you have little choice but to study. Instead, there are hours between classes that you can use profitably or waste away as you choose. On the whole, you are not required to do homework day by day and have it ready for the next class. Rather, you are given some assignments, and nobody checks on whether you did them or not for a week, a month, or even a whole college term. You may have an occasional quiz or hour exam, but in most courses whether you sink or swim depends on how you do in one, two, or three examinations.

What this all means is that you are suddenly thrown on your own. You are now treated like an adult who can be given some general directions and then left to figure out for himself how and when he will do what he is supposed to. This drastically different situation requires long-range, sustained motivation and wise budgeting of time. Many college students simply aren't prepared for this.

Parental Pressure

Making the abrupt change from high school to college is itself a big enough problem for the student, but this usually isn't all. There are plenty of other things to aggravate his problems. One of these, all too frequently, is the pressure put on him by his parents. There are all kinds of parents, nearly all of them well meaning, but some of them don't make the student's adjustment to college any easier.

For one thing, parents often don't understand what we have just explained. They don't realize that the competition in college is keener, that the standard of work is higher, and that their children aren't adequately prepared for the change. They were proud of their offspring's being good students in high school. Being accustomed to seeing A's and B's on the report card, they may be pretty upset when their children's first college grades are several notches below that. At their kindest, they ask why their youngsters aren't doing better, whether they are trying as hard as they might, and so on. At their worst, they threaten to take them out of college if they aren't going to do any better than that.

Thus part of the trouble is that parents don't understand the difference between high school and college. For that reason, we suggest that they read this book to get a better idea of what their children are up against.

Abilities and Interests

There is another important point too. The status attached to college by parents and society, as well as lack of any vocational goal, often attracts students to college who by ability and interests don't belong there—at least not yet. They are propelled there because they are expected to go by parents and friends without having any real intellectual motivation for it. Perhaps they will be ready later after a period of work or military service, but not now. In which case, they should not be there.

It is inevitable also that some young people are not going to be interested in intellectual pursuits or in college life. They would rather be mechanics, sailors, or farmers. There is nothing wrong with such interests, for society needs the kind of people who do not go to college as much as it needs college-trained people. Moreover, college graduates have no corner on happiness or satisfaction in their work. The boy or girl who is really more interested in other pursuits than in going to college should not be pressured into going.

Judging oneself. In considering your prospects for success in college, there is an important point to keep in mind. Students, on the whole, are very poor judges of their own abilities and, indeed, of their own personal traits. Some overrate themselves, others underrate, but mostly they overrate. To prove this, we will cite one large-scale survey of whole classes of high school and college students. Everyone in the class was asked to rate himself on each of a number of items such as speed of reading, vocabulary, note-taking ability, spelling, and grammar by putting himself into one of three groups: the top 20 per cent, the middle 60 per cent, the bottom 20 per cent. The ratings were anonymous; so the students had no one to fool but themselves. If they were good at rating themselves, you would expect their ratings to fall in about the same way, that is, 20 per cent top, 60 per cent middle, and 20 per cent bottom. But that isn't the way the results came out. Instead, only 1 to 8 per cent, depending on the item, put themselves in the bottom 20 per cent, but 35 to 60 per cent put themselves in the top 20 per cent. Obviously the students were unwilling to admit to themselves how deficient they might be in some traits, and they were inclined to see themselves through rose-colored glasses.

This, however, is not true of everybody. Some people are fairly good judges of themselves, some grossly overrate, and some grossly underrate. In one study about 40 per cent placed themselves in the correct category, 40 per cent grossly overrated themselves, and 20 per cent underestimated their own abilities. (See the chart below on which you can rate your own abilities and interests.)

Counseling services. What is one to do if he cannot correctly rate his own traits and abilities? Nowadays students are given many tests throughout the lower grades and, usually, upon entering college. When it is possible to learn one's score, it should be noted and evaluated. To do the evaluation, however, the student must consider the population of people who took the test; that is, the people he competed with. In high school, on an aptitude test, you might have scored at the ninetieth percentile on high school norms; that is to say, you excelled 90 per cent of the students taking the test. However, this same score, compared with only those students who go to college, might be only at the fiftieth percentile. Then, with

SELF-RATING OF TRAITS AND ABILITIES

In the spaces below, check where you honestly think you stand on the traits and abilities listed. After you have done that, discuss your ratings with some other people who know you really well—students, friends, parents, coun-selors—and who might show you where you have overestimated or underes-timated yourself.

In my college, I think I am in the—

Upper fifth	Middle three-fifths	Lower fifth	
			in speed of reading textbooks
			in ability to understand textbooks
			in ability to take notes
			in general preparation for college
			in amount of time I study
			in not wasting time
			in work habits
			in vocabulary (words I know and use)
			in grammar and punctuation
			in spelling
			in mathematical skills

different entrance requirements from college to college, you might find that this same score is something like the thirtieth percentile of the students going to your particular college. Hence the meaning of a score is quite relative to the population in which one finds himself. It is therefore a good idea to learn, if possible, how your ability stacks up at your own college or the college you intend to go to.

To do this, the student may go to his high-school counselor or to his college's counseling service. In recent years, most colleges have instituted such services for testing, interviewing, and counseling students concerning their academic and personal problems. In such offices, there are trained counselors who know not only how to give and interpret tests but also how to put together the whole picture of a student's academic and personal qualifications. Tests by themselves are far from infallible. (Partly for this reason, testing agencies often do not tell students just how they did on a test.) Counselors know this, but they also know how to consider all sides of a student's problem and to help the student in a way that hits his individual case.

Motivation for College Work

Motivation is the most serious problem facing many students. Often students don't seem to have any interest in their courses—or at least in some of their courses. They feel that they ought to be taking their college work more seriously. Very often students feel guilty about not studying, but they don't know how to work up the motivation for it. Lack of motivation is a deadly handicap to effective study. We can't give you motivation, but perhaps we can say some things that will help you develop some.

Lack of Motivation
Why is motivation a problem with college students? Partly it's because of the vast difference between high school and college

that we've already talked about. When someone is at you every day to do your work, hardly any internal push is required. All the motivation is applied from the outside. In college, these external pressures aren't so great, and you are left to move yourself to get your work done.

Another reason has to do with vocational aims. Most students who go to college express some sort of vocational aim. They want to be doctors, lawyers, engineers, salesmen, businessmen, and so on. These aims, though, are pretty vague, and they're shifting constantly. Few students are absolutely sure of what they want to be, and even fewer have any idea of what they must do in college to prepare themselves for their chosen vocation. Vocational counseling in high school and college is growing rapidly, and it will undoubtedly help many students to make up their minds a little earlier about what they want to be. Inevitably, though, many students will be vague and undecided. In fact, it is pretty hard for them to know what they are interested in and can hope to be until they have been in college for a while. Indeed, one of the things college should do for you is help you develop your aims. Even so, vocational choice is often difficult, especially in liberal-arts courses, which are fairly general and far removed from the practical problems of a vocation.

(See the list on the next page, which may help you organize your thinking on motivation.)

We can't do much in this kind of book to help you crystallize your vocational aims. Partly this is your own job, one that you must work out for yourself. Partly it takes time. If you are vacillating and uncertain and if counseling services are available, take advantage of them. The quicker you know what you want to do and what you can do, the faster you'll be able to settle down to college work with a real purpose. Having a definite purpose, you'll find it much easier to take on the habits and skills necessary for effective study and academic success.

Academic and Vocational Success
Even though deciding what you want to do is your job, we might help you out a little by

MOTIVATION FOR COLLEGE

The following questions are designed to help you think about your motivation and to give you some insight into it. Read completely through each group of items; then rank them in importance by using 1 for the phrase that applies best to you, 2 for the phrase that applies next best, and so on.

I. I came (or will go) to college because—

_____ I know what I want to be, and college preparation is necessary for it

_____ my folks wanted me to, even though I didn't

_____ I thought it would be a lot of fun

_____ I wanted to gain a better knowledge and understanding of the world I live in

_____ many of my friends did, and I wanted to be with them

_____ I wanted to get away from home

_____ I am particularly interested in athletics and student activities

_____ a college degree seems indispensable in this day and age

_____ I like to study and am particularly interested in certain subjects

II. I want to make grades that are good enough to—

_____ let me stay in college

_____ meet degree requirements

_____ let me participate in extracurricular activities

_____ put me on the honor list and give me special recognition

_____ make an outstanding record in college

III. My motivation for making grades is to—

_____ prove to myself that I am learning something

_____ secure a good job recommendation

_____ please my family

_____ do better than my competitors

_____ live up to my reputation of being a good student

_____ be respected by my teachers

IV. I sometimes don't study when I should because—

_____ I worry about my personal problems

_____ I simply can't get interested in certain subjects

_____ I am too involved in extracurricular activities

_____ I am bothered by illness and poor health

_____ I get distracted by things going on around me

_____ I tend to keep putting off my work

_____ I am easily tempted to do more interesting things

pointing out some things that are true regardless of what you want to do. If, for example, you are interested in making a good income, look carefully at the following facts:

Those who make the best grades in college are generally those who make the best incomes later on. The member of Phi Beta Kappa, for example, typically earns considerably more than college graduates in general. And people who enjoy the distinction of being in *Who's Who* had, on the average, higher college grades than those who are not there. Many surveys of individuals in various groups have been made, and they all show a rather good correlation between grades in college and later success. For example, some years ago Walter Gifford, former president of the American Telephone and Telegraph Company, wrote an article in *Harper's Magazine* in which he pointed out that the earning capacity of employees in his company showed a very close relation to their grades in college.

There certainly are several reasons why this is the case: One, of course, is that those of the highest ability will be more likely to succeed both in college and in their work. You can't do much about native ability; so you needn't pay too much attention to this one. The other reasons, however, should provide some motivation for studying effectively. Employers are impressed by grades and offer better employment opportunities to those with higher grade averages.

Even more important, however, the same habits and skills that make for college success also promote success later on. In fact, the habits of work we teach in this book are not at all confined to college study. Almost all college-trained people are employed in positions where exactly the same skills are required. They must read rapidly while comprehending and remembering what they read. They must budget their time, much as a good student does. And they must "take examinations" almost daily when they answer the questions of their customers, employees, or associates. Their need for effective study habits is the same as that of the college student. Most people realize how important it is for them to be effective on the job, and many of them wish that they had started earlier to acquire the proper habits and skills. This is the strongest reason we know of for acquiring good work habits in college before it is too late.

Importance of Grades

If you entertain any idea at all of going on to professional school, what we're saying about grades is extremely important. In fact, it probably will decide whether or not you get into a law school, medical school, or graduate school. When you apply to such a school, you can be sure that your grades will be scrutinized very carefully because experience has proved that good grades are the best omen of success. Though a few people with "connections" may be admitted despite mediocre grades, this doesn't happen very often. Most graduate and professional schools have two to ten times as many applicants as they can accept; they can afford to take only the best. In many fields, hardly anyone with less than a B average is considered for admission. Some schools can boast that they seldom admit anybody with less than an A or A— average. If, therefore, you are one who thinks he may want to go on to advanced studies after college, you ought to understand that your grades in college are all-important and work accordingly.

Grades, of course, aren't the sole measure of a man or of his academic success. Almost every teacher in public school or in college describes them as a necessary evil. They are only one somewhat imperfect measure of educational accomplishment. People can learn much and acquire a really useful education without having high grades, and some of the grinds who make straight

A's may have concentrated so much on doing only what is necessary to make grades that they miss a valuable part of their education. On the whole, though, grades measure what one has learned, at least in courses, and what one can be expected to accomplish in the future. In fact, many scientific surveys prove that they predict as well as or better than any other index the success of individuals in more advanced schooling and in the workaday world. So even though we may have some reservations about them, they are good things to work for and good things to get.

Satisfaction in Study

Naturally, there are other reasons besides grades for being interested in improving your study techniques. Learning can be a lot of fun, and knowing what to learn and how to learn makes it even more fun. If you can pick up a book, read it quickly, know how to select the main points, and remember them, you're a lot richer person. Besides acquiring some useful and interesting information, you have a sense of satisfaction and the feeling of pride that a craftsman has in his handiwork. Though you can't see what you've done, you know you've accomplished something worth doing. Having done it once, you're in a better position to do it again. You can read more and more and learn more and more. Learning then becomes an exciting and satisfying process, not a dull, frustrating experience. If you will apply yourself to developing the study methods described in this book, we can almost guarantee that you will come to enjoy studying and that you won't dread it the way so many students do.

How to Study Less

Another thought that might boost your motivation for learning how to study is this: Good study habits are mighty efficient; they let you get more done in less time. From the time you save, you have more left over for other things in college. You will be able to engage in more social and extracurricular activities or perhaps study things that are really interesting to you. If you're one who must earn part of his way through college, you'll have more time for such work without its interfering with your academic success. We can safely make these promises because they have been demonstrated. In many different universities, students who have been trained in how-to-study methods on the average make better grades with less time spent in studying than other students.

Also consider the fact that it is not *how much* you study but rather *how well* you study that counts. When students are divided into groups according to how much they study, it turns out that those who study a great deal, over thirty-five hours a week, say, actually make poorer grades than those who study less. This isn't necessarily because they have poor academic ability; every student knows somebody who seems relatively bright, who studies day and night, and yet for some reason doesn't get the grades he ought to. Educational psychologists who have surveyed students are pretty well convinced that the major factor is *quality* rather than quantity of study time. Though every case is different, the odds are that you too are one who could do more in less time if you only learned how.

Part-time Jobs

Alongside this point we'll put another that may surprise you: College students who work earn on the average grades as good as, or better than, those who don't. In some cases, working students are distinctly better than the nonworking students.

There are probably several good reasons why the comparison turns out this way. Students who have to earn part of their way are likely to be more highly motivated than others. Paying some of their own bills probably makes it seem more important to them to get something for their efforts. Thus they try harder at their studies. Another reason may be that they are forced to budget their time more wisely than other students. Since part-time jobs usually have to be done on a schedule, working students must also study on a schedule or not get it done. They can't afford to dribble away their time. And the management of time, as we said before and will show in detail later, is an important facet of effective study. A final reason should be plain, even though it frequently isn't realized. There are so many hours in a week that there is plenty of time to work a few of them, enjoy many social activities, and still have lots of time for study—*if* the hours are used wisely. This brings us back to the point we started with: It isn't so much how many hours you study as how you use the ones you have. Except in very unusual circumstances, there is ample time to work, study, and play, assuming one knows how to do all three well. (It just *seems* as though there isn't!) And we'll prove it in the next chapter.

chapter 2

ORGANIZING TIME

If you are typical of the majority of students, you have at least one, if not more, of the following troubles:

1. You do not get as much studying done as you should. This is not because you don't try or even because you don't go through the motions of studying, but somehow or other you don't manage to accomplish as much as you know you should.

2. You waste time going from one thing to another. You try to study too many things the same day or evening or even within an hour. Hence you are so disorganized that you do not stay with one thing long enough to get something done.

3. You have difficulty settling down to work. You are always getting ready to study, but for one reason or another, a lot of time goes by before you actually tackle a job.

All these troubles are slightly different aspects of the same thing. When you study, you just don't use your time and apply yourself so that you really accomplish something. Even if you're a student who thinks of himself as studying long and hard, the chances are that you are wasting time. In fact, if you study a lot more hours than other people, it's very likely that half or more of your time is being wasted.

Value of a Schedule

Fortunately, these ills have remedies. The prescription, though, is not just one medicine but several. And they are all things you must do for yourself. Not all of them will work for you, but you must give them your best efforts until you have found the best combination for your individual habits and abilities.

A Schedule Saves Time
The first remedy—and this is something that is likely to be of use to everybody—is to set up a schedule for studying. A well-planned schedule makes time. It keeps you from vacillating about what you are going to do next. It sees to it that you are doing the right thing at the right time so that you aren't so helter-skelter about studying. It will cut out much of the waste motion in attempting to study. If properly managed, it assigns time where time is due, it keeps you from studying something more than it requires, and it lets you spend time where you really need it. With your time thus organized, you will find that you have more to devote to what needs it most and also for more things besides study.

Making Every Hour Count
In the end, of course, you've got to make your own schedule so that it suits your class hours, laboratories, subjects, part-time work, and so on. We can only show you how to go about developing a good schedule. Let's start with the accompanying example. This is a schedule for a typical student carrying a fairly heavy load. He happens to be taking the following subjects: economics, psychology, German, organic chemistry, and English literature. Organic chemistry includes laboratory as well as lecture. The student who has this program is also employed ten hours a week, and his job calls for working two hours each weekday afternoon.

Notice first of all that the schedule is blocked off into one-hour periods. One reason for this is that many of the gaps in any student's class schedule are only an hour long. These hours add up, and only by using them can he keep from wasting a good part of his week. A more important reason, however, has to do with the psychology of work. Psychologists know from extensive research that people get their best work done by working intensively for a reasonable period of time, then resting or changing to something else. There is an optimum cycle of work and rest for every job and every individual. For the kind of work involved in studying and for the typical student, a period of forty or fifty minutes of work at a stretch followed by ten minutes or so of rest or change is just about right. Consequently, an hour used properly is pretty close to the best unit of time for most college study.

When to Study

Notice too that the hours in the schedule are blocked off for specific subjects, not just for "study." That is partly to save the student time he might spend vacillating about what he is going to do and partly to ensure that he has with him all the needed materials for study. (Not being ready to study is one of the most common reasons for wasting time.) You can also see that, by scheduling hours for studying specific subjects, you can make sure you do your work in each subject as it needs to be done. Otherwise, students are always finding themselves behind, cramming on one subject to catch up, but at the same time getting themselves behind in other work.

There are other important reasons for blocking out a schedule for specific subjects:

1. It enables you to assign less time to "easy" subjects than to "difficult" ones.

2. It also *distributes,* rather than *masses,* study time. Psychologists have done an enormous amount of research on the "timing of learning," and this research underscores the need for distributing time spent in learning a particular subject. That is to say, in the long run, you will learn a lot more and remember it better if you spend eight different widely spaced hours studying something than if you spend eight consecutive hours studying it.

3. Finally, there is a best time to study anything, depending on what it is. Certain subjects should be studied at certain times and not at others. As a good general rule, a study period for a particular subject should come close to its class period. This rule does not mean that *all* study time on a subject should be scheduled in this way but only

that some of it should. The rule can be further subdivided into two parts:

(a) If class time is mostly devoted to lecture rather than to recitation, you should allocate a study period immediately *after* class.

(b) On the other hand, if class time is largely spent in recitation, you should schedule a period of review just *before* class.

Some courses are mostly lecture, others mostly recitation, and others a mixture. You should make up your schedule accordingly.

Studying for Lecture Courses

What do you do in a study period placed immediately *after* a lecture? You review the notes taken in class, first of all making sure that you understand them. Don't assume, since you were able to follow all the principal points made by the lecturer in class, that you have in fact assimilated them. It's easy to fall into this trap and to deceive yourself into thinking you have learned more than you actually have.

In most cases, unless the lecturer is unusually well organized and you are a top-notch note taker, you should revise or rewrite the notes. In doing that, eliminate any of the notes that now seem trivial or unimportant, and expand those you now can see are important. You can do this while the lecture is still fresh in mind, but you will find it a hopeless job if you let time pass and with it your memory. In revising your notes, you can also reorganize them so that they are more legible, better arranged, and in a more useful condition for subsequent reviews.

What do you do when a study period is put just *before* a class? If the class is a lecture, you can read the assignment that goes along with the lecture. Lecturers usually want students to read textbook assignments before the lecture, especially in the larger introductory courses. Yet most students don't do this since no one checks up on them. Prereading, however, is a good rule of effective study, for the more you know about what the lecturer is saying, the more you learn in lecture and the better

A SAMPLE SCHEDULE FOR A COLLEGE STUDENT

This schedule is for a typical student carrying a moderately heavy load. Notice that the times set aside for study are labeled for specific subjects. Study time is about twenty-five hours per week; the student is also employed for ten hours a week.

Hour	Monday	Tuesday	Wednesday	Thursday	Friday	Saturday
7-8	Dress, breakfast	Dress, breakfast	Dress, breakfast	Dress, breakfast	Dress, breakfast	
8-9	Econ. lect.	**Study econ.**	Econ. lect.	**Study psych.**	Econ. lect.	Dress, breakfast
9-10	**Study Ger.**	Eng.-lit. class	**Study Ger.**	Eng. class	**Study Ger.**	Org.-chem. lab.
10-11	Ger. class	**Study Ger.**	Ger. class	**Study Ger.**	Ger. class	Org.-chem. lab.
11-12	Psych. lect.	**Study Ger. or psych.**	Psych. lect.	**Study Ger. or psych.**	Psych. lect.	Org.-chem. lab.
12-1	Lunch	Lunch	Lunch	Lunch	Lunch	Lab. cont. or lunch
1-2	Org.-chem. lect.	**Study** or recreation	Org.-chem. lect.	**Study** or recreation	Org.-chem. lect.	Lunch or recreation
2-3	**Study org. chem.**	**Study psych.**	**Study org. chem.**	**Study psych.**	**Study org. chem.**	Recreation or **study**
3-4	**Study econ.**	ROTC or athletics	**Study econ.**	ROTC or athletics	**Study org. chem.**	Recreation or **study**
4-5	Employed	Employed	Employed	Employed	Employed	Recreation
5-6	Employed	Employed	Employed	Employed	Employed	Recreation
6-7	Dinner	Dinner	Dinner	Dinner	Dinner	Dinner
7-8	**Study Eng.**	**Study org. chem.**	**Study Eng.**	**Study for subj. needing "catching up,"** library time	Recreation, make-up **study,** or library	Recreation
8-9	**Study Eng.**	**Study org. chem.**	**Study Eng.**			Recreation
9-10						Recreation

your notes generally are. You know better what is important and unimportant among the things the lecturer says, and the chances are you will be able to identify technical terms he doesn't explain clearly.

Studying for Recitation Courses

If a class is mostly recitation, as many language courses are, you can use the study period just before the class to get ready to recite. If the assignment is such that you can

15

master it in an hour and be sure of it, this can be your principal study period. In many cases, though, this hour won't be enough, and you shouldn't take the chance that it will be enough. To be safe, you should go over the assignment at an earlier time and use the study period for review and for private recitation of what you have previously learned. In this way, you distribute study and bring yourself up to peak performance for the class. Consequently, not only will you do your best in class, but you will probably get more out of the class. Instead of depending on class to get you started in what you should have done for yourself, you now can count on the class to polish off the job you already have two-thirds done.

Incidentally, although students are taught all through school to be prepared, they only too often have not learned the value of practicing the maxim. Not preparing *at the right time* keeps them hobbling through a course. In subjects such as language and mathematics, where knowledge and skills progress a step at a time, the consequences of poor preparation can be calamitous. Because a student hasn't prepared on time, he doesn't know what's going on in class and is hesitant about asking questions for fear he may reveal his ignorance. As the problems become more difficult, he is increasingly baffled both in outside study and in class because he hasn't kept up with what has gone before. The prepared student, on the other hand, takes each step in stride. Also he is no longer afraid of class or bored by it. Knowing what's going on and being the master of it, he finds learning interesting, even exciting. He can participate in classwork and take satisfaction in his progress. Thus he makes headway in the most difficult of all problems, the problem of having sufficient motivation and interest to study.

How to Make and Revise a Schedule

We've explained why a study schedule is blocked out in hours and why certain subjects should be studied immediately before or after their class periods. Now we come to the question of how you should allot time to particular subjects. How do you plan and revise a study schedule? We say *plan* and *revise* because you can't just make up a schedule at the beginning of a term and never change it thereafter. You must revise it in the light of your experience with it. In any case, you must have a schedule, and *you* are the one who must make it.

How Much Time?

The amount of time you allot to particular subjects depends, of course, on how much total study time you think you should budget. This is a highly individual matter. You must evaluate your own abilities and study habits. Most students, as we brought out in the last chapter, tend to overrate their own intelligence, speed of reading, ability to work, etc. It will therefore pay you to be critical of how much you can accomplish in an allotted time, especially if your ambition is high. Make sure, therefore, to budget enough time for your principal job in college, which is studying.

Don't overdo it, though. Leave realistic amounts of time for eating, sleeping, and leisure. Leisure is essential, not only because you must be rested and healthy to get the most out of college but because well-spent leisure is an essential part of a college education. In factories and offices—as well as in studies—when people attempt to put in very long hours, say, fifty-five to sixty hours a week, not only are they less happy and less efficient, they usually get less done than if they didn't work so many hours. That's why, in part at least, the grinding students who work thirty-five to fifty hours a week don't do as well as those who study less. There are exceptions, of course, but don't consider yourself one until you have proved it. Perhaps if you learn to work effectively in a shorter schedule of study, you will later be able to grind away harder and longer if need be. Starting out by trying to do too much, however, often leads one to give up altogether; and it is more important to have a moderate schedule that works than one that goes to pieces because it is impossibly ambitious.

Allocating Your Time

Now about the details of the schedule. Use the pages you will find for this purpose in the back of the book (they can be torn out by using a ruler). Start with the page labeled Provisional Working Schedule. As soon as you know when your classes and laboratories will be, fill these in. Next fill in the amount of time you spend eating and doing other daily routines. Now estimate how much time you will need for studying each of the various subjects you are taking. A good general rule for studying is that one to two hours of study time are required for each hour of lecture or recitation. You must modify this in the light of what you know about the probable difficulty of your courses *for you*.

You can make some estimate of difficulty by considering your own previous experience and training. If languages have always been relatively easy for you and sciences relatively hard, make allowance for that. If you feel your preparation for one course has been strong whereas that for another has been weak, adjust for that difference. This, of course, is obvious advice and most students take these points into account both in choosing their courses and in preparing for them. What they don't do, however, and what you must do, is think these and other questions through carefully at the outset and incorporate your estimates into a study schedule.

When you have made your best guesses about the work various courses are going to entail, you are now ready to fill in the details of your first provisional schedule. In deciding where to put periods for different subjects, keep in mind what was said about the study periods you put just before class and those you schedule just after class.

An Example

To illustrate the process of making up a schedule, consider the sample schedule given on page 15. This student has allotted a total of twenty-three hours a week to study. In addition, he has provided for up to six additional hours to be used to catch up on something or to review for examinations. These "optional" hours, however, are not labeled, for they will be used as the occasion arises.

Of the five courses he's taking, he thinks organic chemistry will be his most difficult because it has a laboratory and requires laboratory reports. Then too, chemistry has never been easy for him. He therefore assigns six of his twenty-three hours to this subject. Three of them he puts immediately following the three weekly lectures. A fourth he puts on Friday to prepare for the laboratory on Saturday. The last two he assigns to Tuesday night in order to have a longer stretch for writing up his lab report.

Of the remaining subjects, he thinks German may be most difficult partly because he hasn't been tops in languages, partly because the German course has a reputation for being one of the more difficult courses, and partly because he knows there is a lot of memorizing and translating to do. He therefore assigns five hours to this and also provides for a couple more that may be spent on it (or on psychology) if necessary. Of the five regularly scheduled hours, he puts three just before the three classes each week because German is primarily a recitation class in which he may be called upon to translate.

In planning for his other three subjects, he thinks economics will probably be the easiest. He comes from a business family, did well in this sort of thing in high school, and has read widely in business magazines. Furthermore, the campus grapevine has it that the text is rather easy reading and that the instructor puts the greatest emphasis on lectures. He therefore assigns three hours a week, about the minimum, to economics and puts two of these hours as close after lecture as he can. He can't do any better than that if he is to give priority to organic chemistry and German, which are his toughest subjects.

So far, he hasn't given too much attention in his planning to English literature because he can study that almost any time.

A DIARY OF TIME

In order to discover how you are now using your time and to help you develop a realistic schedule for yourself, you ought to keep track of your time for at least a week. Make it a typical week of the regular schedule of classes and study. Either carry this book around with you or draw up some charts on cards that you may use for the purpose. Follow the example at the

EXAMPLE			MONDAY			TUESDAY			WEDNESDAY		
Activity	Unit	Time	Activity	Unit	Time	Activity	Unit	Time	Activity	Unit	Time
Sleep	7:30	8:00									
Toilet	7:55	:25									
Break	8:15	:20									
Study French	9:00	:45									
Class	10:00	1:00									
Waste Time	10:25	:25									
Study History	11:00	:35									
Class	12:00	1:00									
Lunch	12:25	:25									
Social	1:00	:35									
Lab.	4:00	3:00									
Work	6:00	2:00									
Waste Time	6:30	:30									
Dinner	7:00	:30									
Reading	7:20	:20									
Study Psychology	8:15	:55									
Waste Time	8:50	:35									
Study English	10:00	1:10									
Recreation	11:15	1:15									
Toilet	11:30	:15									
Sleep	—	—									

left of the table as a guide in keeping the chart. Each time you start an activity, write it down in the column provided. Each time you finish that particular activity, note the time in the box beside the activity. Then by subtracting the time previously recorded from this time, figure out and write down in the right-hand box for the day the amount of time spent in this activity.

THURSDAY			FRIDAY			SATURDAY			SUNDAY		
Activity	Unit	Time	Activity	Unit	Time	Activity	Unit	Time	Activity	Unit	Time

SUMMARY OF TIME DIARY

Add up the times recorded for each activity in your time diary and enter the totals in the spaces below. Thus you'll be able to see just where your time is going and take steps to use it more profitably.

Activity	Monday	Tuesday	Wednesday	Thursday	Friday	Saturday	Sunday	Week's total
Sleep								
Meals								
Classes								
Study								
Work								
Social								
Recreation								
Campus activities								
Waste time								
Miscellaneous								
Total								

The big job in this course will be to read rapidly a great number of pages of outside reading. This material doesn't have to be learned in detail like a textbook, nor will it be difficult to comprehend. He'll just have to read it and know the gist of it so that he'll be prepared for the discussion in class. He therefore sets aside a couple of hours on two evenings each week to get this reading done.

That leaves psychology. He hasn't had any courses before in psychology, for this frequently isn't taught in high school. It shouldn't be too hard, and reports are that it isn't. Moreover, according to the outline of the course he received on the first day of class, his main job is to study the textbook. The lectures, according to the teacher, will be mainly to explain and illustrate the book. So he decides to assign it, like economics, the minimum of three hours a week and to schedule them in the odd spaces he still has

left in his morning and afternoon schedule. He is uncertain, though, whether this will be enough, just as he did not know whether five hours a week would be enough for German. So he sets aside two hours that can be used for either German or psychology, depending on how things go in these courses.

Of course, this is a first approximation of the total amount of time he'll need for studying and of the amount assigned to each course. To play safe, he had better have, say, six additional hours available in case any of his estimates have proved too low. He'll undoubtedly need them when hour exams come around, and perhaps at other times. Otherwise, he can use them the way he pleases. These extra hours are chosen and put down in his schedule as either recreation or study.

Totaling up his accounts, he can expect to be in class or laboratory about seventeen hours a week, studying from twenty-three to twenty-nine hours a week, and working ten hours a week at a part-time job. This is quite a bit; yet he has a good deal of time left over. He doesn't have to burn the midnight oil and, in fact, can plan on knocking off about ten o'clock each night for a snack, bull session, or other recreation. He has leisurely meal hours for restful breaks in his work; there is time for some exercise; and beginning with Saturday afternoon, his whole week end is free. Some of the time, too, he can expect to take one or two extra evenings off a week. Though this schedule calls for more study than most students actually do, it is still one of great leisure compared with the schedule of a doctor, lawyer, or businessman or the one the student himself is likely to have when he is well launched on his career.

Revising the Schedule

Your first schedule for the semester should not be your last. The chances are that you will have planned too much or too little time for various activities. You may have been too unrealistic about how much total time you spend in studying. If so, make a compromise. Use the schedule as a kind of goal to work toward, particularly if you are not doing as well as you should. But, above all, be realistic. Your schedule will do you no good at all if it is so unrealistic that you can't follow it at all in practice. Make a workable schedule, and perhaps after you begin to acquire regular habits of work, you can begin to revise your schedule to make it more like your original goals.

Once you have regular habits of study, you don't need to rely on your schedule as an incentive. You can use it just as a convenient plan for your week's activities.

We have provided four schedule sheets for you to use in making revisions in your schedule. Perhaps you will need more. If so, you can make up some additional ones for yourself. You probably ought not to change your schedule more than once every two weeks, and ordinarily not oftener than every three or four weeks, for you ought to know how one schedule has worked for a week or two before you revise it. And you probably

shouldn't make drastic, sweeping revisions all at once. Any changes should be made by reassigning only a few hours at a time. Otherwise, you'll be so confused you won't have a schedule. When you have a schedule that seems to work well, with or without a few minor changes, make out the Final Working Schedule you'll find in the back of the book.

We should mention incidentally that you ought to keep your schedule where you can refer to it easily. In fact, you ought to have it where you can't miss seeing it several times a day and thus have it as a reminder of what you should be doing. One good place is the front of your notebook, which should be your constant companion. Another, if you do most of your studying in your room, is on the wall above your desk or in a similarly visible place.

How to Use Your Time

Many students set up a schedule and don't find it to be of much help because they can't make it work. They can't seem to do what the schedule calls for. Though they start off with good intentions, they can't manage to study when they are supposed to.

Are You a Dribbler?

Here, for example, is what happened to one student whose schedule was to read English literature from seven until ten o'clock. Determined to do his reading on schedule, he sat down at his desk promptly at seven. First, he discovered that his pencil was out of lead and needed a refill before he could make any notes. Walking across the hall to the room of a friend to see if he had some lead, he found an interesting discussion going on about the merits of Fords versus Chevrolets. Becoming absorbed in this, it was some time before he remembered that he was supposed to be studying English. Starting back to his room, he recalled that there was a good TV program on. With the aid of a little wishful thinking, he convinced himself that he could be studying while watching TV in the lounge. Next, with his attention divided between the TV and the book, he found himself daydreaming about the weekend coming up. And so it went. Ten o'clock came, time to go out for a bite to eat—and still no work done.

This dribbling away of time is the major stumbling block to effective study. Countless surveys of students have shown this to be true; and if you've been in college long, you've no doubt seen it for yourself. If this is a problem for you, and it probably is, try to solve it slowly and carefully. It can be solved, but it takes practice and determination.

Definite Study Periods

Start by making your study periods short, and plan on brief periods of rest or relaxation in between. Instead of trying to study three hours at one crack and accomplishing nothing, settle for one hour at a time. It is much more important to work effectively for short periods than to schedule long ones and fritter them away in aimless procrastination. If you set for yourself a modest target, it will be easier to hit. You won't find the prospects so forbidding, and you'll be more likely to do what you set out to do. Then at least, you will have accomplished something.

If necessary, cut yourself down to very short periods, say, of twenty minutes, and take ten minutes off deliberately, then go back to work for another twenty. Indeed, use any device you can to make yourself work for some definite period of time. The essential thing is to actually work when you are supposed to and to make yourself study with all the concentration you can muster while you are studying.

Once you have gotten into the swing of an easy schedule of work and rest, you can gradually change it. Having experienced the satisfaction that comes from concentrated work, you can then lengthen the periods. Even so, they probably shouldn't be too long. Those who are proficient at studying and creative efforts and who are able to keep at their work more or less continuous for long hours usually find that they need short breaks every hour or so to keep themselves alert and rested and thus able to make the most of their working periods.

Physical Conditions of Study

Good physical conditions of study can help you considerably in your efforts to work effectively on a schedule and to accomplish what you want to do. The best place to sit is at a table or desk, not on a bed. Bed is a little too relaxing and doesn't go along with the work that studying is. Sitting up straight and keeping muscles reasonably tense may require more effort, but it also keeps one alert and in the mood to work.

The table or desk should be clean and clear of everything not connected with the work. It should have no pictures, trophies, radios, or other things that might cause one's mind to wander away from the task at hand. For the same reason, a table or desk that faces the wall or away from other people or objects in the room is a good idea. This position offers better protection against distraction than one facing a window, door, or other people. You just won't see people passing by, or, if you are in a library, the other students around you, and when they see you, they'll know you're working and will be less likely to interrupt you.

Good lighting that floods the entire working area is also an important condition for effective study. If you have to hunch and squint to see your work, you tire easily and give up more quickly. Hence lighting that is adequate, comfortable, and pleasant will keep motivation up longer and make studying a more inviting task.

Where to Study

Wherever you can find the best combination of conditions we've just described is the place to study. If you have a room all to yourself that you can arrange to meet these conditions, and if it is located in a quiet area where other people will not distract you with their noise or conversation, that is a good place. Even if you have a roommate but he is intent on following the same rules for effective study that you are, your room can also be suitable.

On the other hand, it frequently happens that other people in your dormitory, fraternity, sorority, or apartment house are on a different schedule than you, and are no more disciplined than you in getting down to work. They pop into your room and start a discussion, or they have something interesting going on within earshot, and the temptation proves too great. In the war against frittered time, our roommates, friends, and relatives are our worst enemies.

That is why it is usually better to find some place to. work where other people cannot bother you. In a college, the best place is probably the library, near the back and facing a wall rather than near the door. Libraries are set up for people to study in and they have rules against talking and other distractions. They even protect the student against himself, for they have no radios to turn on and no sweetheart's picture to look at, and they make one somewhat more embarrassed to be seen daydreaming. It's no surprise, then, that surveys show that students who habitually study in the library make better grades than other students.

Some students, though, claim they feel uncomfortable in the library. Perhaps that is because they are not really motivated to study or are afraid they'll miss out on a good time at the dormitory or fraternity house. It may be due partly to the fact that studying in strange surroundings is more difficult than in familiar ones. And libraries are indeed strange places to many students. The remedy, of course, is to get acquainted with the library so that it seems like a normal place to be. If then you make up your mind to study in the library and go there only when you really intend to study, you should find it a good place to get some work done.

Although libraries, on the whole, are good places to study, some people can and do study effectively in other places—in their rooms, on park benches, on busses and trains. You probably can too after you have really learned to study. If you are still learning the art, though, it's safer to pick a library or similar place and then graduate later to working under more distracting circumstances.

More and more dormitories, fraternities, and student centers are setting up special places for study which are quiet and well designed for studying. If you have some special prejudice against the library as a place to study, one of these places is a satisfactory substitute.

Concentration

Up to this point in this section, we have been talking about the environment for study—where it is best done and the ideal conditions for doing it. In the end, however, none of these does any studying for you. It is you who must use your mind effectively for learning to take place.

In the chapters that follow we shall describe very specific things you should do in various aspects of study to improve your efficiency in study. But before we do that, we should give you some general points concerning your fitness and your attitudes in study.

Physical fitness. The first one is to be in the best possible physical condition when you study. This means eating meals regularly so that you are not bothered by stomach pangs or feelings of hunger when you try to study. It means getting sleep regularly so that you come to the task well rested and as alert as possible. Don't try to live it up and study at the same time. Save the partying for weekends or periods when you are taking time off from study. If you try to study when you're "beat," you are handicapping yourself in a task which is already difficult enough.

Keeping physically fit also means getting a reasonable amount of recreation and exercise. Many students, particularly those with some sport that interests them, should set aside definite times to play their tennis, squash, etc. But walking, jogging, or tossing the ball around are also good forms of exercise that tend to keep one feeling healthy and fit.

Sleepiness. Sleepiness and mental fatigue frequently get in the way of effective study. If a person gets sufficient sleep regularly, he presumably should not be sleepy during the working day. Study, however, is a quiet activity and, on occasion, it may be boring; both of these are conditions conducive to sleep. So you may at times fight sleepiness when you study even if you have been regularly getting your eight hours of sleep. Such sleepiness may lend you an excuse for saying that you had better put off studying until you are "fresh." But beware of such a rationalization, for this will simply put you off your schedule of work so that later you are behind in it, and still sleepy!

The best approach is to find ways to fight sleepiness. One is to take a five-minute break in which you rest or even nap. Most people snap back very quickly with a short rest. Another is to pace the floor, take a brisk but brief walk, or to recite a lesson out loud. Still another is to schedule boring activities, recreation, or something not requiring concentration, at times when you normally feel sleepy. Each person has a time at which he tends to be sleepy—often after lunch or dinner—and when he discovers it he can schedule his study at other times.

Mental fatigue. Related to sleepiness, but different, is the feeling of being tired. After a period of reading or study, we may feel mentally fatigued. But psychological research has revealed some interesting things about such so-called fatigue. It really is not fatigue similar to physical fatigue; rather it is boredom and represents decreased motivation to study. You can prove this easily when you feel tired by changing your activity. For example, you may be tired of reading history, but you can easily get interested in reading the newspaper.

Changing the activity is, in fact, the cure for fatigue in studying. If you tend to lose interest in history, you can change to something else that interests you more, say, chemistry, and function effectively. This is one of the reasons for scheduling periods that are not too long for the study of any particular subject and to provide deliberately for changes in the topic studied. To help combat fatigue, it is a good idea to schedule first the subjects that interest you the least, leaving until later, when you may be fighting fatigue, the subject that interests you most.

Maintaining interest. In the end, the maintaining of interest in studying, as opposed to interest in football, girl friends, etc., is the goal to be achieved. Anything that will do that should be exploited. Some of the pointers we give in subsequent chapters will help you do that, but each person is unique, and you may be able to discover your own ways of concentrating on your studies. If you are the argumentative type, you may try arguing with what you read. Read it, translating what the author says into opposites, and ask why these are not true.

Try always, in any case, to make studying an active process rather than a passive one. Try to make yourself think all the time you are studying, rather than let the words passively fall on the eyes and ears. Use any device you can to do this. If you succeed in concentrating effectively on whatever you study, you will have won the biggest battle of all. Then the specific things we tell you to do in the chapters that follow will make the concentration pay off in more efficient study, higher grades, and more satisfaction in college.

chapter 3

CLASSROOM LEARNING

Almost at the beginning of this book, we underscored the fact that college is different from high school. Besides being tougher, college also puts a student much more on his own than he was used to being in high school. In particular, the relative emphasis on classes and homework is reversed. In high school, the student spends twenty-five to thirty hours a week in class work and usually no more than a third of that in reading and other outside assignments. In college, the full-time student will spend fifteen to eighteen hours in classes and laboratories, and be expected to spend approximately twice that in preparation outside of class. That is why throughout this book we emphasize the skills needed in study outside the classroom.

All learning in both high school and college, however, starts in the classroom, so that is where we will start.

Classroom Teaching

College courses vary enormously in the way they are taught, and the student's first task is to understand how each of his particular courses will be handled.

Large Classes

First of all, classes vary in size, and this determines many other features of a course. Some small colleges and private schools that have a relatively large faculty-student ratio may maintain class size at thirty or less in number. But most publicly supported colleges, as well as many private ones, do not feel that they can or should keep all classes small. Rather, this decision hinges on the subject being taught.

Lecture courses. You will find, typically, that freshman classes in languages and

English are taught in small sections of less than thirty students per section. This is because such courses emphasize recitation and discussion, and it is not possible to have much recitation in a large class. On the other hand, classes in most other subjects taught at the freshman level will typically be so large that little or no student discussion is feasible. These courses are planned frankly as lecture courses—courses in which the teachers will do virtually all of the talking. This being the case, it really doesn't matter much how many are in the class, for the lecturer can just as easily lecture to three hundred, five hundred, or even a thousand as he can to a hundred. And obviously, it is more economical to put students together in large classes than to teach several smaller ones. Hence, entering freshmen more and more find themselves in classes of several hundred.

Quiz sections. In many courses, attempts are made to offset the one-way communication of the lecture by having the students meet at least one hour each week in discussion or quiz sections. The purpose of these sections is to permit students to ask questions and, through active participation, come to a better understanding of the material than they would have merely by listening to lectures. On the other hand, because such teaching is uneconomical, it is usually done by graduate students or junior members of the staff who are relatively inexperienced in teaching. Moreover, there is rather little new material taught in these sections, so a student who is not particularly interested in the subject and primarily concerned with doing what he must do to earn a grade has little incentive to attend. To provide such an incentive and to motivate students to keep up with their work, quizzes are frequently a feature of such sections.

If you are taking courses having such sections, we can give you no hard-and-fast rule on what to do about them. You will certainly want to find out whether quizzes are given in these sections, and if so, what they cover. Then behave accordingly. You will want to assess, but not too hastily, the competence of the instructor and whether or not he contributes in your particular case to your learning and understanding of the material. What your attitude toward these sections is can also depend on your particular abilities and interests. If you gain little from discussion and otherwise can master well the required material, you may wisely decide not to attend faithfully these sections. In any case, the strategy is something for you to work out in the light of your interests and the way the sections are conducted.

But whether or not there are extra quiz sections, the lecture is the main feature of classroom work in these large classes. Hence some advice is in order for students entering courses of this sort for the first time.

Organization of the Course

Large lecture courses are usually perforce carefully organized. A teacher of such a large group cannot simply assign a textbook, start lecturing, and periodically throw a quiz or hour examination. The organization will usually be presented, at least in part, in an outline or syllabus that lays out the topics to be discussed, along with textbook assignments, for each day or week of the course.

Examinations. The plan of the course will also include a schedule of hour or "mid-term" examinations. The dates of these, because so many people are involved, almost never can be changed once they are set. Hence you should note them in the schedule, and if you have other hour exams coming on the same date or near the same time, you will simply have to plan your preparation to cope with this eventuality. Some instructors will give a weighting for lecture material versus textbook study. They may, for example, say examinations will be

based half on lecture, and half on the textbook. Others are not so clear-cut but will give you a rough idea of the coverage on examinations.

Another feature of large lecture courses is the use of objective examinations. These are examinations in which you write little or nothing in longhand but select alternatives in multiple-choice questions, mark true or false, or match up items. The lecturer usually will tell you early in the course what kinds of examinations you will have, and this will greatly affect, as you will see later, the way in which you do your studying—at least if you are interested in doing your best on the examinations.

Notes. Another thing you need to know about a course is how the lectures are related to the assigned readings. It is fairly typical of courses in the social and natural sciences for the lecturer to have an outline and content for his lectures that is different from the book. (Sometimes he follows a book other than the one assigned.) In this case, you will organize your notes accordingly, having a different set of pages for lectures and for textbook and other assigned readings. Some lecturers simply teach the book. They feel the book contains all they want to teach, but that its explanation and elaboration in lectures is helpful to the student. (A lecturer can only cover about one-third to one-half the ground assigned in a textbook, so his lectures will generally stress the most important or the most difficult points in the book.) In this case, you will want to organize your notes so that the lecture and textbook material can be co-ordinated.

The important thing for the student is to find out at the outset how each particular course is organized. Since the lecturer usually gives this information on the first day of class, it behooves the student to attend the very first day. Getting straight what is expected at the outset can very well save a lot of grief later. For this reason, it is recommended that you attend the first class of any course you think you might take even if you are undecided or have not yet signed up for it. Indeed, it is worthwhile to do this where feasible for the courses you consider taking in subsequent semesters. In that way, you are in a better position to plan subsequent course programs. If, for any reason, you miss the first class, you should find out from the instructor when you do attend class just what he said concerning organization and ask for any syllabus or outline he may have handed out.

Class Attendance

A dedicated teacher, and some who ·are not so dedicated, believes what that what he teaches is important. Hence it is understandable that almost all teachers advise students to attend class faithfully. Occasionally, though, an instructor whose lectures cover the same material as the book will tell students that class attendance is optional. In this event, the student must decide whether his own abilities and study habits are such that he can get the material from the book more economically by attending or by not attending class. In other instances, where the lecturer is giving new material, as he usually is, a student really should go to class regularly.

Our advice to all freshman students would be to attend all classes faithfully regardless of the way the course is organized. Even if the lecture re-covers the ground of the textbook, the teacher's emphasis and explanation are usually of sufficient help to be worth the time. After all, class time is not that crucial in a student's schedule. He can easily spare 15 hours a week out of the 112 that he is awake. And students who cut classes more often than the regular attendees have problems of academic standing. After you have been in college a year or so and know your own strengths and limitations, you may be in a position to decide wisely whether some classes might be cut.

Good Listening

Large lectures can be a boring, even depressing experience. One can feel that he is in a herd that is being talked to—often down to—from a podium. There is nothing for him to do but listen, and so he can easily adopt the wrong attitude toward lectures. He can slump down in his seat, even doze, taking no notes, and just barely listen to what is being said. If he encounters a lecturer who seems boring or dull, this attitude is all the more easily taken.

Actually, good listening, like good studying at a desk, is an active process. You should sit erectly, be mentally alert, and prepare to concentrate as completely as possible on what the lecturer says. If the teacher is not endowed with a good speaking voice, this is all the more important. You should try with eyes and ears to learn all that you possibly can. Your mind throughout should be on what the lecturer says and displays, not on his mannerisms, his speaking voice, the crack in the wall, or anything else in the room. An apparently dull lecturer and dull subject can turn out to be interesting when regarded in this way, especially after you have learned something about the subject. In any case, keep your mind working all the time, digesting and reflecting on what is being said, as well as taking notes (see below), and you will be amply repaid. You will be able to answer questions on the examination that otherwise slid by you and perhaps never got into your notes—even if they are good notes—and you will find the whole experience more enjoyable.

Taking Lecture Notes

Besides good listening, the main job of the student in a lecture class is to take good notes. Hence the rest of this chapter on classroom learning will concern note-taking and the use of lecture notes in subsequent study.

Most students know they should take notes in class, if only to impress the instructor, but many don't know how to go about it. They take either too many or too few, and they don't take the best ones. Taking lecture notes is an art that must be developed by practice. It requires effort and an alert mind. Also involved is additional work after class to edit and, often, to rewrite the notes. But good lecture and classroom notes can be the key to remarkable academic improvement.

Surveying, Questioning, Listening

There is the old saw about the country politician's explaining how he gave speeches. He said, "I tell 'em what I'm goin' to tell them, then I tell 'em, and then I tell 'em what I told them." The first part of this, which should be a part of any good speech, chapter, article, or piece of communication, is a survey of what is to come. When a student reads a textbook, as we shall see, he can make such a survey by skimming the headings and reading the summary of a chapter. When it comes to lectures, he can't do this unless the lecturer does it for him.

Many lecturers, however, *do* give something of a preview of what they are going to say. (This is one reason why it is a good idea to get to class on time.) When they do, be on the alert and make notes very rapidly on the points they say they are going to cover. Then refer to these notes as the lecture proceeds. It permits one to see the orderly development of the ideas, and also to anticipate the point in the lecture at which questions raised in your mind may be answered.

And questioning is one of the things you should do to get the most out of a lecture. Beside thinking of questions as you listen hard, before you go to class, you should think of questions based on your reading of the textbook assignments and on what the lecturer said last time. As soon as you are settled in your chair, get to questioning and thinking and continue doing it throughout class. This is one of the principal ways in which you can participate actively in the lecture process even though you can't talk out loud, and it serves to maintain your interest and alertness throughout the lecture.

Getting the Organization

Somehow or other you must comprehend and note the organization of what the lecturer is saying. This is equivalent to noting the headings in a book. Only here you must often figure out for yourself what the headings are. Some lecturers use the blackboard to write down the topics they're

talking about. If so, fine. It will provide the skeleton for your notes. If not, you must somehow make up or pick out the outline for yourself. Sometimes this is almost impossible, and you will have to write down all that seems to be important and then organize it after class. Even the most disorganized lecturer, however, gives you many clues to his organization if you will only recognize them and use them. One clue may be the statement "The main point is this: . . ." or "Note this: . .," or "Remember this: . . . ."Another clue may be the mere repetition of a statement; if the lecturer takes the trouble to say something twice, he must think it's important. Or he may say essentially the same thing in two or three different ways, which is a kind of repetition, and this may be your clue. Changes of pace may also serve as clues. When a lecturer suddenly slows down and says something as though he specially wanted you to get it, his statement is probably important. Or if his voice changes in tone or loudness so as to give his statement emphasis, that signals an important point.

Lecturers have different styles, and they may use any of these clues in any combination. As soon as you begin taking a course, study your lecturer carefully to see what his particular style is and how he gives his clues. For this purpose, it is often helpful to compare notes with a couple of other students and discuss with them the lecturer's style. Another student may pick up clues you don't, and vice versa.

In one way or another, you should be organizing what the lecturer says and take notes according to this organization. You do it by trying to identify the lecturer's main points. You look for main ideas and then for important details connected with them, just as you do in textbook reading. If you listen carefully, you'll find that there are paragraphs in his spoken words as there are in a book. Your job is to condense these paragraphs into simple phrases and sentences that include the main ideas and important details. You should do this in words of your own phrasing, not in those of the lecturer, in order to make sure that you really understand what he is saying. On the other hand, if he gives you a technical definition or states something obviously intended to be a precise statement, you should take this down verbatim.

Sometimes it is difficult to organize your lecture notes as you are taking them down and even to be sure all the time what the main points are. In this case, you are forced to take copious unorganized notes just to keep up with the lecture. Don't do that unless you can't avoid it. In any event, though, don't spend so much time trying to take neat well-organized notes that you lose the point of the lecture. Almost any kind of note is better than none at all. Still, the more organized your notes are, the more useful they will be later on.

The question of how many notes you should take depends somewhat on the individual, how apt he is at spotting main points, and how rapidly he can write. It also depends on the lecturer and how many main points he has. Some lecturers jam a lot into an hour, others relatively little. Some students do their best by taking many notes, and others do just as well by taking rather few. In general, though, it is best to err on the side of taking too many. You can always sort them out and reduce them later. If you take too few, you may never regain what you have lost.

Reviewing and Revising
Your lecture notes, compared with your textbook, are incomplete, imperfect, and not well organized. It is therefore necessary to review them carefully and frequently to recall and recite as much as you can, thus battling the inexorable law of forgetting. Your first review should be right after the lecture or within a few hours of it. At that time much of what the lecturer said is still fresh in your mind, and you can fill in essentials that did not get into your notes. You can even correct errors that crept in by writing something down hurriedly or before

you understood it. If you wait too long to review your notes, you may easily wind up saying, as many a student has, "My lecture notes just don't make sense."

It may often pay you to rewrite your lecture notes completely. We don't recommend that you do this needlessly, for you can waste time doing it. Some students manage to get neat well-organized notes and need to do only a little editing, making occasional inserts and cross-outs. Students who aren't in this class may be well advised to rewrite almost all their notes. Even the best students may have to rewrite when the lecturer's style defies all attempts to organize what he is saying while he is saying it. You'll have to decide for yourself when and what you should rewrite. If you suspect you need to, you'd better do it. For if you manage to organize more clearly what you've written, you'll be much better off later. And you'll get some valuable recitation and review in the process.

How to Keep Notes

It's hard to say what handicaps students most in their attempts to do college work. A schedule of work, proceeding according to a plan of study, reading with a purpose, and reading rapidly are all important assets. So too are some other matters, and one of them is taking, keeping, and using good notes, both on assigned reading and on lectures. In talking to hundreds of students who have done badly on their examinations, we have found that one of the most frequent and obvious deficiencies in their study methods has to do with their note taking or lack of it. That's the reason we are devoting so much emphasis to this aspect of how to study.

First of all—and not by any means trivial—are the problems of what kind of notebook to have and how to arrange notes in it.

The Well-kept Notebook
The remedy for many ills is to use a loose-leaf notebook, the kind with three

rings, which permits pages to be quickly shifted around or discarded if need be. You should set up such a notebook with distinctive tabular dividers, one for each subject you are taking, and plainly write or print each subject on the tab of the divider. At the end of the book, keep a liberal supply of clean ruled paper. Always make sure to use the kind of paper intended for the notebook. Keep the notebook with you whenever you go to class or study. Make it a constant companion during your class and study hours. Then you'll always have all your notes, and they can be kept in order with no trouble at all.

Probably the best size for such a notebook is letter size, the one that takes pages about 8 1/2 by 11 inches, such as people use in typewriters or for regular business correspondence. This allows plenty of room for all kinds of notes, and it usually will accommodate all the notes you take in a semester or term.

Since your notebook should get a lot of hard wear, don't skimp when you buy it. Pay a little more, and get one with the sturdiest possible binder. The flimsier ones are likely to fray and even lose their covers before you get through a term.

A couple of other words of advice about how to keep notes: Start your notes for a new chapter on a new page. Similarly, start those for each lecture on a new page. By "lecture," however, we don't necessarily mean class hour. Lecturers seldom stay on their planned schedule, and even if they do, they sometimes devote more than one hour to a lecture. Rather, by lecture we mean a topic that corresponds more or less to a chapter in a book. Usually you can tell when a lecturer finishes one topic and starts another even if he is otherwise not easy to take notes from. By starting each chapter or topic on a new page, you can save time later in getting your notes into any order you want and in rewriting them when that is necessary.

Also be sure to *label* each set of notes. For class notes, put down at the top of the page the date and then a brief statement of the topic. For textbook notes, put down the number of the chapter (or group of pages) and the title of the material. It is even desirable to do this for every single page of notes (just as books have running heads at the top of pages) so that you can always tell at a glance what the notes are about.

Make certain too to keep *all notes* in your notewook. If, for any reason, you are caught without your notebook and take notes on separate sheets of paper, see to it that they are entered in your notebook at the very next opportunity. Also each time you go to class or study a particular subject, make sure that all your notes for that subject are arranged in the proper order. It costs you practically nothing to do this, but it will later cost a lot of time and confusion if you don't.

Note-taking Formats

Now let us get down to the details of how one makes notes. So far we have covered only one aspect of note-taking. This is the *recording* of material heard and sometimes seen in a lecture. The way you construct notes, however, should be geared to the study process that will follow and lead up to examinations. There are several ways to describe this process, but Professor Walter Pauk of the Study Center at Cornell University has organized the steps involved into the five R's of note-taking. These are as follows:

1. *Record.* This we have already discussed in talking about writing down the meaningful facts and ideas in a lecture.

2. *Reduce.* This refers to summarizing the ideas and facts that have been put down in lecture. This is a way of clarifying the meaning of what has been recorded, of picking out key terms and concepts, and of providing flags or clues to the details described in the recorded notes. The reduction of ideas and facts produces what some students would call "cram sheets." These are sheets made out to list, usually in outline form, the bare bones of a course. The student uses them in reviewing by looking at the key ideas and then reciting the details of what he has in his recorded notes. The format of each page of notes should provide room for you to write down these clues.

3. *Recite.* As we said earlier, lecture notes should be reviewed very soon after the lecture while it is still fresh in mind. At this point, the student does whatever rewriting of the recorded notes is necessary, but it is also the time to reduce the main ideas and facts to a form suitable for recitation. In each of the formats suggested below, a column about two inches wide at the left of the note page is provided for this purpose. As you first review your notes, you write the key words and phrases in this column. Then, when you have finished, you cover up the recorded lecture notes and look only at your reduced clues. With each clue, you see whether or not you can recite, not in rote form but in your own words, the points you have in the recorded notes. From time to time, you can uncover the recorded notes to see whether you are correct.

4. *Reflect.* This means thinking about the content of the notes. As you are reciting your notes, you usually will have ideas pop into mind that make them more meaningful to you. Perhaps you will think of an example, or you may come to a conclusion, not given by the lecturer. Whatever it is, it will be helpful to you, and make studying more fun even if it does not give you a better grade, to record the results of your reflection.

5. *Review.* Reviewing is necessary to retain what you have learned. Otherwise, in the course of time you forget. To review, merely repeat step three of the five R's. Cover up your recorded notes, leaving only the reduced clues to guide you. Then recite, checking yourself when necessary, from the clue words and phrases.

These five R's, then, constitute tried and proven methods of learning from lecture notes. To implement them, you need to have a prearranged format for your notes. We will show you three that have been found useful

at the Cornell Study Center. Which of the first two you use depends on your preference and somewhat on how wordy your notes are. The third suggested format is suitable for the course in which the lecturer closely follows the textbook.

The 2-5-1 format. The numbers here refer to the number of inches allowed for each of three steps described above: reduce, record, and reflect. Your lecture notes are recorded in a five-inch column. To left of it is a column for you to fill in later with your reduced ideas and facts. To the right is a 1-inch column for your reflections. You use this one by writing sidewise on the column.

The 2-6-2 format. The numbers here mean the same as they do in the first format except that a 6-inch column is provided for recorded lecture notes. This format is to be preferred when notes are taken in sentence rather than in topical form and are relatively wordy. This will depend on the course and the student. In this format, the space for putting down one's reflections is left in a column 2 inches high across the bottom of the note page.

The 2-3-3-2 format. As indicated above, this is the one to use when lecture and textbook material are quite similar and need to be co-ordinated in one set of notes. The 2-inch column, as before, is for reduced clues. The first 3-inch colunn is for textbook notes, for in this kind of course—in fact, in most courses—you should read the textbook material *before* listening to the corresponding lecture material. If you do that, you will find the lecture material much more meaningful, and you will be able to take much better notes. In this format, a couple of inches is left at the bottom of the page, as in the preceding format, for you to record your reflection and synthesis of ideas on the page.

2-5-1 FORMAT

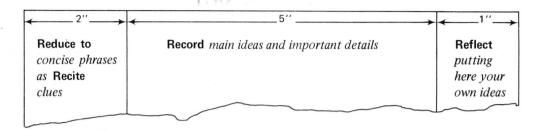

2''	5''	1''
Reduce to *concise phrases* as **Recite** clues	**Record** *main ideas and important details*	**Reflect** *putting here your own ideas*

2-6-2 FORMAT

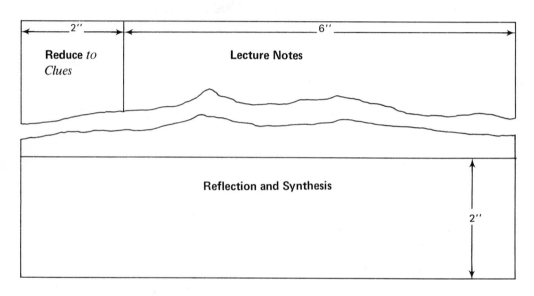

2''	6''
Reduce *to* Clues	**Lecture Notes**

Reflection and Synthesis

2''

2-3-3-2 FORMAT

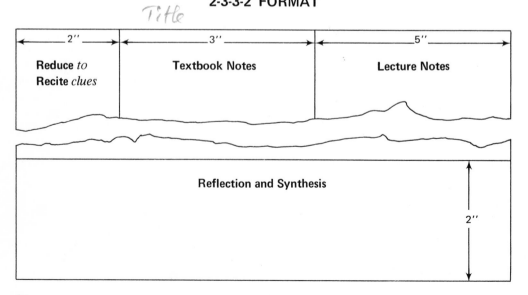

Title

2''	3''	5''
Reduce *to* **Recite** *clues*	**Textbook Notes**	**Lecture Notes**

Reflection and Synthesis

2''

chapter 4

READING BETTER AND FASTER

In the last chapter, we dealt with learning from lectures. In the next chapter, we shall consider learning from textbooks. In this one, we pause to look at the question of how well you read. We do this because the chances are that you do not read efficiently and because you should improve your reading habits before or at the same time as you attempt to improve your methods of studying textbooks.

Nearly every college student has been reading for at least ten or eleven years and for two or three hours a day. In college, he will have to read more than that. Yet the simple fact is that most college students do not know how to read well. They neither read as fast as they should, which wastes time, nor comprehend what they read as well as they should, which impedes learning. The reason why they do not read well is because they have one or more faults that slow down reading and impair comprehension.

To get an idea of what your faults may be, read carefully through the following questions, answering them as honestly as you can. Perhaps in some cases you will not know the answer. If so, keep the question in mind and when you are next reading something—even this book but preferably something more difficult—try to determine whether you have the faulty habit. Any question to which you give the answer "Yes" earmarks a fault. After each question, we have given brief comments indicating the cure for the fault.

1. *Do you move your lips or vocalize when you read?* If you do, try mumbling some irrelevant phrase such as "mamby pamby" or put your finger rightly on your lips as you read.

2. *Do you read each word one by one?* If so, you should try to read whole phrases at a glance.

3. *Are you frequently stopped by an unfamiliar word?* If so, there are two things you should do. One is to increase your vocabulary. The other is to look for the ideas behind words even if you are not sure of the precise meaning of a word.

4. *Do you read all material at the same rate?* If you do, you should learn to distinguish different types of reading material and to set out deliberately to read each one at the pace that is best for it.

5. *Do you back track and reread?* In this case, you should try to concentrate on reading whatever you read only once. If you go back and reread sections of the material, you should concentrate on doing a good job of reading and note-taking the first time you read—as distinguished from skimming or reviewing—the material.

There are other faults besides these, but these are most common ones and are found in some degree in the majority of students coming to college. We have indicated briefly what should be done about each fault, but we shall go into more detail later in the chapter.

Reading with a Purpose

The typical student who has an assignment to do says to himself, "I've got to read this chapter." Then he sits down and reads it—just reads it. He reads everything about the same way, English, history, chemistry, and so forth. He plods through the sentences like a man trudging to work, and when he's through, he says, "I've read it."

That's not the way to do it at all. There are many different ways to read, different things to look for and learn, and different speeds to read at. Which way one reads depends on his purpose. In fact, in studying college assignments, you should "read" the same material two, three, or four times, each time with a different purpose. You must know before you start what your purpose is, and read accordingly.

Skimming

One purpose in reading is simply to find out what something is about. You want to construct a sort of map of where the material goes and how it is structured. You do it simply to obtain an overview or survey of material.

To do it, you simply read for signposts, that is, clues that tell you what the textual detail is about. Most textbooks are carefully constructed to supply this. They have headings of various orders, usually starting with chapter titles, moving down to sectional headings, then on to headings in bold-faced or italicized type. This is done by textbook writers because formal learning is not simply acquiring a host of isolated facts. Knowledge has a certain organization, and this organization is more important than the details that fit into it.

The skimming kind of reading is an important and first step in the reading done by college students. We shall go into it more thoroughly in the next chapter.

Getting the Main Idea

Another purpose, and one important in college study, as well as in business and professional reading, is reading merely to get the main idea. All you want to end up with is one sentence that expresses the nub of the passage. This is one of the things, but only one, that you want to do when you study. It's the thing you're after in the very first stage of studying, which is to survey. In doing this, you scan headings and skim sentences to give you the main topics and ideas of the chapter. It's also what you're after when you settle down to reading the assignment more carefully. Even though you will want more than the ideas, it's essential to pick them out; otherwise, nothing else will be meaningful or remembered well.

How do you find main ideas? This depends on what you want the main idea of—chapter, section, subsection, or para-

graph. Let's start with the paragraph, for this is the smallest unit. The usual definition of a paragraph, in fact, is that it contains one, and only one, idea. Most writers of textbooks know it, and they've usually put one idea in each of their paragraphs. Your job is to find it.

You may remember an old precept about writing: that you begin a paragraph with a topic sentence, then explain it, illustrate it, support it with additional sentences, and finally wind up with a summary sentence. To have the topic sentence, the idea sentence, come first in a paragraph is not, however, always practicable or desirable. Sometimes there has to be a transition or introductory sentence between the idea of the last paragraph and the idea of the present one. Such a sentence shows the student how one idea is connected with another one, but it shouldn't be mistaken for the main idea. Sometimes the author holds back his main idea for artistic reasons.

In looking for the main idea, don't look always for a whole sentence, for the idea is likely to be only a part of a sentence. It may be the principal clause or phrase in a sentence, and you usually can boil it down in your own mind to a couple of words. To see what we mean, pick up one of your textbooks and find some sentences with main ideas. Now try throwing away some of the adjectives and adverbs that don't materially change the meaning and keep only the subject, verb, and predicate. If you remember these key words, you can always supply the supporting words yourself.

When you do this, though, don't be too free and easy. Sometimes qualifiers are essential to the meaning. If we say, for example, "The fast reader is usually the fast learner," you can't omit the "usually." We don't mean that fast readers are always fast learners or that fast reading is synonymous with fast learning. We mean that, typically, often, most of the time, or on the average, fast readers manage to learn faster. On the other hand, if we say, "The person who reads rapidly, scanning each line in three or four glances and not stopping to daydream, is typically the person who learns a great deal in a short period of time," you can eliminate most of these words, translate them, and come up with "The fast reader is usually the fast learner" as your main idea.

We should point out in passing that you may encounter paragraphs in which the main idea is not expressed in a single sentence or even made explicit at all. That won't happen often in textbooks, but it will in descriptive writing, literature, and fiction. A story writer may, for example, spend a paragraph describing in minute detail the clothes one of his characters is wearing. He wants to tell you the kind of person the character is without flatly saying it, and so he leaves it to you to extract the character's personality from a vivid description. In that case, you can't find any sentences or group of words expressing the main idea; you simply have to devise your own summary of the paragraph. Keep this in mind when you're studying literature and, more generally, any descriptive writing. Sometimes a skillful writer of fiction can use this technique of spreading the essential idea over a whole paragraph to suggest many different things at once about a character or event in the story.

Make a habit of finding the main idea in every paragraph you read. When you think you've found it, check your conclusion by holding the idea in mind as you read on through the paragraph and compare it especially with the summary sentence. If you have any doubts about your selection, run through the paragraph again, this time skimming it, to make sure you have the correct idea. Remember, though, that you cannot always find it in a few exact words; you may have to rephrase the idea in your own words (which is a good practice anyway) to have it straight.

Consider next how you find the ideas of larger scope than those in each paragraph, that is, the main ideas of sections and chapters. If you did your surveying well, before you read the chapter and as you went along, you probably have a good general idea of what each section is about. In addition, however, authors usually devote certain paragraphs near the beginning and the end of each section to an expression of the main idea of the paragraphs in between. (See, for example, the first two paragraphs under the heading of the present section, Reading with a Purpose.) Any passage of prose has a hierarchy of ideas: a general one for the whole passage, several less general ones under that one, and so on down to the main idea of each paragraph.

Most students read their assignments at least once, which should be enough to spot the main ideas, but somehow many of the ideas are not recognized when they are read. Almost any student, if he reads to get main ideas, can improve enormously his understanding of what he reads and consequently raise his grades on examinations. In addition, reading to get the main ideas is essential to good outlining, for an outline consists of the main topics and ideas of a passage. And outlining, as we shall see in the next chapter, is an invaluable device for learning and reviewing a subject.

Extracting Important Details

A second major purpose of reading is to locate *important details.* Because students aren't always able to do this, they often think that instructors maliciously look for unimportant or trivial details to ask about in examinations. This complaint, however, is frequently a rationalization for poor reading. So is the frequent excuse "I get the main idea, but I can't remember the details." Although an occasional student may be good at remembering main ideas without the important details, most students are as bad at one as they are at the other because they have not learned how to pick out either. Actually, the main ideas go hand in hand with the important details; one without the other is a structure without supports. The trouble is that each has to be recognized for what it is and not be confused either with the other or with more trivial matters.

What is an important detail? It is the basis for the main idea. Usually it is a fact or a group of facts. It is a fact, though, that is relevant to the main idea. It may be a case in point, an example of the main idea; this is fairly common in textbooks. It may be the proof that makes the main idea worth believing or accepting. It may merely pin down the main idea to something more concrete. In the case of a narrative, it may be the sequence of events in the story.

What is important is, admittedly, a matter of judgment, and no two people are likely to agree on every item. In most factual textbooks encountered in the natural and social sciences, there is usually at least one important detail associated with every main idea. If the student looks for it, he's pretty sure to find it. Sometimes there are so many details that it is difficult to pick out the most important one. However, the detail or group of details that is stressed most by the language the author uses or by the space the author gives to it is usually the most important one. Another criterion is how closely the detail is tied to the main idea. Is it the best example of the idea? Is it the best proof of the idea? Or is it just one more example or just one more item of proof or support for the idea? Tested in this way, the important detail or details will usually stand out from the others. And if a student remembers just one important detail for every main idea and gets all the main ideas, he'll probably make an A on the next examination. (See Analyzing Paragraphs below.)

The first time you read a passage, you can concentrate on main ideas, reading and noting as many important details as you can. The second time, you may simply review and check yourself on main ideas but concentrate on spotting and remembering important details. The third and perhaps last time you read it, you can do it to review both.

ANALYZING PARAGRAPHS

Here are two passages from an introductory psychology book (Clifford T. Morgan and Richard A. King, Introduction to Psychology, 3rd ed., McGraw-Hill, New York, 1966). In the first of these passages, we have analyzed the words and phrases in the paragraph to illustrate what we have been saying in the text. The second passage is one for you to practice on. See if you can pick out the main idea, important details, and summary. Underline important words and write your diagnosis of them in the space provided in the margin.

Main idea

important details

Summary + implication

Genes are contained on the chromosomes, and for our purposes, they may be thought of as the units of heredity. They are complex chemical packets, very probably parts of the large deoxyribonucleic acid (DNA) molecules found in the nuclei of cells. Because of their composition and chainlike construction, these DNA molecules can carry the code both for their own reproduction and for the ultimate production of substances, called enzymes, which control the formation of proteins within a cell. The chain of events through which the DNA of genes produces enzymes is a long one in which there is some uncertainty about the individual links. Various types of ribonucleic acids (RNA) are almost certainly involved in this chain. For instance, it seems likely that one of these RNAs, "Messenger RNA," may be constructed according to the code in the nuclei DNA; then "messenger RNA" may carry the information from the nucleus of the cell to the microsomes—the areas in the cytoplasm where proteins are synthesized.

Color blindness is a good example of a sex-linked characteristic. It happens to be recessive, but it is carried on the X chromosome. So whenever a male has a recessive gene for color blindness, he is color-blind, without exception. If he marries a normal woman carrying no genes for color blindness, all his sons will be normal because they will receive their father's Y chromosome and their mother's X chromosome. All his daughters, however, will be carriers without displaying any color blindness, for they will receive a dominant X from their mother and a recessive X from their father. When the carrier mother marries, the possibility of her children being color-blind depends upon whether their father is color-blind and upon which of her X chromosomes, the dominant or recessive one, is passed on to the offspring.

Other Purposes in Reading

We have described three purposes in reading. These three are the important ones in studying textbooks. Obviously, these can be done at different speeds. If one is only scanning, he can "read" thousands of words per minute, for in fact he is not looking at most of the words. If he is reading for main ideas, he can still do it at a very good clip because when he has found the main ideas he can skip over details. Even the reading for important details, which does require reading *everything,* can usually be done at several hundred words a minute. Much depends, however, on how closely packed the material is, that is, on how many important details there are in each paragraph. Students should learn to judge this and to read different material accordingly.

In addition to the three kinds of reading most important in studying textbooks, there are other kinds of reading that at one time or another will be used in college study.

Questions and answers. One purpose in reading is to find answers to specific questions. Questioning is an important aid to effective study in reading textbooks as well as in listening to lectures. In studying textbooks, you must think of the questions as you go along; they are suggested to you by headings and things you read. Then, as you find the answer to one question, this in turn raises questions to guide you as you read further.

Reading for answers to questions is also appropriate for certain other kinds of material. It is what you do when you do library research to write a paper on a particular topic. Having chosen the topic, you raise certain questions about it, then seek books, articles, and literature that answer these questions. Of course, more questions come up as you read, but you are throughout trying to find material that addresses certain questions. When you do find it, you will read it carefully for main ideas and important details. When you do not, you skip over the material and go on to something that may be relevant. Hence reading of this kind goes in skips and spurts, sometimes being extremely rapid and sometimes fairly slow. This kind of reading is what scientists typically do when they are reading articles describing particular experiments. They try to determine, usually, whether an article answers particular questions in which they are interested.

Evaluation. Another purpose you may sometimes have in mind is to *evaluate* what you read. This is most appropriate where you are reading controversial materials, interviews, news stories, and other things that cannot be taken at face value. It is also of varying usefulness in the things you study. When you read a textbook, you can, of course, usually be sure that the writer knows what he is talking about. On the other hand, you'll find that what is said in textbooks, especially of psychology, education, and social sciences, often does not agree with your beliefs or preconceptions. Usually you're wrong and the author is right, and getting your ideas corrected is part of your education.

To make the most of your opportunities, however, you shouldn't take these corrections passively. On the contrary, when you read, read with the purpose of comparing what the book says with what you've thought or believed. When there's a difference, ask right away why the author goes against your views. What is his evidence? Why does he come to his conclusion? Where were you wrong? How wrong? Why? In essence, be critical. Evaluate carefully the author's statements. At the very least, this is a way of keeping yourself alert, of picking out main ideas and important details, and of having them make an impression on you. With this frame of mind, you'll learn more. More important, you will be training yourself for reading, and forming your own opinions about, more controversial material. You will learn how to use your head, not merely to soak up what a writer says.

Critical reading to evaluate ideas is particularly appropriate for material that has some point of view or ax to grind. Most newspaper stories, magazine articles, and advertising materials are slanted in some degree by the bias of the writer or by the purposes of publication. They are designed to persuade us in a particular direction. In evaluating material of this sort, you must consider carefully the possible motives of the writer and what is known about the background of the author or the periodical. In reading this kind of material, one should watch especially for loaded words designed to evoke emotional rather than logical reactions, the misuse of facts, and logical inconsistencies between different things being said.

Applications. Another purpose, finally, to have in reading is to *apply* what you read to your own problems and to the world you live in. The writer doesn't have the space or inclination to point out applications for everything he says. Besides, you live in your own world and have knowledge and experience of your own. In the end, the usefulness of anything you learn depends upon your ability to apply it, and that is your responsibility. If you start thinking about and using what you learn in college, you will later be able to put your college education to much better use.

Applying what you read can be a very personal sort of thing. In the case of this book, we hope it is. It was not written, as textbooks are, to teach either main ideas or details for their own sake. It was prepared to help you. As you've been reading it, your paramount purpose should be to see what applies to you. Some things will and some will not, for every student is different. Each has his specific deficiencies in how to study. We have selected for teaching the things we know many people need to know, but the application is up to you. You must decide or discover how it can be of most help to you. Hence the purpose of reading to apply what you read to yourself is particularly appropriate in the case of reading this book.

Using Your Eyes

You know, of course, that you read with your eyes, but you probably don't know just what your eyes are doing when you read. You can't be blamed for that, because the activity of the eyes is so intricate and minute that it can be observed only with special equipment. One apparatus consists of an eye

camera so designed that it photographs the stop and go of the eyes when they are trained on a particular passage of reading. Eye cameras of this kind have been used to record the eye movements of tens of thousands of readers, ranging from very poor ones to very good ones. From the data obtained with these cameras, we know that eye management is pretty important in reading. In fact, you can't hope to be an effective reader unless you learn to use your eyes efficiently.

Eye Pauses

When you read a passage of printed matter, your eyes move along the line. You know that, but you may not know that they move in quick jerks with stops in between. In fact, you can't see anything while your eyes are moving. If you did, it would be a blurred swish, like a whip whizzing past. This would probably be so annoying you couldn't stand it, but fortunately you don't have to. The brain has a mechanism for blanking out this part of eye activity. When your eye jumps from one spot to another on the line, this mechanism keeps the perception of movement from being registered in the brain. Hence you are unaware of the moving blur that you would otherwise see. The important point is that you can perceive words only when your eyes are still, not when they are moving.

Recognition Span

Your eye is so designed that is sees most clearly what it fixates, what it is looking at. If you look at the word "stop," you see all the letters in it quite clearly. On the other hand, you *can* see the words on either side of "stop", which are "word" and "you." You don't see them so clearly because they fall on a part of the eye that is not quite so sensitive as the part you are using to look at "stop." The point, though, is that you can see and comprehend these words if you try. The number of words you see at one glance is called your *recognition span*. If you see only one, your recognition span is one word, and that's pretty small. If you see two or three and sometimes more, your recognition

In the picture is an ophthalmograph used for photographing the movement of the eyes in reading. (American Optical Co.) The film shows a record of eye movements made with such an instrument. (New York University Testing and Advisement Center.) The lines of print show the difference between a good reader and a poor one. Each vertical bar accompanied by a number represents a fixation. The good reader makes relatively few fixations and does not retrace a line.

span is larger. People with large recognition spans are more likely to be good readers.

There are a number of differences between good readers and poor readers, but perhaps the most important has to do with this matter of recognition span. The poor reader takes in only one word at a glance. Consequently, he is a word-by-word reader. He has to pause for every word on the line. And that's a lot of pauses. For a line like this one, it's eight pauses a line. Obviously, the reader can't read very fast because he is pinned down to each word. Instead of romping down a line, he trudges along it in laborious steps.

But good readers don't do that. They've learned to take in at a glance an average of two words or better. They do this by making use of the words they can see but poor readers ignore. They have practiced at enlarging their recognition span. (A little later in this chapter, we'll show you how you can do that too.) As a result, they don't have to make half the stops the poor reader does, and they whiz down a line twice as fast as the poor reader. Improvement in recognition span cuts reading time in half.

Saving Pause Time

Good readers also have a couple of other advantages over poor ones. For one thing, they don't dally as long on a pause. There is a limit to the possible brevity of a pause. You can't, on the average, make your eyes stop and start again in less than 1/5 second. So it takes this long to perceive and hence comprehend the words that can be seen in one stop. Poor readers, however, haven't cut their stop time to a minimum. They keep their eyes in one place longer than they need to. The savings to be made here aren't usually as enormous as they are for reducing the number of stops, but they can be appreciable. The good reader, who makes the shortest possible stops, probably saves a third or more of the time spent by poor readers on stops.

Reading Straight Ahead

Another characteristic of poor readers is that they retrace their steps. Instead of going forward all the time, they often are going backward. Their eyes get part way down a line and then move back a few words to where they were before. (These retracings are called "regressions" or "regressive movements.") This habit occurs partly because poor readers aren't alert when they read and therefore don't comprehend the words they've looked at. They keep missing the meanings when they pause even though they've looked right at a word. When they get farther along in a line or sentence and find they don't understand it, they have to go back and get what they've missed. Partly, though, regressions are just bad habits acquired in sloppy reading. The reader isn't reading with a purpose; he's dawdling. Hence his eyes wander back and forth aimlessly, just as his mind does.

Such regressive movements are unnecessary and wasteful. There are times, especially in very technical reading, when even the best reader has to go back to check something, but the good reader does very little of it. Hence he saves a lot of time by going straight ahead. He also has another advantage: By moving along at a good speed, he goes fast enough not to forget what was at the beginning of the sentence by the time he's reached the end. The poor reader spends so much time meandering back and forth with his eyes that what he has read is pretty stale by the time he has arrived at the end of the sentence. Faster reading, without retracing, actually helps the comprehension of the good reader.

At this point, before we go on to show how you can improve your reading, let us interject an important but neglected precaution. In order to be a good reader, you've got to have *good* eyes or good corrective glasses. If you don't have the best possible vision, the words around the word you're looking at will be blurred and you won't be able to perceive them easily. If you haven't had a thorough eye examination recently, better get one. Don't take the slightest chance that your eyes may not be in good condition. By making certain that any slight defects you have are corrected, you will give yourself the opportunity to read at your very best. The dividends you'll get back in time saved and in improved grades will be tremendous compared with the money and time required to look after the matter.

Before reading the next section, we suggest that you take the reading tests, How Fast Can You Read?

HOW FAST CAN YOU READ?

Following are two short selections that you can use to get a rough idea about how fast you can read. Before you read them, get a watch or clock with a second hand so you can time yourself. When you are ready to begin, write down the exact time at the head of the passage like this:

> *[Hour]   7   :[minute]   23   :[second]   15*

Then read the passage as rapidly as you can. Do not, however, read so fast that you do not understand and remember what you read because you will want to check yourself on the comprehension test we have provided for each passage. When you are through reading, mark down the exact time at the bottom of the passage. Then go directly to the comprehension test. Do not look back at the passage while taking the test. You should get nearly all the items right on the test (at least nine). If you miss too many items, you have not read carefully enough. You can find a rough index of your speed of reading by checking the following table against the time it took you to read the passages:

Minutes	Seconds	Reading speed words per minute
6	9	80
4	54	100
4	6	120
3	30	140
2	48	170
2	27	200
2	2	240
1	40	280
1	31	320
1	22	360
1	13	400

Passage 1   Starting time

The effort to treat sufferers from chronic kidney disease by machine, which once promised to save thousands of lives a year, is foundering for lack of financial support.

High costs have plagued the so-called artificial kidney program from the outset. Hospital bills for the twice-weekly machine blood "washings" that take over the kidney's vital function of removing blood wastes and adjusting body chemistry now run from $10,000 to $20,000 annually per patient. That's the main reason only about 1,700 Americans currently receive the treatments, while an estimated 8,000 people will die this year for lack of them.

But even this far from adequate situation is deteriorating. Federal Grants have been running out at the 14 hospitals designated by the U. S. Public Health Service about three years ago as demonstration centers for the process; without Government help, some of them have had to reduce the number of cases they handle.

Some private hospitals have been forced into similar cutbacks because of difficulties in attracting donations to support patients who can't pay the cost themselves. Indeed, private support of any kind has been slow in coming.

"The cost per capita of the treatment is an overwhelming drawback when we approach organizations for help," says Dr. Frederic B. Westervelt, director of the kidney care demonstration center at the University of Virginia School of Medicine in Charlottesville. "They say, 'Look what we can do for $10,000 a year—we can give 20 people an artificial leg.' When they measure what they think is the greatest good for the greatest number, we come out second best."

As a result of this lack of funds, hospital committees that once spent weeks agonizing over which artificial kidney candidates would receive the life-giving treatments, called emodialysis or simply dialysis, now find the decision has been taken out of their hands. "Who gets the care here now is determined purely by ability to pay—we don't like it, but that's the way it is," says Dr. Daniel Leb of the Louisville (Ky.) General Hospital's kidney center, run by the University of Louisville School of Medicine.

Physicians' chagrin over the financial obstacles to the treatment is heightened by the highly advanced state of artificial kidney technology. The prototype of the present artificial kidney machine, which resembles a squat old-fashioned washing machine, was developed in 1943 in Holland by Dr. Willem J. Kolff, who now is a resident of the U.S. The patient is connected to the machine, and his blood is pumped through a series of tubes, coils, and filters.

The key element of the device is a thin cellophane membrane immersed in a saline solution. Through the process of osmosis, wastes in the blood that otherwise would accumulate and cause death pass through the membrane into the solution. At the same time, vital chemicals normally added to the blood by healthy kidneys pass from the solution into the blood. The "cleansed" blood then is returned to the body.

Time finished

(From Jim Hyatt, "The Cost of Living," Wall Street Journal, March 10, 1969. By permission of Dow Jones & Co., Inc.)

Comprehension Test on Passage 1.

Mark each statement either true or false.

1 About 1700 Americans receive artificial kidney treatments.
2 Machine blood washings must be made daily.

3 The life-time cost of treatments with a kidney machine could easily reach a half-million dollars.

4 One can give 40 people artificial legs for the cost of one year's kidney machine treatments.

5 Federal grants continue to support many patients treated with the machine.

6 Private donations to support patients who can't pay their own costs have been meager.

7 Hospital committees still spend weeks agonizing over which artificial kidney candidates should receive the life-giving treatments.

8 Artificial kidney machines provide a treatment called hemolysis.

9 The prototype of the present machine was developed in Belgium by Dr. Daniel Leb.

10 Who gets the care now is determined entirely by ability to pay.

11 Through osmosis wastes in the blood pass through a cellophane membrane.

(The key for scoring the questions above is as follows: (1) T, (2) F, (3) T, (4) F, (5) F, (6) T, (7) F, (8) F, (9) F, (10) T, (11) T.

Passage 2   Starting time

Shock waves are rolling through the U.S. educational community over a frank and startling reappraisal of differences in classroom performance between whites and Negroes.

In a lengthy article, taking up most of the winter issue of the "Harvard Educational Review," one of the nation's leading educational psychologists, Dr. Arthur R. Jensen of the University of California at Berkeley, presents these major findings:

Negro scores averaging about 15 points below the white average on IQ tests must be taken seriously as evidence of genetic differences between the two races in learning patterns.

Research suggests that such a difference would tend to work against Negroes and against the "disadvantaged" generally when it comes to "cognitive" learning—abstract reasoning—which forms the basis for intelligence measurements and for the higher mental skills.

Conversely, Negroes and other "disadvantaged" children tend to do well in tasks involving rote learning—memorizing mainly through repetition—and some other skills, and these aptitudes can be used to help raise their scholastic achievement and job potential.

Unfortunately, big programs of "compensatory" education, now costing taxpayers hundreds of millions of dollars a year, are doomed to failure as long as they pursue old approaches stressing "cognitive" learning.

Pointing to many admissions of failure in huge "compensatory" education programs for the poor, he asked:

"What has gone wrong? In other fields, when bridges do not stand, when aircraft do not fly, when machines do not work, when treatments do not cure . . . one begins to question the basic assumptions, principles, theories, and hypotheses that guide one's efforts. Is it time to follow suit in education?"

A fresh look at the whole problem of inequalities in the classroom must begin with a re-examination of what "intelligence" really is. As developed over the years, the "intelligence test" is a sampling of abilities, oriented toward the middle-class child, by which testers can forecast likely performance in school and in occupational status and job capacities—not precisely, but within a small margin of error.

The crucial ability in this sampling is "cognitive" or "conceptual" learning—the capacity for abstract reasoning and problem-solving through classifying of similarities and dissimilarities.

Can intelligence centering on the "cognitive" factor be raised as much as environmentalists claim? Dr. Jensen's reply is No. Of especial interest are studies of identical twins—those who develop from a single fertilized ovum and therefore have identical genetic endowment. These studies show that such twins, even if reared apart in dissimilar environments, still tend to develop IQ's almost as similar as those of identical twins reared together.

Furthermore, children adopted shortly after birth are far more similar in IQ to their natural parents than to their adoptive parents.

Such studies, Dr. Jensen said, make it clear that "brain mechanisms which are involved in learning are genetically conditioned just as are other structures and functions of the organism." Altogether, heredity accounts for about 80 per cent of those individual variations as against only 20 per cent resulting from environmental influences.

Time finished

(From "Can Negroes Learn the Way Whites Do?", US News and World Report, March 10, 1969. By permission of the publisher.)

Comprehension Test on Passage 2.

Mark each question true or false.

1 Dr. Jensen Brown presented his findings in the Yale Review.
2 Cognitive learning is learning by rote or memorization.
3 Negroes and "disadvantaged" children tend to do well in tasks involving rote learning.
4 Cognitive learning forms the basis for intelligence measurements and for higher mental skills.
5 "Compensatory" education is doomed to failure so long as it pursues old approaches stressing "cognitive" learning.
6 The fact that Negroes average 15 point below whites on IQ tests is largely due to environmental differences.
7 An intelligence test is a sampling of abilities, oriented toward the middle-class child, by which we can forecast school performance and occupational status.
8 The crucial ability in test sampling is ability to learn by rote or memorization.
9 Identical twins, reared apart in dissimilar environments, tend to develop dissimilar IQ's.
10 Children adopted shortly after birth are far more similar in IQ to their natural parents than to their adoptive parents.
11 Heredity accounts for about 80 per cent of individual variations in intelligence as against only 20 per cent resulting from environmental influences.

(The key for scoring the questions above is as follows: (1) F, (2) F, (3) T, (4) T, (5) T, (6) F, (7) T, (8) F, (9) F, (10) T, (11) T.

How to Improve Your Reading

With some knowledge of how your eyes serve you in reading, you are in a position to improve your reading. We shall first give some general guidance for better and faster reading and then prescribe specific things you can do to improve.

Stop Talking to Yourself

Probably the reason many people read word by word is that they first learned to read out loud. Children who are just learning to read do this, and it helps them to get started. Later, of course, they are taught to read silently, but they often do this by talking to themselves. They continue to move their lips when they read and go through all the motions of oral reading without making any noise.

You often can tell whether a person is still talking to himself by whether or not he moves his lips. If he does, it is a sure sign that he is a slow reader; if a person reads at the same rate he talks, he is reading far more slowly than he can and should. Ordinary speech is delivered at a rate of 100 to 125 words a minute. Good readers should read at 200 or more words on difficult textbook material and up to 600 words a minute on easy, storylike material. Nobody can make this speed moving his lips. If you are a lip mover, you've got to get out of the habit.

To develop the ability to read without moving your lips, there are two things you can do: At first, you can place your finger on your lips. This not only tells you when you are moving your lips, thus drawing your attention to your fault, but also acts as a brake on them. It keeps them from moving as they do in talking. The best cure, however, is to practice rapid reading. Try to read so rapidly that there isn't time to move your lips. This advice, admittedly, is a little circular: We want you to stop moving your lips so you can read faster, and we advise you to read faster in order to stop moving your lips. Nevertheless, by deliberately trying to read faster, you can break loose from the lip-moving habit. After you've done that for a while, you'll find you can read faster without its being so much effort.

Read "Thought Units"

Another way to improve your reading is to concentrate on thought units. Though the unit out of which sentences are built is the word, words group themselves together into larger units. These thought units are the more natural units for comprehending the meaning of a sentence, for it is possible to take in each thought unit at a glance.

What is a thought unit? A noun and its modifying adjective. A verb and its qualifying adverb. A prepositional phrase. A relative pronoun and its associated verb. The article together with the noun or adjective it precedes. These are the major thought units in a sentence. For example, in the last sentence, the major thought units might be broken down as follows: "These are—the major—thought units—in a sentence." Each pair or group of words belongs together, and the good reader takes in each group at a glance. You don't have to read every word in that sentence; you can take it in four gulps.

It's not necessary to know precisely what a thought unit is to be able to attend to them. In fact, what it is depends on the difficulty of the material and how familiar you are with it. The first time you read relatively difficult, unfamiliar material, you may have to take it in rather small units. On rereading the same material or on reading something you already are fairly familiar with, you can group more words into each thought unit. A good reader averages close to two words in a unit for difficult material, and three or more for very easy material. We say "averages" because all units are not the same length. Sometimes the unit is only one word, more often it is two, and sometimes it is three or four. The important point is to try to read more than one word at a time and to do it in terms of the natural grouping of words into thought units.

Practice Reading Faster

Getting rid of lip movements and concentrating on thought units will not by themselves get you to read appreciably faster. They'll only help. The only sure way to improve your reading speed is to practice fast reading and to practice it so faithfully and for so long that it becomes an ingrained habit. You cannot practice in fits and starts because you'll relapse, in between, into your old habits. You've got to have a systematic program and one that you do not interrupt until you really have mastered the art.

First of all, you should devote a special period every day to training yourself in fast reading. This can be at any time, so long as you can count on it and don't run the risk

of having other activities interfere with it. We suggest, however, that it be just before you go to bed. This is a time of day you can count on. It's a time, presumably, when you've finished your studying and can concentrate on something else for a while. It's also a good time for doing a little extra, unrequired reading. Figure on spending about a half hour—certainly no less than ten or fifteen minutes—on your practice in fast reading.

At first choose some light materials that are relatively easy, the kind you might do for the fun of it, for example, *Life* magazine or *Reader's Digest*. The latter is particularly good because it contains many short articles, each of which can be read in a few minutes, and because its pages are uniform enough to tell quickly how many words you have read. A full page of *Reader's Digest,* at this writing, usually contains about five hundred words, but you should make allowances for illustrations or other material that is not part of the text. You had also better check this in case *Reader's Digest* subsequently changes the size of its pages, lines, columns, or type face.

Select an article that interests you. Get a watch or clock that has a second hand and note the time to the second when you start reading it. Read as rapidly as you can and still get the meaning of what you read. When you have finished it, note the time again. Subtract the first time from the second, and divide the number of words by this result to get your rate of reading in words per minute; record it in the chart provided for the purpose. To make sure your comprehension hasn't suffered, ask yourself what you have read; then run back through the article to see that you have gotten all the main ideas and important details. If you have missed any of them, you've probably been reading too fast for your *present* reading ability. Don't let this bother you. Keep on trying to read fast. Only try at the same time to concentrate on getting the main ideas and important details.

If you are using *Reader's Digest* or something like it that has rather short articles, you can probably read three or four articles each night. Time yourself on each one, and record your rate in words per minute. Continue doing this each night for a couple of weeks, trying to pick out articles that are about the same in difficulty from night to night. Practicing on easy material is the best way to break away from your old habits of reading everything at the same speed.

After practicing nightly on reading such easy material, you ought to reach some maximum rate of reading speed within a couple of weeks. You'll be able to tell this from the records you keep of your reading rates. This is probably not the best you can do after you have become an accomplished reader, but it is good enough for the time being. Then it is time to start practicing on material that is more difficult, something that is more like the textbooks you study.

At this stage, we suggest you turn to periodicals such as *Saturday Review, The Atlantic* monthly, or *Harper's Magazine*. These contain interesting and informative articles; yet their style of writing is more challenging. The words are bigger, the sentences longer, and the content more complicated. The level of difficulty is more like that of your textbooks. We suggest that you provide yourself with several copies of one of these magazines and continue your nightly exercises by reading articles in them. Count all the words on one typical full column or page of text so you'll know how many words there are on a page. From this you can easily estimate the number of words on other columns and pages broken up with titles or other material. Then continue your reading as you have before, trying to read as rapidly as possible and keeping track of your speed.

At the same time you are carrying on these nightly reading exercises, you should, of course, be trying to read your regular assignments more rapidly. We suggest separate exercises so that you can have a regular time of day to train yourself and so that you can follow a plan of reading material at about the same level of difficulty. The primary purpose, though not the sole purpose, of such exercises is to help you study more effectively. Hence you should waste no time applying your improved reading skills to your regular studies. In fact, in so far as possible, you should consciously attempt to read faster and faster every time you read anything, no matter what it is.

In reading your study assignments faster, remember that reading speed varies a lot with the kind of material you are reading. You should read most rapidly in history, literature, and philosophy—those things that are most storylike and where main ideas are the important things to get. More technical material that is phrased rigorously and contains many important details must be read more slowly. For example, if you are reading directions in a laboratory manual for doing an experiment, you should read the specific step-by-step instructions very slowly, making sure not to miss any detail. You will have to judge for yourself how fast you can go, but you must expect to read different things at different speeds.

Your objective, of course, is to accomplish your reading purpose at the greatest possible speed. That is to say, you must make sure to comprehend what you read and not sacrifice comprehension for speed. If you try to push yourself too fast, you will undoubtedly lose something in comprehension. This is no reason, though, to lapse back into habits of word-by-word reading. You might slow down a trifle because you cannot increase your reading speed all at once. It has to be done gradually, just as a typist or stenographer gradually increases the number of words she can get down. But make sure to go as fast as you possibly can and still comprehend what you are reading. If it turns out that you are going too fast, you can always reread the material again at your top speed to glean what you missed the first time. This will prove a lot more efficient than continuing to trudge along at your old rate.

We should like to insist, in case you have any doubts, that these instructions for reading faster actually do work. It is hard to get data on people who learn by themselves to read faster, for we usually cannot measure them before and after self-training. There are, however, hundreds of cases in which students, after following the advice given here, have reported that they have greatly increased their reading speed, usually by 50 or

100 per cent. In courses that have been given to thousands of college students, business executives, and other persons, nearly everyone has improved some, and the average improvement has come close to doubling the previous reading rate. People in such courses naturally have the advantage of being prodded by the instructor and paced by the course. Yet they still must train themselves. Only by practicing outside the class what they have been instructed to do in class and in books do they actually improve. You can do the same thing!

We should add that there are some fine manuals available for use in improving reading skills. These provide various exercises at different levels of difficulty. Two that can be recommended are *Increasing Reading Efficiency* (rev. ed.) by Lyle L. Miller (Holt, Rinehart & Winston) and *Tactics in Reading* by O. S. Niles et al. (Scott, Foresman and Co.).

RECORD OF PRACTICE IN READING

Use this chart to keep track of your progress in your daily practice in reading faster. For instructions see text (to find reading rate, multiply the number of pages by the number of words per page and then divide by time).

Magazine or book	Pages	Time	Rate

Building a Vocabulary

If you want to be a top-notch student, you must pay attention to another important but sadly neglected matter, your vocabulary. Many tests of students at various levels, including the college level, indicate that good students almost always have a better working vocabulary than poor students. Good students not only can recognize and define more words than poor ones but also can discriminate meanings of words. This helps them read faster because they perceive the meanings of words at a glance, without thinking, and they end up comprehending much more of what they read. Hence part of learning how to study and to read faster is to become a master of the words you read. There are several ways to do this.

Paying Attention to New Words

Look and listen for new words. When you see a new word or encounter one that is only vaguely familiar to you, don't pass it by, thinking you can get along without it. That's not only laziness, it's sheer suicide as far as study is concerned. The meaning of a whole sentence may hang on the new, unfamiliar word. And this may be the sentence with the main idea or an important detail. If that's not true in this case, still the new word may turn up somewhere else as a key word in an idea or detail. And if you are going to read efficiently, you need to know well all the words you read, whether they are key words or not. So cultivate new words. Use them as steppingstones to better reading and understanding.

Using the Dictionary

Once you've spotted a new word, an old word in a new context, or a word you think you know but are not sure of, the first thing to do is look it up in a dictionary. In brief, *get the dictionary habit.* Have a good dictionary handy at all times when you study, and don't be lazy about using it. Once you understand the meaning of a new word, it's part of your personal property and can be yours to understand and use. If you're a poor student, you particularly need to get

the dictionary habit, but good students ought to have it too. Accomplished writers, who probably have a better command of English than most people, usually have half a dozen dictionaries for different purposes within arm's reach. They're always looking up new words and even words they've been using all their lives, simply to sharpen their use of these words for particular purposes.

Vocabulary Cards

One specific technique of learning new words and refining the meaning of familiar words is the use of vocabulary cards. The common index card, 3 by 5 inches, can serve this purpose. Carry some around in your pocket, and when you come on a new word, or a word about whose meaning you have a question, write the word on the index card. It is advisable to write not only the word but also the phrase or sentence in which it is used so that you can know its context. When you do this, underline the word. Then at some convenient time when a dictionary is handy, look up the word and write its definition on the other side of the card.

Keep a batch of cards made out in this way in your pocket or pocketbook. At odd times, even when you are walking down the street, take out the batch and look at the side with the new word. With this as your cue, see if you can rehearse the meaning of the word, then turn to the other side to see whether you are correct. Some people using this system keep tabs on themselves by putting a dot on the corner of a card each time they miss a definition. This warns them to pay particular attention to the words they have trouble with.

General vs. Technical Terms

In building your vocabulary this way, however, you must bear in mind the difference between general words and technical words. General words are most commonly found in literature and history and in newspapers and magazines to describe and interpret things of general interest. They're in the dictionary. Technical words are those used to express concepts, laws, and the special meanings of a particular subject. You'll find plenty of

WHAT YOU CAN LEARN FROM A DICTIONARY

Here is a reproduction of the entry for "memory" in Webster's New Collegiate Dictionary. Besides giving pronunciation, the entry gives part of speech (n. = noun) and etymology (OF. = Old French; fr. L = from Latin), then a series of definitions, and finally under synonyms (Syn.) a number of words with meanings that are similar to, but not identical with, those of "memory." Reading and studying carefully this one entry can teach the correct use of a half dozen words. (By permission. From Webster's New Collegiate Dictionary, copyright 1960, 1961, 1963, 1965, by G. & C. Merriam Company.)

mem·o·ry /'mem-(ə-)rē/ *n* [ME *memorie*, fr. MF *memoire*, fr. L *memoria*, fr. *memor* mindful; akin to OE *mimorian* to remember, L *mora* delay, Gk *mermera* care, Skt *smarati* he remembers] **1 a** : the power or process of reproducing or recalling what has been learned and retained esp. through associative mechanisms **b** : persistent modification of structure or behavior resulting from an organism's activity or experience **c** : the store of things learned and retained as evidenced by recall and recognition **2 a** : commemorative remembrance **b** : the fact or condition of being remembered **3 a** : a particular act of recall or recollection **b** : an image or impression of someone or something remembered **c** : the time within which past events can be or are remembered **4** : a component in an electronic computing machine into which information can be inserted, stored, and extracted when needed

syn REMEMBRANCE, RECOLLECTION, REMINISCENCE; MEMORY applies both to the power of remembering and to what is remembered; REMEMBRANCE applies to the act of remembering or the fact of being remembered; RECOLLECTION adds an implication of consciously bringing back to mind often with some effort; REMINISCENCE suggests the recalling of incidents, experience, or feelings from a remote past

---

them in natural sciences like biology, chemistry, and physics but also a good many in other subjects, including literature, languages, history, and the social sciences. You won't find most technical words in your ordinary desk dictionary, at least not until they have become so prominent and important in everyday affairs that they should be known by any educated person. (Then they become general words.) Of course, you will be able to look up a great many more technical terms in an *unabridged* dictionary—a book that has a lot of diverse information other than that pertaining strictly to definitions—but the size and cost of such a book usually make it more suitable for the library than for a student's desk.

Textbook writers are supposed to give you a definition of a technical word when they first introduce it. That's one way of finding out what they mean. Sometimes the writer forgets to do that, or he assumes you already know it because you are supposed to have had it in your previous preparation. Or perhaps he did and you missed it, only to run into the word later in the book. In any of these cases, first try the book's glossary if it has one; if not, use the book's index, looking for the word and the subentry under it called "definition" or, in lieu of that, any extended discussion of the particular word.

If this doesn't get you a good definition of the word, try one of your more elementary textbooks in the same subject, again using the index to find the word. If you're still unenlightened, try any special dictionary in the subject. There are one or more dictionaries for almost all technical subjects, and you usually can find them in your library by looking up the subject, for example, psychology, chemistry, or economics, and then scanning the cards for "dictionary" or by doing the reverse, looking first for "dictionary" and then for the subject.

Some textbooks have a glossary in the back. This is a dictionary of important terms used in the book. Don't neglect it. The author went to a lot of trouble to prepare it just so you could easily find the correct definitions of the technical terms used in the book.

The importance to effective study of learning technical terms cannot be stressed too much. In some courses, half or more of the subject matter is either a matter of technical terms or can be mastered by knowing these terms. Topnotch students almost always have some way of listing and studying such terms. Sometimes they have a separate place in their notebooks just to enter technical terms as they are encountered in the course. Sometimes they merely underline the words in their notes. However they do it, they make sure to have a pretty complete list of the terms, to know their meanings, and then to review them systematically before an examination. You should do that too.

Dissecting Words

You can do much to develop your mastery of word meanings by paying attention to the structure of words and their history. The English language, and particularly the part of it derived from Latin, is built of certain elements. There are compounded in various ways to make the words we now use. In general, the elements are of three kinds: prefixes, suffixes, and roots. Each of these has a meaning that runs through all the words in which it is used. If you know Latin (and this is one of the best reasons for knowing it), you can translate each element into English, put the elements together, and have a pretty good idea of what the word means. Even without a knowledge of Latin, the meanings of the elements are constant enough for you to learn from the English alone.

In a separate table, we have given some of the more common prefixes and suffixes. Study the meaning of these, and then when you encounter a new word, try to figure it out from your knowledge of these prefixes and suffixes. We have also provided a brief list of fairly common root words. If you can recognize the prefixes and suffixes, you can pull the word apart and bare the root word. This, you'll find, is usually familiar to you. Then you can put the three meanings together to obtain the "translation" of the whole word. We should warn you, though, that this process doesn't always give you the precise meaning of words. That often has been modified through usage. Translating the elements only helps you fix the meaning of the word or to make sense of it in terms of how it came about historically.

COMMON PREFIXES AND SUFFIXES

The following prefixes and suffixes occur frequently in English words. All are listed and defined in Webster's New Collegiate Dictionary and in many other dictionaries. You can help yourself build a bigger vocabulary by looking up their meanings and writing them in the space provided.

Prefixes	Meaning
ab-, abs-, a-	
ad-, a-, at-, ap-	
be-	
bi-	
co-, com-, con-	
de-	
dis-	
en-	
in-, il-, im-, ir-	
non-	
per-	
pre-	
pro-	
re-	
sub-	
un-	

Suffixes
-able, -ible, -ble
-al
-ance
-ent
-est
-ful
-ing
-ion
-ity
-ive
-ize
-less
-ment
-ous

To illustrate the way root words and prefixes and suffixes in various combinations account for a great many words, we have taken the Latin word *mitte,* which means send, and given a list of words that represent some of these combinations. In this list are most of the prefixes and suffixes given in the table. We have chosen only examples. If you take all possible combinations, more than a hundred familiar words can be made from the one root word. These various words apply to many different phases of life—religion, business, radiation, war, education, and government. You can do the same thing with any other root word in the list. There are in fact more than ten thousand relatively common English words that have as their parts the prefixes, suffixes, and roots listed here. By studying the meanings and uses of these components, you can make some pretty good inferences about the meanings of the words in which they are combined.

One way to understand better how words are derived from components is to use an historical or etymological dictionary. This

SOME COMMON LATIN AND GREEK ROOTS

The accompanying list, consisting of ten Latin verbs and two Greek words, provides roots for 2,500 or more English words. (After S. Stephenson Smith, The Command of Words, Crowell, New York, 1935, p. 67.)

Root word	Meaning
capio	take, seize
duco	lead
facio	do, make
fero	bear, carry
grapho	write
logos	word, speech, knowledge, thought
mitto	send
plico	fold
pono	place
tendo	stretch
teneo	hold, have
specio	observe, see

is a dictionary that breaks words down into their elements, much as we have described in the process above, and then shows you the original meanings of these elements. Such a dictionary also frequently tells you when the word was first used in the English language and what it meant at that time. A good example of such a dictionary is the *Oxford Universal Dictionary.* If you are not familiar with it, you'll probably find one in your college or local library. Spend a half hour with it, looking up any words that interest you. You'll be surprised at how interesting it is, for every word has a history and a story behind it. You'll enjoy learning about them while you make progress building your vocabulary.

---

mitte—send

admissable
commitment
committee
dismissal
emission
emissary
missile
missive
mission
missing
permissive
promissory
remittance
submit

chapter 5
STUDYING TEXTBOOKS

Let us assume that you have read the four preceding chapters and have done as much as you can to carry out the advice given there. You have worked out a schedule, found a good place to study, and are in good physical shape to do it. You thoroughly understand the plan of the course you are taking, have set up a notebook in a format suited to the course, and have begun to take lecture notes. You have tested yourself on your reading ability and have a definite program laid out for improving your reading speed and vocabulary.

You have obtained promptly a copy of the textbook designated by the instructor, you have it at your library table or desk with all the other materials you will need, including a notebook and writing implements, and you are now ready to proceed with the reading of the assignments in your textbook. Now your problem is how to make the best possible use of the time you have allotted for this study so that you will have learned the important things and bypassed the trivial, and remembered what you study. Let us now consider the best way to go about studying your textbook.

As a disclaimer at the outset, we must point out that every student has his own approach and his own techniques. Two different students, each outstanding, will often go about studying the same material in somewhat different ways. That is to be expected, for different techniques are suited to different people. There are, nevertheless, general rules for effective study of books. People who are good at studying make use of these rules, in one way or another, whether or not they realize it. They will differ mainly in their individual styles and in the degree to which they rely on different rules.

What are these rules? One way of phrasing them simply has been worked out at Ohio State University in an elaborate program for analyzing and treating student's academic problems. In this program, the essential rules are condensed into the following formula: *Survey Q3R* or merely *SQ3R*. Say this over to yourself a few times in order to commit it to memory because it is a good slogan for carrying out a course of effective study.

This phrase is a way of summarizing five specific steps in effective study:

- Survey
- Question
- Read
- Recite
- Review

The *Survey Q3R* program has been soundly tested. It has been shown to describe not only what good students do but to be a safe guide for improving enormously the work that all students, good and poor, can do. This chapter will consider in detail each of its five steps.

Before we go on, however, we should point out that some experts have developed variants of this program. One authority (Miller), an expert in reading and study, speaks of the *SQ4R* program. His wrinkle is an extra *R* inserted between Recite and Review. This *R* stand for Repeat, and refers to repeating steps two, three, and four for each section of a chapter studied. This is merely a matter of emphasizing that the first and last steps refer to the chapter as a whole, while the middle steps are taken a section at a time.

Another expert, Professor Walter Pauk, who directs the Reading Study Center at Cornell University, speaks of the OK4R system. These stand for Overview, Key Ideas, Read, Recall (Recite), Reflect, and Review. His Overview means the same thing as our Survey. His *K* for looking for Key Ideas is a way of emphasizing what one looks for in reading, and we shall consider his advice on this point under the heading of "Read." In his scheme, he puts relatively less emphasis on questioning while one is reading and more on reflecting on what has been read. But this is a matter of emphasis rather than any basic difference in philosophy. Indeed, those who have done research on study methods and who have had extensive experience with helping students improve their study methods are in surprisingly close agreement. They all arrive at just about the same prescription. Hence, although you might find a somewhat different outline if you read another book on how to study, the advice will be about the same.

Survey

The first of the five main steps is the *survey* (or getting an overview). In this step you should get the best possible over-all picture of what you are going to study before you study it in any detail. Such a perspective is important in study for the same reason that people consult maps before they drive unfamiliar roads, that expert golf players want to walk around a new course before they actually play it, or that a road builder makes a detailed survey of the terrain before he starts the construction of a road. In each case, the person wants to know what he is going to run into before he starts; he needs to know the general picture before he can make intelligent decisions about the details.

Surveying a Book
Surveying a book must proceed in steps, from big ones to little ones. When you first pick up a book, a good thing to do is to survey the whole book. Start the survey by reading the preface, for in it the author quickly gives you an idea of why he wrote the book and what he will attempt to do in it. By reading what the author has to say, you can find out what kind of book it is and whom it is for and not for. It may even tell you what preparation and knowledge is required for reading the book. In any case, the preface usually gives some clear picture of what is to come.

Next in any book comes the table of contents. Look at it, go through it slowly and thoughtfully, find out from it as much as you can about what the book contains. Moreover, you should do this repeatedly as you progress through the course. The farther you read in the book the more meaningful the table of contents becomes.

To conclude your survey of the book as a whole, there are two further things to do. One is to leaf through it, and the other is to read the summaries of the chapters (if there are summaries). In two or three hours you can turn every page of a substantial textbook, glancing at the headings and reading occasional sentences under them. And it is well worth the trouble since it gives you a feel for the book and an understanding of its over-all organization. If your book has summaries, read them all as part of your initial survey of the book. The bird's-eye view you obtain in this way is of incalculable value.

Surveying a Chapter
Now let's turn from the initial survey to what you do when you sit down to read an assigned chapter. You should survey the chapter, but more carefully than you've done for the book, and this time with an eye especially on the headings.

When most authors write textbooks, they go to some pains to organize their words under various headings. In fact, the time they spend planning their headings, putting them in the right places, and phrasing them so that they will tell as much as possible is often a good chunk of the time they spend in writing. They do this partly so the student can know what to expect as he reads—in other words, survey—and partly to make later reviewing much easier. In most textbooks you will find scarcely a page without a heading on it.

Yet many students ignore the headings and try to read textbooks the way they would novels. When they do that, they ignore much of the author's careful work, and more important, they throw away the most significant and useful clues to the contents of the book.

One important precept, then, is *use the headings*. They give you the author's organization, they tell you how the material is put together, and they make it clear how topics go together and follow each other. Most important, they make it clear what the main subject of each section is going to be. When you finish reading a section, you should have located certain points that bear on the heading. Anything else in the section will be secondary or relatively unimportant.

You should also pay attention to the *order of headings*. Most textbooks use two or three orders. This one, for example, has two: main headings on separate lines and run-in side headings. There are two or more side headings under each main heading, and this arrangement tells you what topics are subordinate to the main topics. In many textbooks, there is still another (lower) order of heading, indicated by a different kind of type, usually italic. These indicate sub-subheadings under the subheadings, which in turn come under the main headings. Note the kinds of heading used, for they are the key to the structure of the subject you are studying.

We have told you in detail about headings because you must use them at several stages in the study process. You use them in making a general, initial survey of the book, and then you go over them again as part of your detailed survey of an assigned chapter. The first thing to do, in picking up a textbook to read a chapter, is to run through the headings in the chapter. In this way, you learn generally what the chapter is about and know what to expect. It is also a good idea to skim some of the sentences here and there in the chapter and to look at some of the pictures and charts.

In addition, if there is a summary, read this as part of your chapter survey. It will give you the most important points of the chapter before details begin to clutter up the picture.

This concludes what we have to say about the survey step in *Survey Q 3R* methods. We have dwelt on it and emphasized it for two reasons: First of all, we know from experience and systematic research that most students do not do enough surveying. They have acquired habits of plunging into the woods without first getting a map of the footpaths in it. Secondly, we know that survey methods pay great dividends. In several programs in which thousands of students have been taught to use survey methods, the students have made remarkable gains, by actual measurement, in their ability to comprehend and learn new material.

Question

The *Q* in *Survey Q 3R* means question, and it emphasizes the importance of asking questions for learning. Most things worth remembering in textbooks or in life, more generally, are answers to some sort of question. Moreover, people seem to remember what they learn in answer to a question better than things just read or memorized.

Questions help learning because they make us think about what it is we want to know about what we are reading or studying. They give a purpose to our learning. A person with a question is a person with a purpose. The answers to our own questions make an impression on us because they make what we are studying more meaningful to us, and we always remember something better when it means something very specific to us.

Your Questions

If you make use of the question technique in reading this book, you should already have a number of them about this section: Why does the author have a heading about questions? What do questions have to do with studying? What good are questions? How can I use them in studying? Whose questions? Where do they come from? How do I know when they are answered? These are some of the questions you might have asked by now. Some of them are already partly answered, and if you keep them in mind, you will find that the rest will be answered shortly.

Who asks the questions? The best source is yourself. You are the one who is

THE USE OF QUESTIONS

Here is a sample paragraph from a textbook (Clifford T. Morgan and R. A. King, Introduction to Psychology, 3rd ed., McGraw-Hill Book Company, New York, 1966, p. 44). The kinds of questions you would want to ask about this material are written in.

What is intelligence?
How is it measured?
What does I.Q. mean?
How is it inherited?

Intelligence is a general term covering a person's aptitudes in a wide range of tasks involving vocabulary, numbers, problem solving, concepts, and so on. It is measured by standardized tests, which usually involve several specific aptitudes, often with emphasis on verbal aptitudes. A test score on an intelligence test can be converted into an intelligence quotient, or IQ, which indicates the individual's relative standing in the population independently of his age. Since an intelligence quotient reflects several aptitudes, not just one, and each of these is itself fairly complex, we should expect that the inheritance of intelligence would be multiply determined; that is, it would depend on many genes rather than on one or two pairs.

Here is another passage from the same source (p. 49). Try writing your own questions. See how they compare with the questions listed below.

The endocrine glands mature slowly. This may be explained in part by the fact that the supply of hormones furnished to the fetus by the mother makes it unnecessary for the fetus to secrete its own. Then, too, many of the hormones of the endocrine glands are not needed until later in life. The sex glands are a good example of endocrine glands which mature late. They do not mature until puberty, when boys and girls at the age of twelve or thirteen begin taking on the characteristics of men and women. Some of the changes that take place then, such as the growth of the beard and change of voice in boys and the development of the breasts in girls, are brought about by sex hormones. So, too, are changes in sexual motivation and the emergence of patterns of sexual behavior. This connection has been established in experiments with many different kinds of young animals by injecting sex hormones into them and noting the appearance of sexual behavior at a considerably younger age than that at which it would otherwise appear. This is just one kind of evidence that the schedule of maturation of sexual behavior is controlled by the maturation of the sex glands.

YOUR QUESTIONS

The following are the sorts of questions you can ask in studying the passage above.

What are endocrine glands?
How do they mature?
Why?
Example?
What effects do hormones have?
How do we know?

---

trying to learn and who will be helped by asking them. Every time you see a heading, questions should come rushing to mind. At the very least, you should ask what the word or phrase means. If you know its dictionary definition, you should be curious about its meaning in the present context.

Now you might be asking yourself a new question, "I know I'm supposed to be asking questions, but I'm not used to doing that. How do I acquire the skill?" The answer to this one, like answers to so many such questions, is "It takes practice." Knowing that questions are aids to study, you should begin working at the technique in everything you study. At first, to emphasize the method, you might write down questions when you survey a chapter, as you are running through the headings and skimming the topic sentences of paragraphs. This is laborious and too time-consuming to be done as a regular thing, but it might get you off the ground. When you have cultivated the questioning frame of mind, you may simply think your questions out to yourself as you survey and later as you read the chapter. Eventually, the art of asking questions becomes so ingrained that you don't have to stop to formulate them. They flood in as you read along; as they get answered, the answers raise new questions without your consciously trying to ask them.

The Author's Questions

You can secure some help in acquiring questioning skills from textbooks and workbooks. Authors occasionally ask questions as part of their teaching technique and in some cases start off each chapter with a list of questions to be answered in the body of the chapter. Be alert to them and use them. In some textbooks, authors have listed questions at the end of each chapter. Such questions are usually the most neglected part of a textbook, for students do not realize their value in studying. You should read them as part of your survey of a chapter, then again after you have finished reading it. Used in this way, the questions help you study the chapter, providing a means of testing yourself. If you test yourself before the instructor does, you do much better when faced with a formal examination.

Now stop for a second. In starting to read this section, did you pause to ask questions? What are author's questions? Are they in the book? Where? Where are the answers?

Nowadays many textbooks are accompanied by student workbooks which the student can obtain and use separately. Very frequently the workbook contains several kinds of questions, some to be used in studying and in reviewing and others that are samples of the kind of examination you can expect to take. When such questions are available, make the fullest possible use of them. Faster learning, more fun studying, and better grades are practically guaranteed!

Read

The next part of *Survey Q 3R* is to read. This is the part too many students put first, for they mistakenly think that studying is mostly a matter of running their eyes over the textbook. The book is, of course, to be read, but this is neither the first, last, nor even necessarily the most important part of studying. It's only the trip through the woods made after the terrain has been surveyed and the path mapped out by questions. It enables one to mark the big trees and the points of interest so that they can easily be found later when the trip is made more hurriedly (review) or be pointed out to someone else (recitation and examination).

Read Actively

When you read for studying, do not read passively as you would an adventure novel. Such novels are for entertainment, and they are written without any concern for whether you remember the details. Most textbooks, on the other hand, have structures that must be explored. You can't just walk through them; you must be alert to your surroundings every step of the way. To avoid passive reading, read to answer the questions you have asked yourself or the questions the instructor or author has asked. As you go along, keep challenging yourself to make sure that you understand what you read.

Every once in a while, remind yourself of your task: to understand and remember what you read. If you do, you will no longer voice the familiar complaint "I forget what I read as soon as I am through."

Some of the really important novels, incidentally, deserve the same kind of reading that textbooks do, even though some of the specific recommendations for avoiding passive reading that you will find in this section will not apply to reading novels and stories.

Read for Main Ideas and Important Details

At this point, we should remind you of the discussion of the purposes of reading in the preceding chapter. Of the several possible purposes in reading considered there, two are particularly important in studying a textbook. One is to read for main ideas, the other to read for extracting important details. Rather than repeat ourselves, we suggest that you go back and see whether you can recall what was said there.

Note Important Terms

Notice especially any words or phrases that are italicized. Authors use these, like headings, to emphasize important terms, concepts, and principles. They are a warning to stop and take heed—that here is something more important than the rest the author is saying. Say these terms to yourself a few times. Make sure you know how to spell them (instructors get a little impatient with students who can't spell even the important words). Then make sure you note and understand what is said about them.

Read Everything

When you read, too, read *everything*. That means tables, graphs, and other illustrations as well as the main text. They are there for a purpose, not just to make the page attractive or to fill up space. Textbook writers never have enough space to cover all they want to say, and when they use their precious space for tables and illustrations, they think these will teach better than words. They actually will if you use them. Sometimes a mere glance at an illustration will tell vividly what a whole page of the book is about. In other cases, illustrations convey information that cannot be expressed easily in words, no matter how many of them were used. Remember the old adage "A picture is worth a thousand words"? Sometimes this is very true, and the same is true of tables. Although tables are not so easy to grasp as pictures, they tell a story if you only take the trouble to read and compare carefully the different columns in the table.

Recite

Recitation is an old, well-established way of learning and of examining. Before books were invented and in areas of the world where books are still scarce, it is the heart of learning. The teacher says something to his pupils and then asks them questions about

what they have learned. They recite their answers. Oral recitation is a particularly handy teaching device when something must be learned by rote. We've probably all done it at one time or another in the lower grades of public school memorizing the multiplication table, in learning the catechism of a church, or even in learning foreign languages in college.

Value of Recitation

What most students don't realize, however, is that recitation is also an effective device for learning while reading a book. So long as you just read a book, you have the comfort of thinking that you understand and can remember what you read. It is an unpleasant fact, as you no doubt have discovered at one time or another, that you do not necessarily remember all you feel you easily understand and remember. And the only way you can really find out what you remember is to recite to yourself. Because recitation can reveal your ignorance to yourself, it is one of several reasons why recitation is such an effective study method.

To make certain that you understand and remember, you should stop periodically and try to recall to yourself what you have read. This is recitation. At this point, for example, you might ask yourself what you have read so far in this chapter. Try to recall the main headings and the principal ideas under each heading. Can you give a synopsis of your reading without looking at the pages? Try to do it; then check yourself. See whether you have covered everything. If not, note your omissions and errors. Then a little later, recite again.

The general rule, then, is as follows: As you read, stop at intervals to recite the substance of each major section of a chapter. When you review for examinations, again make recitation a substantial part of your study procedure.

Don't think, though, that this is merely a good but rather incidental rule. Recitation can make all the difference in the world in how much you remember. If you read a prose passage such as this straight through, the chances are that you will remember *when you finish* no more than 50 per cent of the points made in it. The forgetting process has been going on even while you were reading. It continues, of course, to do its destructive work, and a day later you remember no more than 25 or 30 per cent. After that, memory fades more slowly, for there is less to lose, but at the end of two weeks you will probably remember no more than 10 per cent.

VALUE OF RECITATION

Each solid line represents the forgetting of a group of high-school students. All groups read the same material, but each group had different opportunities to recite what it had learned. The numbers indicate the number of recitations each group had. The top solid line, for example, represents a group that had three recitations, one immediately after learning, a second seven days later, and a third one sixty-three days later. (*Redrawn from H. F. Spitzer, "Studies in Retention," Journal of Educational Psychology, Vol. 30, pp 641-656, 1939.*)

This is the course of forgetting when you don't recite. The actual percentage retained depends on how much you read, what kind of material it was, and on individual differences in memory ability. The percentages given above, however, were the ones actually obtained in a study of several thousand high-school students who were given tests to measure how much they remembered at different times after reading passages of prose. Some of the groups in this study, however, were "recitation groups." They recited what they could remember from their reading, two groups immediately after reading (one of these recited twice) and other groups at later times. When they were tested three weeks later, the group with two recitations immediately after studying remembered 80 per cent of what it knew when it finished reading, but a group with no intervening recitation knew only a sixth as much. Another way of stating these results: The no-recitation group forgot more in one day than the recitation group did in sixty-three days! This difference was produced by a relatively brief recitation immediately after reading.

How Much Recitation?

How much time should you spend on recitation? This depends on what it is you are studying. If what you are learning is disconnected and not too meaningful, recitation should run as high as 90 or 95 per cent of your study time. If, for example, you have to learn a number of rules, items, names, laws, or formulas, then recitation will be your principal form of study. On the other hand, for well-organized, storylike material, such as one may find in history or

THE INTERPRETATION OF GRAPHS

The above graph is fairly complicated as graphs go, and for that reason makes a good exercise in the study and interpretation of graphs. Here are some questions you might ask and answer in studying the graph. Write down your answers.

1. How much was retained after one reading of the material?

2. What does the dotted line represent?

3. When does recitation do the most good? When does it do practically no good?
4. What is the general shape of a curve of forgetting? How does recitation change it?

59

philosophy, less recitation is needed. In this case, recitation might be no more than 20 or 30 per cent of the study time. For textbooks in psychology, economics, political science, and the like, something of the order of 50 per cent is a good estimate, though even in these subjects books can vary quite a bit in "meaningfulness."

This you can be sure of: The time spent in recitation pays off. In one study, for example, students who spent up to 80 per cent of their time on recitation did better than people who spent the same time reading without reciting. You can also be sure that time spent in recitation actually saves time. The amount you remember by reciting is so great that you don't have to spend nearly so much time later in rereading the material and in reviewing it for an examination.

When to Recite

When should you recite? To wait until you have finished a chapter is usually to wait too long. You are already too hazy about the chapter's contents. Forgetting has taken its toll. On the other hand, stopping to recite after every paragraph or two may break up the material into too many disconnected pieces. For most prose like this, the section set off by a heading is probably the best unit. Each time you see a new heading come up, stop and recite the material in the section you have just finished. Do this for each side heading; then double up when you come to a main heading.

Besides improving your memory and saving time, recitation has other benefits: One is that it serves to keep your attention on your task. While you are merely reading, you may attend with only "half a mind" and even find your eyes moving along without learning anything. On the other hand, you certainly can't daydream while you are trying to recall something. In the second place, recitation lets you correct mistakes. It shows you where you missed something or where you misunderstood it. If you make notes of these mistakes when you recite, you know what points give your memory or understanding the most trouble. You can

then concentrate on these when you later reread or review the material.

Review

The fifth and final precept of *Survey Q 3R* is review. We don't need to emphasize this because most students do review, especially before an examination. Many of them even review things they haven't read before! There are a few comments worth making, however, about what review is and when it should be done.

Survey

Review isn't, of course, really very different from the other things that have gone before! In fact, it is all of them put together. A review is, first of all, a survey. Only it is a survey of what one is supposed to have done, rather than what he is going to do! It is done in much the same way as the original survey except that it can be combined with other steps in *Survey Q 3R*. When you now skim over the headings of the book, you can ask yourself what they mean and what they have under them. Under each of the headings, you can recite the points that you have previously read and that you hope you remember.

Rereading

You should reread enough to check yourself and see either that you haven't left anything out or that your memory is refreshed. The same is true when you now review the summaries. Instead of reading them as you did originally, you now see if you can recite them, and then you check yourself by rereading to see how well you know what is in the summaries. In reviewing, you will also go over notes you have taken on the book and on classroom work. (We haven't said anything yet about taking notes because we have reserved that for page 62.)

Timing of Reviews

If you have followed well the first four precepts under *Survey Q 3R,* you won't have much trouble knowing what to do when you review. You may not know, however, just when you should review and how often you should review. At least, most students don't. They review at the wrong times, and they don't review enough. They usually wait until they are face to face with an examination before they do their reviewing. That's a good time for a final review, but not for the first review.

The first time to review is immediately after you have studied something. For example, after you have read a chapter, reciting between each of its sections, you should immediately go back and review it. This means trying to recite the important points of the whole chapter and rereading as necessary to check yourself. It also means reading over and then reciting the notes you have made on it (see Chapter Five). This first review may be fairly brief, for there has been little time for forgetting; and as we have implied, it should be mainly one of recitation.

It will pay you, though, to have one or two reviews between this first review and the final review for an examination. These intervening reviews usually should emphasize rereading more than recitation. They are to remind you of some of the fine points or examples that go along with the main points you have in your notes and, presumably, in your head.

The final review, the one just before an examination, should, like the first review, emphasize recitation. It should be more intensive—and usually is. In this, you go over all you are responsible for on the examination, paying special attention to the earlier material, which has had more of a chance to fade away. But plan your time so that you review *all* the material, and don't run out of time when you are about half through. It should go without saying, too, though many students need to be reminded of it, that reviewing should not be crammed into the last few hours before an examination. This practice makes the final task too hard. And it never gives you at the time of the examination the mastery you could have with a few well-spaced reviews.

The five steps in *Survey Q 3R* have been tried with thousands of college students in how-to-study programs. Students who have learned them and applied them have improved their grades—sometimes enormously—and have found satisfaction in study that they never knew before. You can too, even if you are already a fairly good student!

There are different ways of balancing the *Survey Q 3R* methods for your particular courses. French takes a different approach than physics, and English a different combination than psychology. In later chapters we'll come to some of the problems of studying such different subjects.

Underlining and Outlining Textbooks

We have assumed in presenting the *Survey Q3R* program of studying a textbook that you would be doing some *combination* of underlining your textbook and making notes in a notebook along with your reading. In fact, in the end such underlining and note-taking is the final product of the program. Only with it can the student find an effective way to recite and review. We have, however, put off the question of note-taking to this separate section, for it needs a coherent discussion not intermixed with the steps in reading the textbook.

Underlining

The typical practice of the poor student is to sit down with a chapter in front of him, read away rather listlessly, and then, when he thinks he sees something important, put a line under the prominent words.

He does this without surveying the chapter or asking questions. The result is a hit-or-miss selection of passages, one that represents what interests the student most or seems to him, without any very good basis for judging, to be important. Unfortunately, he is then stuck with what he's done. He thinks he has underscored the important points and uses them later as he studies for an examination. He will have missed many of the really important points and selected others that aren't. In reviewing he doesn't think to check his underlining to see whether it is right; and even if he does, he finds it unfeasible to erase lines and put in others, especially if he has underlined in ink, as so many students foolishly do. When he comes to the examination relying on his poor underlining, he's studied many of the wrong things.

Incidentally, the fact that so many students underline too indiscriminately and in ink is important to consider in buying a used textbook. If you are buying a secondhand book, insist on getting one that has not been underlined; otherwise, buy a new one, for the handicap of someone else's distracting and misleading underlining is far too serious to be worth the small amount you save by purchasing a used book.

Now, as we said, underlining has its place, but it must be done wisely, at the right time, and according to a plan. The plan is this: First you must survey a chapter, and then you ask yourself questions about it and try to answer these questions as you read. In this first reading, it is best not to underline. As your questions are answered or as you think you spot main ideas and important details, put a check mark or a bracket in the margin next to the seemingly important lines. The next time you read, read for *main ideas* and *important details* and for *technical* terms. It is these you want to underline.

Even on the second, careful reading, don't underline the sentences as you read them. Underline only after you have read one or two paragraphs at a time. Then go back and decide exactly what it is you are going to underline. As a guide, use the check marks or brackets that you made previously. If these now don't seem like the most important points, feel free to change your mind. In any case, select with care what you underline only after you have read all the surrounding sentences.

Then don't underline sentences wholesale. Many of the words in the sentences that contain the main idea or important detail are, as we said earlier, relatively unimportant. Decide which these are and leave them out. Underline only the individual words and phrases that are essential. Underline words so that, when you

go back later at reviewing time, you can read merely the underlined words and comprehend immediately the ideas, important details, and definitions.

If you follow these rules in underlining, you probably won't underline as much and as unnecessarily as many students do. On the average, a half dozen or so words per paragraph will do the trick, though the amount certainly depends on the nature of the material. You will also have underlined the best set of words, and you won't find yourself in an examination having "studied the wrong things." Underline lightly. A book heavy with underlining is hard to read and sometimes confusing. A light thin line made with a hard pencil will do.

Why Take Notes?

For most subjects, though possibly not for all of them, you should also take separate notes in outline form of the material in your textbook. There are several good reasons for taking such notes:

In the first place, it forces you to participate actively in the learning process. If you try to write down briefly what the author says, you can't help but make it part of your own mental processes. You can't fool yourself about knowing what you've read. You've got to find the structure of his discourse and pick out the main ideas and important details. And you must learn them—at least temporarily—to get them down on paper. Hence the chances of your remembering what you read are increased manyfold.

A great deal of research, incidentally, proves that we all remember much better the things we actively do than those that we merely experience. That's why recitation is so valuable an aid to study. In fact, taking notes is one way of forcing oneself to recite.

A second important reason for taking notes on reading assignments is that it makes reviewing so much easier and more effective. If you carefully outline a chapter, you reduce to three or four pages what covers twenty or thirty in the book. Now you've got it without all the extra words the author

UNDERLINING A TEXTBOOK

The following passage illustrates the use of underlining to pick out the main points in a series of paragraphs (from C. R. McConnell, Economics: Principles, Problems, and Policies, 3rd ed., McGraw-Hill Book Company, New York, 1966, p. 47.

Extensive Use of Capital Goods

All modern economies—whether they approximate the capitalist, socialist, or communist ideology—are based upon an advanced technology and the extensive use of capital goods. Under pure capitalism it is competition, coupled with freedom of choice and the desire to further one's self-interest, which provides the means for achieving a rapid rate of technological advance. The capitalistic framework is felt to be highly effective in harnessing incentives to develop new products and improved techniques of production. Why? Because the monetary rewards derived therefrom accrue directly to the innovator. Pure capitalism therefore presupposes the extensive use and rapid development of complex capital goods: tools, machinery, large-scale factories, and storage, transportation, and marketing facilities.

Why are the existence of an advanced technology and the extensive use of capital goods important? Because the most direct method of producing a product is usually the least efficient.[2] Even Robinson Crusoe avoided the inefficiencies of direct production in favor of "roundabout production." It would be ridiculous for a farmer—even a backyard farmer—to go at production with his bare hands. Obviously, it pays huge dividends in terms of a more efficient and, therefore, a more abundant output to fashion tools of production, that is, capital equipment, to aid in the productive process. The best way of getting water out of a well is not to dive in after it!

But there is a catch involved. As we recall our discussion of the production possibilities curve and the basic nature of the economizing problem, it is evident that, with full employment and full production, resources must be diverted from the production of consumer goods in order to be used

[2] Remember that consumer goods satisfy wants directly, while capital goods do so indirectly through the more efficient production of consumer goods.

in the production of capital goods. We must currently tighten our belts as consumers to free resources for the production of capital goods which will increase productive efficiency and permit us to have a greater output of consumer goods at some future date. The Russian citizenry, for example, has paid for an accelerated rate of industrialization in terms of a standard of living below that which might have otherwise prevailed.

Specialization

The extent to which society relies upon specialization is astounding. The vast majority of consumers produce virtually none of the goods and services they consume and, conversely, consume little or nothing of what they produce. The hammer-shop laborer who spends his life stamping out parts for jet engines may never "consume" an airplane trip. The assembly-line worker who devotes eight hours a day to the installation of windows in Chevrolets may not own a car, or if he does, it may be a Ford. Few households seriously consider any extensive production of their own good, shelter, and clothing. Many a farmer sells his milk to the local creamery and then buys oleomargarine at the Podunk general store. Society learned long ago that self-sufficiency breeds inefficiency. The Jack-of-all-trades may be a very colorful individual, but he is certainly lacking in efficiency.

In what specific ways might human specialization—the division of labor—enhance productive efficiency? First, specialization permits individuals to take advantage of existing differences in their abilities and skills. If caveman A is strong, swift afoot, and accurate with a spear, and caveman B is weak and slow, but patient, this distribution of talents can be most efficiently utilized by making A a hunter and B a fisherman. Second, even if the abilities of A and B are identical, specialization may prove to be advantageous. Why? Because by devoting all his time to a single task, the

used merely to illustrate or explain his points. If your outline is a good one, most of your review can be simply a matter of making sure you know what is in it. And since you wrote it, the chances that you do know it or can quickly relearn it are good. Then the underlining you've done in the book serves to fill in details and to give you the correct phrasing of the points you have in your notes. Any rereading you do at that point is just to refresh your memory or make clear what your notes mean. You won't get lost in the woods and fail to see the trees.

Methods of Outlining

What is the best way to outline? How do you go about outlining? The very first job in outlining is to pick out the structure of the author's outline. If he has used headings liberally, as many textbook writers do, you can get the skeleton of your outline from these headings. Remember, though, that most headings in textbooks are not sentences; they're just a few key words. They're what we call *topical* headings: the kind a person uses who already knows, and knows very well, what he is going to say. The notes an instructor uses for lectures are probably of this kind, for all he needs is a few words to remind him of what he wants to say next.

A student, on the other hand, must use headings to learn and to remember things not just to remind himself of things he already knows. It is advisable, then, for the student to make sentences out of the textbook headings. Having found the main idea of the section under a heading, he should rewrite the heading so that it contains this main idea. Some students with excellent memories manage to get along without doing this; but unless you know you are one of the few who can, you had better use a sentence structure, not merely topics, in making your outlines.

Once you understand the author's order of headings and can supply more of your own, you should indicate this order in your notes by two simple devices. One is to indent one order under another. The highest order of heading starts at your left margin, the next order is indented under that, the next under that, and so on. Don't indent either too much or too little. If you indent too much, you'll find you often don't have enough space left on a line for writing out your notes. If you indent too little, you won't be able to tell what is indented and you'll get confused about the order of headings. The best amount of indention is two or three letters, or about half an inch.

The other way of indicating structure in your outline is to use a consistent system of lettering and numbering the different orders. There are two or three different ways of doing this, and if you already have one that you use consistently, there is no need to change it. If you don't, we suggest that you use Roman numerals (I, II, III, . . .) for the highest-order headings, capital letters (*A, B, C,* . . .) for the second order, Arabic numerals (1, 2, 3, . . .) for the third order, and lower-case letters (*a, b, c,* . . .) for the fourth order. If you need additional orders, you can use parentheses around Arabic numerals, for example, (1), for the next order, and parentheses around lower-case letters, for example, (*a*), for an even lower order.

If you consistently use both indention and such a system of lettering and numbering, you'll have nicely structured outlines in which the relationship of things to each other is easy to see at a glance.

Content of Notes

What do you put into your notes? We've already said that topical headings should be rephrased to include the main ideas of the sections they head. Beyond that, you should include main ideas and important details at each level of the outline. One system that we recommend is to construct your outline from main ideas at different levels and then add after each main idea, either as additional sentences or in parentheses, whatever important details are relevant. Definitions, which are very important details, can also be inserted in parentheses after you've stated the main idea. Sometimes, of course, a definition *is* the main idea and should be outlined accordingly.

We add one general warning: Write legibly enough to be able to read your notes many days after you've written them. Even people who have a good hand get in such a hurry when they take notes that they later can't read their own scrawl. There's no advantage to hurrying at the sacrifice of legibility, for legible notes are so valuable to you later that the time you take to make them so is fully repaid. If your writing is hard to read anyway (unfortunately this is the case with far too many students), make a special effort to improve it when you take textbook notes. Perhaps by practicing at this time you may learn to write well enough for

OUTLINING A CHAPTER

Here is an outline of Chapter Four. It illustrates the general form in which
outlines of chapters (or lectures) should be written.
Source: How to Study, Chapter Four, Reading Better and Better.

Date: October 15

Most college students do not read efficiently because they have one or more of the following faults:

1. Lip moving or vocalizing
2. Stopping for unfamiliar words
3. Reading word by word
4. Reading everything at the same rate
5. Backtracking and rereading.

Their reading efficiency can be improved by making use of the following facts and principles:

I. All material should be read at any particular time with a specific purpose in mind.
A. Skimming tells one what something is about.
   1. Skim to survey a book
   2. Skim material that you do not need to know in detail.
B. Read to get the main idea.
   1. Find main ideas by looking at paragraphs as units.
   2. The main idea is usually part of a sentence.
   3. Usually qualifiers can be neglected.
   4. In some kinds of writing, often in literature, the main idea is not made explicit by the author.
   5. Finding the main ideas is essential to outlining.
C. Read to extract important details.
   1. Important details are usually facts that form the basis for main ideas.
   2. In factual textbooks, there are usually one or more important details associated with each main idea.
D. Occasionally, you may have other purposes in reading.
   1. One is to find answers to specific questions.
   2. Another is to evaluate material critically, especially in the case of controversial writing that has a point of view.
   3. Another purpose is to apply what you read to your own personal life and problems.

II. How one uses his eyes is important to efficient reading.
A. You perceive words only when your eyes pause in between their movements from one place to the next.
B. The number of words you see at each pause is your recognition span.
   1. Poor readers take in one word per pause; good readers perceive several words at a time.
   2. Reading can be improved by enlarging recognition span.
C. Reading can be speeded by shortening pause time.
D. In efficient reading, the reader reads straight ahead without backtracking.

III. Both reading speed and comprehension can be improved in the following ways:
A. Stop reading to yourself.
   1. Good readers read much faster than they can talk.
   2. To stop talking to yourself, put your fingers on your lips, and practice fast reading.
B. Read "thought units."
   1. A thought unit is a noun and its modifying adjective, a verb and its qualifiers, a prepositional phrase, a relative pronoun and its associated verb, etc.
   2. Good readers average two words to a unit for difficult material, three or more for easy material.
C. Practice reading faster.
   1. Devote a special period each day to training yourself in fast reading.
   2. At first, choose light materials, then progress to more difficult reading.
   3. Time yourself, and keep a record of your progress in reading faster.
   4. Try not to sacrifice comprehension as you increase your speed.
   5. While you are carrying on these exercises, try to read your regular assignments faster, remembering that reading speed should vary with the kind of material studied.
   6. Make use of manuals that have been prepared for the purpose of training people to read faster.

IV. Reading speed and comprehension are improved by building a better vocabulary. To do this:
A. Pay attention to new words.
B. Use the dictionary.
C. Use vocabulary cards for reciting the meaning of new words.
D. Distinguish between general words encountered in history, literature, and general reading which may be found in a dictionary, and technical terms encountered in the sciences that are defined in textbooks or specialized encyclopedias.
E. Dissect the words you meet.
   1. English words are compounded from prefixes, roots, and suffixes.
   2. By learning the meaning of the prefixes, roots, and suffixes, you can frequently infer the meaning of unfamiliar words.
   3. An etymological dictionary, which indicates the elements from which a word is derived, can help you learn the history of words and from that gain a clearer idea of their meaning.

the instructor to read your writing; you would be surprised to know how many grade points that is worth.

Making outlined notes of textbook material will help you understand what you read and then to know it when examination time comes. There are some kinds of material however, for which you should not make outlines. You don't do this, obviously, for some stages in learning a foreign language, especially where the job is to learn vocabulary or for the exact translation of a passage. Some textbooks, particularly in the physical sciences, are already in outline form, and it is hardly worth your while to copy an outline from a book. In such cases, you will use techniques other than outlining. We shall describe some for the study of foreign languages in a later chapter. Where the book is already practically an outline, you'll do better to emphasize good underlining and to put a lot of emphasis on recitation rather than on outlining.

Format of Notes

In the chapter on *classroom learning*, we have suggested several ways of making a format for keeping lecture notes. The same general advice holds for note-taking from textbooks. If the instructor is "teaching" the textbook, your notebook should have a format that provides for lecture notes and textbook notes to be parallel with each other. In this case, we emphasize that you almost always should read and outline the textbook material before going to lecture. Then the lecture notes will be a matter of emphasizing what is already in the textbook notes plus any new material introduced in the lecture.

In most lectures, the lectures are different enough from the textbook that the student should keep a separate set of notes for his notebook. Even so, there will be some relation, and the student will do well to read the textbook before the lecturer covers corresponding material. But in this case, a 2-6 format will be appropriate for most textbooks. The 6-inch column should be used for the outline we have described above.

Because the student can construct this outline at leisure, having surveyed and read in advance, his textbook notes should be much better organized and have a better proportion of main ideas and important details than lecture notes. The 2-inch column at the left can be reserved for clues to be used in reviewing. It can contain a topic outline of key words that can be used to test whether or not the student knows what he has put into his outline. In some instances, the 2-5-1 format will be appropriate. These will be cases in which the notes form a highly condensed summary of many details. Here the separate column on the right will permit the student to write more general ideas or summarizing statements than are contained in the outline.

Writing Summaries

There are other instances in which you should take notes but not necessarily in outline form. Often, when reading literature, for example, you are not reading for a number of specific points. Rather, you want a synopsis, or summary, or even an interpretation of what you've read. In this case, your best method of taking notes is to jot down important points as you go along; then at the end you can compose a summary that tells the gist of the story. Consider what interpretation the author is trying to convey about the story he tells. There are many ways of telling a story (see Three Ways to Summarize a Story). Why does the author tell it in the way he does? Is he trying to convey a feel or atmosphere? Is he ironic? Why is he ironic?

There's another occasion too for writing summaries. This is in the case of textbooks that have no summaries at the end of the chapters. Some authors, in fact, do not provide summaries because they think the student will profit most by constructing his own even though he loses the benefit of a summary in surveying the chapter. Hence if your textbook doesn't have summaries, take advantage of the opportunity to learn something by writing your own.

Don't try to write the summary until you've first outlined the material. Then,

THREE WAYS TO SUMMARIZE A STORY

Here is an account of the same event told in three different ways. Notice how they differ in order, style, and content.

The Newspaper Story

The family of Mr. and Mrs. John Doe of Millvale Road miraculously escaped injury and possible death last night when the frantic barking of the family dog aroused Mr. Doe. A fire had broken out in the basement, filling the house with smoke and fumes. The family escaped through a second-story porch window. James Doe, 8, and Jane Doe, 10, were treated for smoke inhalation at City Hospital. The fire is believed to have started in a defective furnace motor. The interior of the house suffered considerable damage.

The Insurance Adjustor's Report

The residence at 210 Millvale Road, owned by John and Mary Doe, insured under Policy No. 218956, suffered damages from fire and water incidental to smothering the fire on the evening of 15 June 1957. Damages to the premises, furnishings, and personal apparel insured under the above Policy are appended in Report A. The statement as a result of investigation by the Fire Inspector of the City of Springdale established the origin of the fire as a short circuit in the blower motor of the oil furnace, under service contract held by the Springdale Fuel Company. A detailed report of the condition of the motor is appended in Report B. No personal injuries resulted either due to fire or action of the fire department.

Mrs. Doe's Letter to Her Mother

Dear Mother,

A terrible thing happened last night. Our house caught on fire! Everybody is safe, and the insurance adjustor tells us the damages are completely covered by our policy. We lost a lot of valuable things, of course, but we thank heaven no one was hurt. We all have Skippy to thank. He woke us up by whining just as the smoke was getting very bad upstairs. We all got out just in time; I think we would have suffocated if we had been much longer. As you can imagine, we are all tired and upset. I'll write details tomorrow.

Love,

Mary

These versions say somewhat different things, but they also differ in style and individual words. The newspaper account uses words like "miraculously" and starts right out with the rescue by the family dog (dramatized a little by the substitution of "barking" for "whining," which would have been more accurate). The prosaic insurance adjustor mentions first the address and the policy number and then soberly recites the facts of interest to his company. The letter is informal and not well organized; it stresses the personal feelings and condition of the family rather than the facts.

---

after reviewing the outline and using it as a guide, write a series of paragraphs, usually no more than one or two pages long, summarizing the chapter. You'll probably make out best if you let each paragraph stand for a major item in your outline. The main idea of a section, in fact, can be your topic sentence. The other sentences in the paragraph can then be the main ideas of the subsections under the main section. Writing such an outline is one form of recitation and has all the attendant benefits we have described. It is also good practice for writing essay-type examinations, where you must organize succinctly the main points on a question or topic.

A SUMMARY

To illustrate the writing of summaries, we give below a summary of Chapter Four, Reading Better and Faster. Compare the statements in this summary with the headings and main ideas of the chapter. Also, by referring to the sample outline on page 65, note in what ways a summary differs from an outline.

Most college students cannot read well; they take too much time and don't learn what they should. By heeding the following points, however, they usually can enormously improve both their speed and their comprehension.

All reading should be done with certain purposes in mind: (1) One is to get the main idea of each paragraph, subsection, and main section. (2) Another is to select important details; these are statements that explain, prove, illustrate, or exemplify the main ideas. Other purposes are (3) to answer questions raised by teacher, author, and student himself, (4) to evaluate the reading in terms of what the reader otherwise knows and believes, and (5) to apply the reading to one's daily life and to his general understanding of the world.

When a person reads, he moves his eyes along in quick jerks with stops in between; all perception occurs during the stops. In order to manage his eyes most efficiently, there are three things to do: (1) increase his recognition span by taking in two or three words at a time, not just one; (2) try not to dally so long on each pause, cutting stopping time to a minimum; (3) keep his eyes moving forward all the time, never letting them wander backward along the line. He should also make sure either that his eyes are good or that he has the proper corrective glasses.

To improve further his effectiveness in reading, he should practice the following things: (1) reading without moving his lips, for lip moving holds reading rate down to a quarter of what it should be; (2) learning to read in thought units—the natural grouping of words into phrases of two, three, or four words; (3) practicing reading faster by devoting a special period every day to reading exercises, starting out with easy materials and progressing to more difficult materials and keeping a record of his progress in these exercises; (4) in trying to read faster, however, making sure that he comprehends what he reads—comprehension should never be sacrificed for reading speed.

The ability to read rapidly and to remember what is read depends to a great extent on vocabulary. You should constantly strive to build up your vocabulary by stressing the following: (1) Always look and listen for new words—unfamiliar words or words whose meanings are hazy–and look them up in a dictionary. (2) Make a point of using new words at the next opportunity in studying, talking, or writing. Pay special attention to technical terms in textbooks, noting their definitions when they first appear and looking them up in glossaries, dictionaries, or other textbooks. (3) Dissect words into their component prefixes, suffixes, and roots; where possible, look up their history to see how they are derived from French, Latin, Greek, or other languages.

SUMMARIZING A CHAPTER

To practice what we have been teaching, the time to recite what you have read in this chapter is now. Take a piece of paper and write a synopsis of the chapter. Make it in outline form with plenty of space between the lines. When you have written down all you can recall, run back through the chapter and see what you have left out or not gotten quite right. Then make the appropriate additions and corrections in your synopsis.

chapter 6
TAKING EXAMINATIONS

Having read the title of this chapter, you may say, "Ah, that's what I want to know: how to take examinations." You may even harbor the hope that we know some way to pass an examination without studying for it. That's a bit of magic, however, that no psychologist has yet produced. Nor should he, for the basic purpose of examinations is to measure how effectively you've studied beforehand. If you have already done the things we've outlined to improve your studying habits, you've done most of what is necessary to be ready for examinations. Still, there are a number of pointers that we can give you to bring you to top efficiency in taking examinations.

Preparing for Examinations

The only good general rule for taking examinations is "Be prepared." This means being prepared for the kind and scope of examination you are to take and for all the questions you may be asked, not just some of them. It means having a thorough mastery of your subject matter, not a hazy acquaintance with it, and having it so well organized that you can tap it in any way that is called for. It means being rested, emotionally stable and calm, and in the pink of mental condition. Let's look into these matters in more detail.

The Final Review
If you've done your studying as you should, preparing for an examination is largely a matter of review. You review the notes you've taken in class and on the textbook, the main ideas and important details you've underlined in the textbook, and lists of technical words you've acquired as you study. This review should be more intensive than any you've done since you reviewed right after first studying the material. It should,

however, be a review and not an attempt to learn things that you should have learned earlier. If just before the examination you are still reading material for the first time and making notes on it, you're already seriously handicapped. You'll be trying to do too many different things at once and in too short a time. Though you *might* be bright enough to scrape through by doing things this way, you'll certainly do a lot better if you've already done your reading and note-taking and need only to review.

In some subjects, you may want at this time to make some new notes, especially for the purposes of review. If you have a lot of material to cover and have a great many notes, you can make a set of summary notes in three or four pages that will extract the essence of your more detailed material. In constructing these summary notes, you distill the most important ideas and details from your other notes, referring to the book occasionally to check on a point. You end up with a summary of a summary. In this way, you can make sure of the very important points, you then have something to run over before examination, and you obtain the advantages of additional recitation.

Scheduling Reviews
Contrary to what most students do, or think they should do, the period of review before an examination need not be long. For weekly quizzes, it need be no longer than a few minutes; for a midterm hour exam, only two or three hours; and for a final exam, five to eight hours. That's assuming, of course, that all you need to do is review. The periods of reviewing, moreover, should be pretty short, an hour or an hour and a half, interspersed with periods of rest or recreation. If you work too hard at reviewing a lot of material, you'll get confused and actually remember less than if you follow a less strenuous schedule.

SCHEDULE FOR PERIOD OF FINAL EXAMINATIONS

When you know your schedule of final examinations, enter it in the chart.
After that, enter specific subjects you will review in the hours available.
Again, however, make sure to leave time enough for meals and recreation.

Time \ Day						
8:00						
9:00						
10:00						
11:00						
12:00						
1:00						
2:00						
3:00						
4:00						
5:00						
6:00						
7:00						
8:00						
9:00						
10:00						

You should plan definite periods for review in your study schedule just as you schedule your regular hours of study. Find out as early as you can when a quiz or examination is to be given. Then make out a slight revision of your study schedule for the week or two before the examination, writing down particular hours for review. Try not to disturb the hours you'll need to keep up with regular studying for your other subjects. Instead, set aside some of the hours regularly assigned to the particular subject and some of the "optional" hours in your schedule. In addition, you may, if necessary, take a few hours otherwise devoted to recreation, but don't cut into them too deeply.

They're necessary to keep you in good shape and to keep you from overdoing the reviewing.

This brings us to another subject on which many students need advice: In the long run, it does not pay to go without food, sleep, and a reasonable amount of recreation to cram for examinations. Staying up half the night or even all night may seem like the thing to do when you're behind in your work, but you pay (and pay dearly) for it. In the first place, you don't have all your wits about you in an examination; you can't organize material or recall it as well on a written examination, and you're not so sharp in discriminating the right and wrong answers

SCHEDULE OF REVIEW FOR FINAL EXAMINATIONS

Plan carefully the time devoted to review for final examinations. Enter the days of the week in the spaces at the top of the columns. Then write in the squares the specific subjects you plan to study each hour of the day. Leave a reasonable time, however, for meals and recreation.

Day / Time						
8:00						
9:00						
10:00						
11:00						
12:00						
1:00						
2:00						
3:00						
4:00						
5:00						
6:00						
7:00						
8:00						
9:00						
10:00						

of an objective test. You also must make up later for your lost sleep, with the result that you break up your schedule of work, cut classes, and fall behind in your other work. The whole thing becomes a vicious circle. Once you start cramming for examinations, letting other studies and your sleep get shortchanged, you have to do it more and more and never get out of the circle.

Of course it is the fashion to talk about how much cramming you did, to boast about how little sleep you got and how you lived on coffee and booster pills. Most students do more bragging than cramming, but the fact is that any amount of such frantic, helter-skelter studying is inef-

ficient and harmful. Take the boasting of your fellow students with a bit of skepticism, and organize your own life to be cool, collected, and efficient.

You should therefore do everything possible to live a normal life during times of preparation for examinations. Get your meals, sleep, and recreation and do other studying on schedule. You can and should work a little harder than usual, but don't let it throw everything out of gear. If you've done a reasonable amount of reviewing, a good night's sleep will net you more points on an examination than staying up late trying to learn a little more. In fact, the best advice for reviewing is to review two or three hours the day before, take the evening off, and get to bed early.

How to Review

In reviewing for an examination, you should keep rereading to a minimum. Rather, your review should emphasize recitation. In reviewing a chapter, try to recall the main ideas of the chapter without referring to your notes. Then check your recollections against your notes. Under each main heading of the chapter, do the same thing again; try to recall the points under this heading, then check. If there is something you have difficulty recalling or something you don't quite understand, go back to your textbook and reread the passage covering it. That's about all the rereading you should do. If you attempt to do much more than that, you spend so much time rereading that you lose sight of the important points or you skip around so aimlessly that it does you little good.

Another bit of advice is good if you follow it completely; otherwise, it may mislead you. This is to *predict* questions you may be asked on the examination. Ask yourself as you review: "Is this something that could be a question?" "Has this been emphasized?" "How could a question be asked on this topic?" Also take advantage of the clues furnished by instructors. Most of them give some hints directly or indirectly about specific questions they are likely to ask. Such hints may be found in the importance an instructor attaches to certain points he makes or in the time he dwells on a particular topic. They may be contained in advice he gives about studying for the examination.

One way or another, you should be able to spot a great many questions that subsequently appear on the examination. Since you've predicted them, you've rehearsed for them, and you're ready for them. Later, after the examination, if it is not a final, you can study the questions you failed to predict and use your misses as a guide for predicting questions on future examinations.

We must emphasize, however, that this advice can be misleading if you carry it out in the wrong way, that is, trying to outguess the instructor on the questions he'll ask and then studying only the things you think he'll ask. One variation of this faulty approach is to study only the things that appeared on examinations the term or two before. If you thus limit yourself to the few items you guess will be asked, you may luckily hit on some of them, but most of the time you'll miss enough to pull your grade down several notches. Very few instructors are oblivious to this guessing game. Most work pretty hard to ask questions that are not easily anticipated. Therefore, when you predict questions you will be asked, predict all that could be asked, not just a few you hope or guess will be asked. Otherwise you may be saying those famous last words, "I studied the wrong things."

Types of Examination

Generally speaking, the examinations you'll take in college fall roughly into one of two categories: One is the *objective* examination. This doesn't require you to write anything. All you have to do is decide whether certain statements are true or false, which of several statements is true, or how statements should be matched. Such an examination stresses your ability to *recognize* correct answers, not your ability to recall or organize answers. The other type of examination is the *essay* examination. In this, you must *recall* what you have learned. You are asked a question and must then choose and organize the material you consider to answer it best. In other cases, such as mathematics and physics, you may be given problems to solve. Like essays, problems stress your ability to recall, rather than recognize, information. In between, of course, are other possibilities such as the completion test, in which you merely fill in a word, a phrase, or a brief statement. Again, though these don't emphasize ability to organize a lot of information, they do stress recall.

Should you study differently for these different kinds of examination? The answer is both "yes" and "no." You should prepare somewhat differently for each type but not so differently as many students think. Objective examinations seem easier because they require you only to select (or guess at) the right answer. Consequently, students often don't study as hard for them as for essay examinations. It is just as difficult, however, to make good grades on one type of examination as on the other for the simple reason that all students have the same advantages or disadvantages. On the average, therefore, a student ends up in the same relative position—and thus usually with about the same grade—on one examination as on the other.

Students also feel that objective examinations tend to emphasize details more than essay examinations do. This feeling, however, is largely an illusion. It's due to the fact that the detailed statements of an objective examination stare them in the face, but the student taking an essay examination rarely realizes just how many details he should have known to write a good examination. If you feel that objective examinations tend to cover trivial points, compare the next such examination you take with the headings and important points in your textbook and notes. You'll find they correspond pretty well, and it is these points you *should* know if you're organizing an essay question. Actually, in both types of examinations, the instructor is trying to test your knowledge of main ideas and important details. You should therefore study these regardless of the type of examination.

The principal difference between the two types is not so much one of details as one of *organization.* You simply don't have a chance to organize your knowledge in an objective examination, and you do on the essay test. Thus it is perfectly clear that you must give more attention to organization when you prepare for an essay test. This means somewhat more recitation to enable you to recall in outline form what you know. On the other hand, don't neglect organization entirely when you study for an objective test. Some of the questions will be so phrased that they will test your knowledge and understanding of the relationships between various parts of the material.

There is no question but that the objective examination puts a higher premium on recognition than on recall. Our memories are such that we all can recognize many things we cannot recall. This fact leads to the conclusion that, in studying for an objective examination, we should try to be ready to recognize points that we wouldn't be called upon to recall in an essay examination. This means that the final review before an objective examination should include more rereading of the text and, particularly, of notes and somewhat less recitation than are appropriate for an essay examination.

Although there are these differences, we must emphasize that you should not go to extremes in your preparation. All reviews should include some rereading and some recitation. You only do a little more of one than the other for one kind of examination. All reviews too should stress knowledge of the main ideas and important details.

Attitude toward Examinations

In a moment we will discuss the specifics of taking examinations, but first we ought to say something about emotions and attitudes regarding examinations.

Students tend to think of examinations as being among the trials of life, ordeals that can't be escaped and must somehow be survived. They look forward to tests with fear and trembling and often are terribly upset both before and during an examination. This negative, fearful attitude is unfortunately reinforced by the fact that grades depend on exams. The student who is not doing very well can easily feel that the exam is an ax poised to cut him down and out of the academic life.

There is really no need, in most cases, for taking this attitude toward examinations. If one has cultivated good study habits, he should do well enough to have no fear of "flunking out," and he should approach an exam with an air of confidence and anticipation. The examination, after all, gives him a chance to show how much he knows and to receive his reward for the studying he has been doing. The examinations that come early in a course are opportunities to learn something about one's preparation and to correct any deficiencies in it. By profiting from them, the student is in a much better position to study effectively for the final examination and to do well on it. Instead of considering the instructor who gives many quizzes an ogre, the student should be grateful that the instructor is willing to spend so much of his time helping his students learn.

One of the nasty things about examinations is that students frequently "blow up" and get so tense and unnerved that they do much less than their best. They forget things they knew just a little while before, make silly mistakes, and lose all sense of what is important and unimportant.

Probably the best medicine for this disease is to be prepared. If you go into an examination prepared as well as you can ever expect to be, you don't need to get upset. You'll do your best, and that's that!

This point has an important psychological sidelight. Many a student does not realize that going to pieces during an examination is frequently an alibi he has given himself. He blows up not only because he isn't prepared and knows he isn't prepared but also because he then doesn't need to feel guilty about not being prepared. Test anxiety is often a childish defense the student puts up against taking the blame for his own lack of preparation.

Besides being well prepared, there are a few other things you can do to quell your excitement or anxious feelings. One is to allow yourself plenty of time to do what you need to do before the exam and still get there a little ahead of the bell. Don't let yourself get in a rush; this merely aggravates your excitement and further disorganizes you. A second thing to do is to relax deliberately just before the examination and while you are waiting for it to be handed out. Don't try to do a last-minute review, skimming through your notes or your book. Don't get into arguments with other students about some fine point in your notes; this merely upsets you. Remember you can't do anything worthwhile in such a short time; all you can do by hectic, last-minute reviewing is confuse yourself with details and get yourself more excited. Rather, spend the few minutes just before an examination in small talk, reading the newspaper, or doing something that takes your mind off the "ordeal."

The last and most important thing you can do to keep yourself in hand is to have a plan of attack. It has been demonstrated over and over again in emergencies that people who know what to do and what they are going to do seldom get upset or panicky. The same applies to examinations. You probably know about what kind of examination to expect. There's a good sensible way to go about taking each kind. Know what it is, and be prepared to carry out your plan as soon as you get the signal to go ahead. We're going to describe these plans below. The important point, though, is that with a definite plan in mind you can keep calm and collected and thereby do yourself justice.

Taking Objective Examinations

Your plan in taking an objective examination is somewhat different from what it would be in taking an essay-type examination.

Surveying
When you pick up an objective test, first flip through the pages to see how many different kinds of question are being used: true-false, multiple-choice, matching, . . . ? See how many there are of each, and thus get an idea of how to divide your time during the examination. Usually, when the instructor uses more than one type of objective question, he segregates those of one type into one part, and this part is clearly labeled. By surveying the parts at the outset, you know what they are and thus what to expect.

Knowing the Ground Rules
Now begin taking the first part. It will have some directions. Read these carefully, and make sure you understand them. (You'd surprised how many students don't.) Indicate your answers in exactly the way specified in the directions. If you don't, you may cause the instructor a lot of trouble and,

more important, lose points merely because your answers aren't clear to the instructor.

Also when you tackle the questions in each part of the examination, make sure you understand the scoring rules, for these determine your strategy in taking the test. If there is no penalty for guessing, note that fact, and then proceed with the intention of answering every single question. Otherwise you are bound to lose points by leaving some questions unanswered. If there is correction for chance, note that rule. In a true-false test, for example, you have a 50:50 chance of getting an answer correct simply by guessing. To correct for chance, an instructor may take a point off for a wrong answer and give only one point credit for a correct answer. (One formula for doing this is to score papers by taking the number right minus the number wrong.) This really isn't a penalty for guessing; it's merely a correction for chance. In such a case, your strategy should still be to guess and consequently to answer every question, for on the average your guesses will be more often right than wrong. On the other hand, if the scoring rule is to make a definite penalty for guessing, say, by taking two points off for a wrong answer while giving only one point credit for a correct one, then you must follow a conservative strategy. You should then answer only the questions of which you are reasonably sure.

The same principles apply to other types of objective examination. It is possible to score them so that there is no penalty for guessing or so that there is. The formula is usually too complicated to explain easily in an examination. Hence the instructor usually reduces it to a simple direction such as: "There is no penalty for guessing" or "Don't guess, for wrong answers will be penalized." Whatever the instruction, understand it and follow it carefully.

Answering Easy Questions First

Having gotten your instructions straight, you can proceed to read and answer questions. You must be prepared, however, to find some questions that are easy *for you* and others that are difficult. You must handle these questions differently. Those that are relatively easy you answer as soon as you've read them carefully and are sure of the answer. Those that you find more difficult and aren't certain about should be checked and passed by. Don't let them bog you down. If you struggle with them, you may waste precious time and later find yourself rushing through other questions, making mistakes on those you otherwise could get right. Instead, any time you are not certain you know the answer, put a check mark in the margin next to the question. After you've answered all the easy ones, you can come back to these. Knowing how much time you have left and how many tough ones there are, you can properly apportion the time available to spend on them.

The basic reason for this strategy is simple enough. In objective examinations, all the questions of the same kind usually count the same. You get no more credit for a difficult question than you do an easy one. You therefore don't want to become flustered by difficult ones or let them lower your score on the easy ones. We know from experience that this plan of taking objective questions can net a good many points; yet many students haven't learned it.

Analyzing Qualifiers

There is an art to reading and deciding on the correct answer to objective questions, and you can improve your examination results by learning it and practicing it. The following points should help you to do your best on objective questions:

True-false questions are usually constructed by taking two things or qualities and stating their relation to each other. The bare skeleton of the statement might be "Roses are red," "Attitudes are learned," or "The stock market crashed." Any such statement is usually true some of the time and not true at other times. You can't be expected to answer anything so ambiguous. The instructor never intended that you should. He is interested in knowing whether you know when and under what circumstances something is or is not true. So the statement usually is provided with qualifiers,

EXERCISE IN KEY WORDS

The following quiz (from Clifford T. Morgan, Introduction to Psychology, McGraw-Hill, New York, 1961, p. 2), specifically designed both for students who have had a course in psychology and for those who have not, illustrates the importance of key words in objective questions. Take the quiz, picking out the key words and writing them in the space provided. In most cases, there is only one key word, but in a few instances, there are two or three. Also indicate in the right-hand column whether you think the statement is true or false. When you are finished, look below for the correct answers.

1. Geniuses are usually queerer than people of average intelligence.
2. Only human beings, not animals, have the capacity to think.
3. Much of human behavior is instinctive.
4. Slow learners remember what they learn better than fast learners.
5. Intelligent people form most of their opinions by logical reasoning.
6. A psychologist is a person who is trained to psychoanalyze people.
7. You can size up a person very well in an interview.
8. When one is working for several hours, it is better to take a few long rests than several short ones.
9. The study of mathematics exercises the mind so that a person can think more logically in other subjects.
10. Grades in college have little to do with success in business careers.
11. Alcohol, taken in small amounts, is a stimulant.
12. There is a clear distinction between the normal person and one who is mentally ill.
13. Prejudices are mainly due to lack of information.
14. Competition among people is characteristic of most human societies.
15. The feature of a job that is most important to employees is the pay they get for their work.
16. It is possible to classify people very well into introverts and extroverts.
17. Punishment is usually the best way of eliminating undesirable behavior in children.
18. By watching closely a person's expression, you can tell quite well the emotion he is experiencing.
19. The higher one sets his goals in life, the more he is sure to accomplish and the happier he will be.
20. If a person is honest with you, he usually can tell you what his motives are.

ANSWERS FOR EXERCISE IN KEY WORDS

The key words for each question were as follows: (1) usually, (2) only, not, (3) much, (4) better, (5) most, (6) psychoanalyze, (7) very well, (8) better, (9) in other subjects, (10) little, (11) stimulant, (12) clear, (13) mainly, (14) most, (15) most important, (16) very well, (17) usually, best, (18) quite well, (19) sure, happier, (20) usually. All the statements are false. The reasons for their being false can be found in the book from which they were taken or, very likely, in any general course in psychology.

and it's these qualifiers you should scrutinize carefully. Remember that in Chapter Four (page 34) we told you to retain essential qualifiers when you select main ideas and important details.

There are, of course, an infinite number of possible qualifiers, but a good many of them fall into one of the following series:

All, most, some, no
Always, usually, sometimes, never
Great, much, little, no
More, equal, less
Good, bad
Is, is not

If you run into a qualifier in one of these series or a qualifier that means essentially the same as one of these, your best way of testing whether the statement is true is to see whether you can substitute one of the other members in the series. If your substitution makes a statement that is better than the one you have, the question is false. If your substitution does not make a better statement, the question is true. Let's for example, take "Some roses are red." The alternative statements are "All roses are red," "Most roses are red," and "No roses are red." The two extreme statements are obviously less true. You may have doubts whether "Most roses are red" is true; but even if it is true, "Some roses are red" would also have to be true.

Picking out Key Words

This way of analyzing qualifiers should be helpful in examinations even though real questions are naturally more complicated than these examples. It won't always work, but whether it does or not, it should help you find the *key* word or words in a statement. And there is always such a key. It may not be an adjective or adverb, but it will be a word or group of words on which the truth or falsity of the statement hinges. All the other words in the statement could form a statement that is either true or false depending on the key word(s). Look for this and don't worry about the possible exceptions to the other words in the statement.

Some students have picked up the idea that certain words automatically make a statement true or false. They know that it is difficult to construct true statements with such words as "no," "never," "every," or other sweeping qualifiers. They therefore mark such statements false whenever they occur. This is a dangerous practice, however, for instructors are just as aware of any giveaways as students are—usually more so. Consequently, they usually steer clear of statements that can be answered correctly by taking a cue from these simple extreme modifiers. On the other hand, they can sometimes construct statements containing these words that are, in fact, true. In some cases, especially in the natural sciences, blunt unqualified statements are true. Such statements will catch (and they properly should) the student who isn't judging them on their merits.

The best true-false questions usually are one-clause statements, but occasionally they may be constructed in two clauses. Then they are really two statements, not one. If you encounter such a question, judge each of the two statements separately. If one of them is false, even if the other seems true, mark the question false. Usually, though, both statements are either true or false.

Reading Multiple-choice Questions

Multiple-choice questions are basically true-false questions arranged in groups. A lead phrase or clause at the beginning of the question combines with three or more endings to make different statements. Sometimes the questions are so constructed that any number of the statements in a question can be true or false. Then the question is really several true-false statements, and all that we have said above applies. Make sure, however, to read directions carefully so that you can answer the questions as they are supposed to be answered.

Most typically, the multiple-choice question differs from the true-false item in that only one alternative out of the group is to be selected. Hence your job is to pick the alternative that is *more nearly true* than the others. It's a relative matter, not one of absolute truth or falsity. This fact dictates certain tactics in dealing with the question.

Read carefully through the question once and spot those alternatives that are clearly false. To help dispose of them, you can cross out the letter or number that precedes these false statements. Now concentrate on those that may be true. Read them again, note and test the key words as you would in a true-false statement, and compare the items to see which seems to be the more nearly true. Once you've made a decision, mark the answer in the appropriate space and go on to the next question. If you can't make up your mind, place a check mark at the side of the question and leave it until you can come back later to work on the more difficult questions.

Reading Other Types of Question

Similar methods are applicable to *matching questions*. Read down all the items to be matched in one question in order to get an idea of the range of possibilities you're up against. Then take the first item on the left and read down the items on the right until you find one you're sure is the best match. If you're not certain, leave the item and go on to the next one. The general idea is to fill in first all the matches you are sure of. That then reduces the number of possibilities for the difficult matches and simplifies the job. Some matching questions consist only of words or brief phrases to be matched. Others may contain whole clauses similar to those in true-false or multiple-choice statements. In this latter case, try to spot key words and test them as we have suggested above for true-false and multiple-choice questions.

One type of question used fairly commonly in large courses is the *completion question*. This provides a statement much like a true-false statement except that one word or a phrase is left out and you must supply it. When you answer such questions, choose your words carefully, for the instructor has something pretty specific in mind: a technical term or a key word in some main idea or important detail. Try to find the answer that really belongs. On the other hand, if you cannot think of the answer that is called for, write down something that represents your best guess. Often such answers, even though they're not exactly what is wanted, get complete or partial credit.

The Course Is the Context

One general bit of advice about objective tests seems in order because we've had so many occasions to tell it to students in examination situations: Always remember that the context of the questions is the course you're taking. In answering a question, ask yourself how this question should be answered in the light of your textbook or what has been said in class. If possible, identify its source, from textbook or class. If you can't do that, search your memory for anything you've learned in the course that's relevant. Don't answer the question according to the latest magazine you're read, your personal opinion, or some other course you've taken. Sometimes that would give you a different answer, for all answers are relative to a given context and source of information. The instructor, in framing his questions, cannot be responsible for your personal reading habits, but he can reasonably expect you to answer in terms of the course he is giving you.

Finishing up the Examination

We've said that you should read through an objective examination, answering the easy questions and coming back later to the hard ones. When you start to work on the hard ones, see how much time you have left and allocate it among the questions you still must do. However, in planning this time, leave some for a final rereading of your examination. Before you turn in your examination, you should read it through again carefully just in case you have made any foolish mistakes, like putting down a different answer than you intended or leaving some questions unanswered.

When you reread your examination, you may be tempted to change some of your answers. If you do, do not do it hastily or impulsively. You put some thought into choosing an answer in the first place, and you ought not to change it without good reason. To have such a reason, you ought to read the entire question again carefully and weigh the various alternatives. If you do, you may recall something relevant that you didn't on the first reading, or you may perceive more clearly the meanings of the alternatives. In that case, it is quite all right to change the answer, and in so doing you probably will increase your chance of being correct. The point is to avoid helter-skelter changes. Make sure the final choice is the one you feel most sure—even though that may not be very sure—is right.

Taking Essay Examinations

We'll use the term "essay" to refer to any examination in which the questions themselves are relatively brief and most of your work is in composing answers to these questions. Essay examinations may consist, at one extreme, of short-answer questions, which require you to write down a rather specific list of things. At the other extreme are discussion questions, which ask you to cover a rather broad subject at some length. In Chapter Nine we'll consider examinations that involve working out problems.

Planning Your Time

In taking essay examinations, even more than objective tests, you must plan and allocate your time. Even if you're not an outstanding student, you have sufficient knowledge to write much more than you have time for and you may get carried away on certain questions you know the most about. Hence, if you're not careful, you can spend far too much time on some questions and end up giving others short shrift. If you do this, you'll usually draw a low grade on some questions, for the instructor rightly expects you to budget your time and give each question its proportionate share.

To strike such a balance in your examination, read the whole examination through before you start to write anything. See how much time you are expected to spend on each question. If this isn't stated, make an estimate of the time you think should be spent on each, and try to stick to it as you work.

If the examination offers you options

permitting you to take some questions and omit others, make a tentative decision at the outset. Choose and mark the questions you're sure you can write on. If you're in doubt about any, let these go until you can think about them a little and make a decision. Be sure to number correctly each question you answer.

Following Directions

Essay questions, like objective ones, have key words. But in this case, the key words are really instructions to you for writing on the question. The key words are usually those such as "list," "illustrate," "compare," and "outline." Each means something different from the other, and the instructor chose the one he wanted for a good reason. Students are tempted to write around a subject and to tell what they know about it whether they were asked to or not. They do this especially if they aren't prepared to do exactly what the key word calls for. This, however, is a waste of time, for the instructor usually ignores what he doesn't ask for and considers the student to be evading the question that was put to him. You should therefore note the key word in the question and then stick as closely as possible to what it implies. If it is a "list," don't discuss or illustrate, except possibly as a way of adding pertinent information to your list. If it says, "illustrate," illustrate; don't list, discuss, or compare; and so on.

Being Explicit

Students commonly make the mistake of expressing their points in brief, sketchy language and then expecting the grader to know exactly what was intended. They often choose their words carelessly, and the grader, not being a mind reader, isn't sure whether the student actually knows what he is talking about or is just bluffing. For that reason, it is important to nail down every point you make. Say it as precisely as you can the first time, but then give an illustration or an important relevant detail or something that makes it clear that you know what you're talking about. Thus you can convince the grader, whereas otherwise you won't be credited for something you may really know.

IMPORTANT WORDS IN ESSAY QUESTIONS

The following terms appear frequently in the phrasing of essay questions. You should know their meaning and answer accordingly. (The list and the sense of the definitions, though not the exact words, are adapted from C. Bird and D. M. Bird, Learning More by Effective Study, Appleton-Century-Crofts, New York, 1945, pp. 195-198.)

Compare

Look for qualities or characteristics that resemble each other. Emphasize similarities among them, but in some cases also mention differences.

Contrast

Stress the dissimilarities, differences, or unlikenesses of things, qualities, events, or problems.

Criticize

Express your judgment about the merit or truth of the factors or views mentioned. Give the results of your analysis of these factors, discussing their limitations and good points.

Define

Give concise, clear, and authoritative meanings. Don't give details, but make sure to give the limits of the definition. Show how the thing you are defining differs from things in other classes.

Describe

Recount, characterize, sketch, or relate in sequence or story form.

Diagram

Give a drawing, chart, plan, or graphic answer. Usually you should label a diagram. In some cases, add a brief explanation or description.

Discuss

Examine, analyze carefully, and give reasons pro and con. Be complete, and give details.

Enumerate

Write in list or outline form, giving points concisely one by one.

Evaluate

Carefully appraise the problem, citing both advantages and limitations. Emphasize the appraisal of authorities and, to a lesser degree, your personal evaluation.

Explain

Clarify, interpret, and spell out the material you present. Give reasons for differences of opinion or of results, and try to analyze causes.

Illustrate

Use a figure, picture, diagram, or concrete example to explain or clarify a problem.

Interpret

Translate, give examples of, solve, or comment on, a subject, usually giving your judgment about it.

Justify

Prove or give reasons for decisions or conclusions, taking pains to be convincing.

List

As in "enumerate," write an itemized series of concise statements.

Outline

Organize a description under main points and subordinate points, omitting minor details and stressing the arrangement or classification of things.

Prove

Establish that something is true by citing factual evidence or giving clear logical reasons.

Relate

Show how things are related to, or connected with, each other or how one causes another, correlates with another, or is like another.

Review

Examine a subject critically, analyzing and commenting on the important statements to be made about it.

State

Present the main points in brief, clear sequence, usually omitting details, illustrations, or examples.

Summarize

Give the main points or facts in condensed form, like the summary of a chapter, omitting details and illustrations.

Trace

In narrative form describe progress, development, or historical events from some point of origin.

Elaborating your point in this way, however, is not the same thing as padding. Students often bring in extraneous points or say the same thing in slightly different ways just to bulk their otherwise slim answers. Most graders, having read hundreds of papers, can spot this sort of thing quickly, and they don't have a kindly attitude toward it. It's better to be brief than to pad with irrelevancies. That way you don't reveal your ignorance or seem to be bluffing.

Handwriting and Good English

Far too many students have atrocious handwriting. Some student hands are almost impossible to read, and others can be read only with difficulty. If you have one of these, try to do something about it. You may never write a clear, beautiful hand, but you can at least be legible. And it is important that you do, for instructors feel that a student should be able to write legibly; they can't give him credit for something they can't read. Some instructors will try hard to decipher illegible writing, but others have no patience at all with it and summarily mark down the illegible or poorly legible paper. In one research, for example, a group of graders twice graded the same papers, once when the papers were difficult to read and at another time when they were written in a clear hand. The graders' instructions were to pay no attention to handwriting in arriving at their grades. Nevertheless, the grades assigned to the legible papers were a full grade higher than those given to the hardly legible papers, though the two sets contained exactly the same answers. If your writing is hard to read, remember that it may make the difference between a C and a D or an A and a B. That's a lot. If your writing is hard to decipher, you'd better start practicing better handwriting.

You should also take pains to write good English, that is, to use good grammar, punctuate properly, and spell correctly. Aside from making a good impression, all are necessary for easy reading and even to understanding what you are trying to say. To the grader, poor grammar implies disorganized, confused thinking and inadequate command of the subject matter. Poor spelling, especially of important words, reflects not only careless reading and study but inadequate knowledge and understanding of the material. Hence it is only natural that mistakes of this sort will pull your grade down whether the grader intends them to or not. So in your hurry to write an answer, don't foreget to observe the elementary rules of good English.

Learning from Examinations

We'll wind up this chapter on taking examinations by pointing out that you can learn a great deal from them. When the typical student gets his paper back, he looks to see whether the instructor made any error in marking his paper and whether there is anything to quibble about. Then he puts the paper aside and does nothing more with it. Sometimes errors in grading do occur, and a student should point them out to the instructor. More important, however, by studying his paper carefully, the student can learn a lot about his past preparation and his ways of preparing for the next examination.

Where you've made mistakes or lost credit, look the matter up in your notes or in the book to see exactly how this came about. Did you misinterpret something in the course? Did you fail to get something important into your notes and study it? Did you fail to note the important qualifiers? Did you misread the question? These and other queries can be answered by studying your examination paper. In this way, you may uncover characteristic faults in your study habits and then proceed to correct them. All of us probably learn more by correcting our mistakes than we do from our successes, and an examination paper is a concrete record of mistakes. You'll be wise to profit from them.

ORGANIZING ESSAY ANSWERS

Here are two examples of brief answers to an essay question. Read them to see what you think of them, and then compare your judgment with our comment at the end. The question is: What were the important results of the (English) revolution of 1688?

The first answer

I will summarize the most important results of the revolution under three headings:

1. *Parliament's victory.* The most direct result of the revolution of 1688 was the final victory of Parliament in the conflict between it and the crown that had gone on all during the 17th century. Parliament, by declaring the throne vacant because of James II's desertion to France, finally established that the king ruled by choice of the people and Parliament and not by divine right. Parliament established a Bill of Rights, which said that the king was not above the law but was himself subject to the law. In the early years of the reign of William and Mary, many additional acts were passed which curtailed the powers of the crown.
2. *The end of religious conflict.* The revolution itself did not entirely end the religious troubles of the 17th century, but Parliament passed a Toleration Act which brought an end to many of the difficulties of the Dissenters. The Catholics, however, were still subjected to many infringements of civil liberties.
3. *A New political class.* The important general result of the resolution and the victory of Parliament was the beginning of a long era during which political power in England was divided between the landed gentry and the merchant class.

The second answer

The revolution of 1688 was very important. It was so important that it is sometimes called the "glorious revolution." Parliament won, and it passed a lot of acts which were against the king, and it invited William and Mary to rule jointly in England. William and Mary still had to fight though, especially in Ireland where James II was finally defeated. William and Mary cooperated with Parliament so there wasn't so much trouble between the King and Parliament. James II was very unpopular because he was a Catholic, and Parliament made it so no Catholic could ever become king again, although parliament made things easier for the Dissenters. This was the end of the Divine Right of kings in England, though at first the country was ruled mostly by the aristocracy and the rich merchants. Real democracy didn't come until much later, so the revolution of 1688 wasn't a completely democratic revolution.

Notice that these two answers differ more in organization than they do in content. The first answer is not perfect, but it is balanced, clear, and factual. The second is much the poorer because it is vague, disorganized, and full of irrelevancies and loose statements.

chapter 7

WRITING PAPERS

Previous chapters cover pretty well the general problems of college study. But you will run into some specific matters that we haven't dealt with yet. In the next few chapters, we'll try to give you guidance in handling some particular problems that are likely to come your way. We begin in this chapter with the writing of themes and reports.

Most freshmen are required to take a course in English composition. Its purpose is to help you learn to write accurately and understandably; if you give it half a chance, it generally will. Usually, in a course of this sort, you write a number of themes or compositions, and the instructor corrects these, not so much for the purpose of giving you a grade as to point out to you what things you are doing wrong.

For many students, this business of writing themes is an odious and frustrating task. For some who don't do well in it, it spells doom to their college career. Those who merely get through the course move on to their upper classes only to find that they have more themes and papers to write. Finding the task unpleasant, they put off writing the paper until the end of the term and then do it hastily and inadequately, with disappointing consequences for them and their instructors.

Such discomfort and failure don't have to be. Few of you will become professional writers, but just about all of you who graduate from college will find that your jobs and positions in the community require you to write well enough to be able to communicate something to other people. Even a sales report is better if it is well written. In short, you can and should learn to write well if you are going to make the most of your college education.

In this chapter we will try to provide some help for writing term papers and themes. We won't say everything that could be said about writing because most of you will sometime take a course in English composition, and there are also a good many handbooks of composition and manuals on writing that can help you. We will mention some of them later in this chapter.

Steps in Writing

In this section, first of all, we will go over, from beginning to end, the steps that are involved in writing a good paper. After that, we have a section on using the library, which you will almost always have to do in preparing your paper. In the final two sections, we will give you some advice on how to improve your writing and how to take research notes.

Choosing the Subject

The first step in writing a paper, of course, is to choose the topic you will write about. Sometimes topics are assigned, but usually you have some freedom in deciding what the topic will be.

In the case of themes in English composition, you sometimes have complete freedom to write about anything that interests you. More often, though, you must pick a topic within the limits of the course you are taking.

Selecting a topic is one of the hardest things about writing a paper. If you pick one that is too trivial, too big, too personal, or too controversial, you are likely to run into trouble. Most instructors will warn you of the troubles you will have if you choose a topic that is too big or too difficult. You might also be warned about taking a topic that is too limited or one that is too emotionally loaded for you. (The instructor and other people are not likely to share the prejudices you reveal when you write about emotionally loaded or controversial issues.) But better than telling you about the things to avoid would be to tell you about ways to find a good topic.

One of the best ways to find useful and important topics to write about is to thumb through the indexes of textbooks and treatises already written on the subject. Suppose, for example, you are taking a course in human genetics and you want to write a paper about the relationships between race and genetics. Find a book like Boyd's *Genetics and the Races of Man,* and look through the index. The chances are you will find a few entries that will give you some ideas for a paper. Just for practice, why don't you pick up a textbook that is handy and see how many interesting topics for a paper you can find in just a few minutes? Another index you can use to hunt for ideas is one in the abstracts for special fields that we mention below. The topical indexes in such volumes suggest important and worthwhile topics; by looking up the summaries referred to in the indexes, you can see what articles and books there will be on a particular topic.

For some kinds of papers, of course, this approach won't work, but another one will. One instructor, for example, frequently has his engineering students write articles on the design of common household articles. The student must find something ordinary like a stove, a sink, or a hand tool and describe both what is wrong with it from the engineering point of view and how it might be improved. Here the trick is to find something that really needs improvement. The instructor's purpose is not so much to get the student to redesign something as it is to alert the student to engineering problems in common, everyday things. If you had a topic like this, what would you choose to write about?

The point we are trying to make is that your daily experience is full of things to which you can apply the ideas you have gotten from your academic education. These are frequently excellent topics for term papers.

Another source of ideas for papers is the connection between various subjects you are interested in. Suppose you are a psychology major taking a course in aesthetics. Why not consider a paper on the properties of design and expression in abstract art and the categories psychologists use in projective testing? These kinds of topics are not easy to do, but they nearly always are interesting, both to you and to the instructor.

Choosing a topic that probably will be interesting to the instructor is, incidentally, a good ground rule. You can get some hints about his interests from his special area of training and from the things that make him enthusiastic in class. If you aren't too sure about his interests, then at least try to select an important area to write about rather than something so trivial that few people could get interested in it. We make this suggestion not to encourage apple polishing but as an instance of the more general principle that you should always consider the interests of your reading audience both in choosing a topic and in working out your approach to it.

Gathering the Material

After you have chosen the topic, you are ready to gather the material. Where you start to do this depends on the subject you are writing about, the length and complexity of the paper, and the type of paper. Occasionally, you may need to do very little reading, and may write "off the cuff" on a topic of personal interest. More often, however, a major purpose of the paper is to have you learn something and communicate what you have learned in the paper. In this case, you will make extensive use of the library and be taking research notes—both topics that we will cover later. We shall simply assume for the moment that you know how to do both of these things.

To get started, you will have to get some background for specific readings on the topic. Perhaps your textbook will supply this, or perhaps you have read portions of books related to the topic in the course of deciding what it will be. If you are stuck, your instructor can probably help you. He can clarify or limit the topic and suggest general, background sources for setting the stage for your reading. In many cases, this background reading will furnish a bibliography that will lead you to other materials. In other cases, you may go to abstracts, indexes or special bibliographic sources to compile a list of the things you should read. And of course, once you get such a list, you will follow your nose. One article will reference others in the domain of the project.

Constructing an Outline

Let us assume that you have completed most, if not all, of your reading and are ready to begin writing. The next step is to construct an outline, even if tentatively, of what you are going to write. Very few people can write about a complicated topic without an outline. Those who can are able to do so only because they can keep an outline in their heads. In working up an outline, think first of two, three, or four main divisions, the principal points or topics that you want to cover. The best way to begin is to put these as headings on separate pieces of paper so that you have plenty of space to fill in below. Then under your main headings write the specific points you have in mind. Depending upon how complicated your paper is, you will want to carry the outline out to third- or fourth-order headings. A simple theme will probably be outlined with one or two orders of headings. Under the lowest order of heading, you can jot down notes and reminders about what to say.

After you begin writing, you will probably find that you want to revise your outline. Do so in such a way that the revised outline can serve as a kind of table of contents for your paper. Indeed, you will want to preserve your outline in the form of headings throughout the paper.

The First Draft

Very few people can get by with just one version of what they write. Usually a first draft, and sometimes another draft, before the final version, is necessary. You will want to write your first draft from your notes on cards arranged in the order of your outline.

Try to write it pretty much the way you want the final version to be, but be less concerned about the right way of getting your ideas on paper than about just getting them down. After you have them in front of you, you can work them over more easily.

One important point to remember in writing the first draft is to leave plenty of room for correction. If you type—and you will be much better off if you can type even your first draft—leave at least two spaces between lines and perhaps even three. If you handwrite your first draft, write on only every other line.

After you have written the first draft, go over it once for corrections. Then put it aside for a while. This is an important step. Many students fail to give themselves enough time to write papers so that they must do their drafts and final version all bunched together. Time between the original draft and the final version allows you to get a fresh approach so that a lot of things that were difficult or obscure in the first draft can more easily be corrected.

Revising the Paper

When, after a few days, you pull out your first draft and go to work on a final version, you must take a fresh look at what you have done. It is this fresh look that is aided by putting the paper aside for a while. In the intervening time, you have forgotten some of what you have written, you have gotten out of the forest of detail engaging you while you were writing, and you are better able to read the paper in the way somebody else would. In taking this fresh look, there are some things you should be particularly careful about.

The first is coverage. You ask whether the paper really covers the topic properly. Are there relevant things you have read but left out in the first draft because they didn't seem to fit then or because you were tired? Was your reading really complete? Are there subtopics that ought to be covered on which your reading was inadequate? Are certain topics too thin because you did not include enough important detail? Your answers to these questions will determine what you do, whether you go over your notes to supply additional information or go back to the library to dig up additional material. In any case, consider carefully at this stage whether your paper covers well the subject chosen.

Secondly, you should check the organization of the paper. Does the outline make good sense? Are your headings and subheadings in the right places? Do thoughts flow in the proper order? Are there good transitions and guideposts throughout the paper to make it read smoothly? If you are not satisfied with any part of the paper, make the necessary revisions. Sometimes this will involve "cut and paste" to transfer paragraphs to better positions. Sometimes it means rewriting paragraphs, rewriting certain sentences, and in general doing any repair work that seems necessary. This stage is one that any writer, even those who are expert in doing articles and books, always goes through, and it is essential to achieving a polished product.

Thirdly, look very carefully at your mechanics. Is your sentence structure good? Is your punctuation and spelling correct? When in doubt consult the dictionary, and other sources we will mention below, to check on whether or not you are correct.

Finally at this stage, you prepare "copy" for your bibliography. In the humanities, references are usually arranged as footnotes, while in the sciences they are customarily given at the end of the paper in the alphabetical order of the last name of the first author. Whichever system is appropriate to your paper, you do the mechanical things necessary to provide a correct set of references. You see that the proper numbers or names are included in the text and that the cards on which you took your notes are arranged in the proper order with numbers or some system of tying them to the references in the text of your paper.

The Final Draft

At this point, you will probably feel that you have finished the paper. You probably have—almost. But if you put the paper away again for a few days, then go over it for the last time, you will undoubtedly catch a few rough spots that you missed in the first and revised drafts. Now you are ready to have the paper typed up to hand in. Here are some of the things you should keep in mind in typing the final draft.

One is to prepare a title page on which you record your name, the class, and any other information the instructor needs for identifying the paper and returning it to you.

The paper should be typed according to whatever specifications are appropriate. Your instructor may have given specific directions for this. If not, it is customary to double-space typed papers in a column of about six inches wide on letter-size paper of 8 1/2 by 11 inches.

If the paper is a long one, you probably should provide a table of contents so that any reader can see beforehand the topics covered; that is, survey the paper.

Once the paper is typed, be sure to proofread it carefully for any mistakes that were made in typing or carried over from the preceding draft.

Finally, it is good practice to make a second copy for your own keeping. This is to guard against loss of the original or to offset the possibility that the teacher will not hand it back to you. Nowadays, with copying machines generally available, you may make a copy from your original on such a machine, usually found in the library or in some place providing copying machines. Otherwise, you should make a carbon copy when the original is typed.

Using the Library

The library is the place for you to go to gather your materials for writing a paper. Everybody uses the library once in a while; but if you have not written a paper before in college, you may not know all the things that even a small library can do for you. If you do no more than go to the library to study, to take out a book, or to hunt down an assigned reading, you really do not yet know how to use the library. Hence we should tell you about some of the things you will find in the library that are absolutely essential for writing good papers.

Layout of the Library

The first thing you should do is learn the layout of your library or libraries. We say "or libraries" because many colleges have more than one library. As colleges and universities become larger, there is a general trend toward the decentralization of libraries. This may go only so far as to break up the main library into principal divisions corresponding to groups of departments, such as psychology and education, business and economics, etc. Or, in many large universities, it has been carried to the departmental level so that each department has a library housed in its main building. In this case, the departmental library is probably not a complete library and may duplicate books found in the main library, but it will serve well the needs of a student writing a paper in the subject of the department.

To start familiarizing yourself with the organization of your library system, go to the main library and look around. Do this within the first few weeks of college when you have no specific assignment and have not yet gotten under the pressure of examinations and deadlines for papers. Most larger libraries have directories posted at various points in the library, including the entrance or main desk, to guide you to the various collections. Some publish manuals that list their various departments and services. Study whatever information of this sort is available. In addition, just walk around all the places not closed to students, noting what appears to be in each area of the library. From such an exploration, you should get a picture of how the main library and any divisional or departmental libraries are laid out. Some schools have guided tours as part of the orientation of freshman students; if yours does, take advantage of them.

Card catalogue. In the course of either a guided or unguided tour, there are certain things you should look for and note. One is the location of the card catalogue, for this is the backbone of the library and the place you will usually start when you begin library research or hunt for almost anything in the library. We have a section below on the use of the card catalogue.

Reading rooms. Another part of the library to look for is the reading room or rooms. Large libraries usually have several reading rooms, one for each of several functions or subjects. Smaller libraries may have one general reading room. In any case, this room or rooms will be the place in which you will lay out your notebook and do the reading associated with your project. It may also be, as we suggested earlier in this book, the best place for you to do your other studying.

Reference works. Another thing to look for in your library is the arrangement of books and bound volumes. These may be divided into three general categories: regular books, periodicals, reference works. Reference works are almost always kept separately from the other two. They may be all together in a reference section or room of the library, or they may be found in a reading room along with books, say, in the social sciences. These reference works will often be a place to start in getting background for a paper.

Periodicals. Periodicals are usually kept in stacks along with regular books. *Stacks* is the library term for books arranged on shelves one above the other, and in large universities the stacks may occupy several floors. The stacks may be *open* or *closed*. Open stacks are those available to all users of the library; closed stacks may not be entered without a special *stack permit*. Such a permit is usually issued to faculty members and sometimes to graduate students, but it is not often given to undergraduates. In this case, you secure something in the stacks by presenting a card at the desk and waiting for one of the library attendants to fetch it for you. There are advantages and disadvantages to each system depending on the size of the library and other features of its layout, but we will not go into them because the system will be whatever it is in your particular library.

Classification. All books and periodicals, in fact all reading matter in a library, are classified according to some system. This classification is expressed by some combination of letters and numbers. Two systems are widely used. One is the Dewey Decimal Classification in which numbers are used to divide documents into general categories and then into more specific categories. The general divisions of the system are given in a separate table. The other widely used system is the Library of Congress Classification. It uses letters of the alphabet for its general divisions, and numbers for finer distinctions. Then within each subject category a letter is used for the author's name and then a serial number to distinguish books in this category with the same initial. Separately, we list the principal divisions of this classification and give examples of categories within each division. There are a few libraries that have devised their own systems, although they are tending to change over to one of the two general systems above. You might note what system your library uses, and then learn the general categories represented in the system.

Reserve shelves. Another thing to note in your tour of the library is where the reserve shelves are. As a freshman, you may have little occasion to use these shelves, but when you can't find a book in the regular stacks it may be because it is on the reserve shelf. Such a shelf is used to make books available to students who have had them assigned in a course, but to keep them on the open shelf rather than in closed stacks or out of the library. The library usually has rather rigid rules, in the interest of fairness to students, about how long the books may be borrowed by a student even to read in the library. You might note what these rules are so that you can plan your use of such books.

Special collections and facilities. Another thing to note about your library is what it possesses in the way of special collections and facilities. Even with open stacks, most libraries have some materials, especially those which are valuable, that it keeps in closed stacks or special rooms. Nowadays, in order to conserve space, many periodicals and some rare books are being placed on microfilm to be read with the aid of a special microfilm reader. You might note whether your library has such a collection and facilities. Also coming into use are tapes and phonograph records for the study of languages and other special subjects. Note whether your library has such a facility, for it may come in handy at the right time.

Card Catalogue

The card catalogue is the index to your library. It tells you what may be found in the library and, by means of its classification, where it is. The way you use this catalogue depends on what information you already have, for books are catalogued in three different ways: by *author,* by *title,* and by *subject.* Which of these you look for depends on what you already know about the book. In the early stages of library research, you will probably look under the subjects for which you are likely to find documents of interest. In this way, you can compile quite a list of books. Later in your research, when you have already done some reading and are acquiring references from this reading, you will probably use the author as your point of entry.

Here are some of the points you should know in order to use the catalogue most efficiently:

(1) Cards appear in alphabetical order according to the first word at the top of the card, whether or not this be the author, title, or subject. In the titles of books, however, articles such as *the, a,* and *an,* are neglected, hence you look for the first significant work in which you are interested.

(2) In alphabetizing titles and subjects consisting of more than one word, some libraries alphabetize word by word, and others do it letter by letter without regard to the spacing between words. As a test of which system is being used, you can look for New York and Newark. In word-by-word filing, New York comes first; in letter by letter, Newark does.

(3) In addition to regular subject cards, the card catalogue also contains cross reference cards to related subjects. These appear

DEWEY DECIMAL CLASSIFICATION

000-099	General works: bibliographies, encyclopedias, periodicals
100-199	Philosophy: metaphysics, psychology, logic, ethics
200-299	Religion: Bible, theology, Christian churches
300-399	Social Science: political science, economics, education
400-499	Philology: comparative philology, English language, various languages
500-599	Pure science: mathematics, physics, chemistry, biology
600-699	Applied science: medicine, engineering, agriculture
700-799	Arts and recreation: architecture, sculpture, painting
800-899	Literature: American literature, English literature, other literatures
900-999	History: geography, biography, ancient history, modern history

at the end of all the cards on a given subject. These are particularly useful to the young person doing library research because they give him ideas for subjects to look under.

(4) Historical periods are filed in alphabetical order, so that books on the Civil War would appear before those on the reconstruction period. The subject headings in this case would probably be History—U.S., Civil War, and History—U.S., Reconstruction Period.

(5) Titles of books that begin with numbers are alphabetized as though the numbers are spelled out.

Periodical Indexes

The card catalogue indexes volumes, and it will give you the titles of periodicals in particular subjects. It will not, however, index individual articles in periodicals. Yet much of your paper writing, especially in more advanced courses, will require you to ferret out this sort of material rather than rely entirely on books. To find articles, you need a different sort of index, an index to periodical literature.

There are several such indexes, each covering a different sort of publication. For current events of a newsworthy sort, the *Reader's Guide to Periodical Literature* is your most useful index. It covers articles appearing in popular magazines and less technical journals. For more scholarly articles, particularly in the humanities, arts, and social sciences, the *International Index of Periodicals* is the source to use. Beyond that, there are more specialized indexes, such as *Engineering Index*, *Index Medicus* (for medical

literature), *Education Index*, and several others.

Abstracts

Most professional societies, at one time or another in their history, have published an index to literature in their subject. In some cases, however, they have decided that merely indexing literature is inadequate. It should, in addition, be abstracted so that a person reading an abstract could both be informed and evaluate an article before seeking it out to read. The outcome of this is that in a number of fields you should look for abstracts rather than for indexes. The best examples of such abstracts are: *Chemical Abstracts*, *Biological Abstracts*, *Psychological Abstracts*, and *Sociological Abstracts*. In each case, however, the abstracts are provided with indexes at annual or semiannual intervals. Hence to find articles in these fields, you secure the index number, jot down abstract numbers, then turn to the abstracts to see whether you think you are interested in the article. If you are, you can then take down the complete citation from the abstract and, after looking up the journal in the card catalogue to find its call number, go to the journal for a reading of the original article.

If your subject is such that newspaper articles need to be located, a different approach is required. Newspaper articles are not indexed in the sources we have named above. Here the *New York Times Index* is your best bet. This index covers all important articles published in that newspaper. Having the reputation of printing "all the

LIBRARY OF CONGRESS CLASSIFICATION

A.   General works. AC, collections; AE, encyclopedias; AY, yearbooks; AZ, general history.
B.   Philosophy-religion. BC, logic; BF, psychology; BL, religions.
C.   History-auxiliary sciences. CB, civilization; CS, geneology; CT, biography.
D.   History and topography. DA, Great Britain; DC, France; DK, Russia; DU, Australia and Oceania.
E.-F. America. E., America (general) and United States (general); F, United States (local) and America except the United States.
G.   Geography. GC, oceanography; GN, anthropology; GT, manners and customs; GV, sports and amusements.
H.   Social sciences. HB, economic theory; HD, economic history; HE, transportation; HF, commerce; HG, finance; HM, sociology; HQ, family, marriage, home; HT, communities; HV, social pathology, philanthropy.
J.   Political Science. JA, general works; JO, theory of the state; JX, international law.
K.   Law.
L.   Education. LB, theory and practice; LC, special forms; LD, United States.
M.   Music. ML, literature of music; MT, musical instruction.
N.   Fine Arts. NA, architecture; ND, painting; NK, industrial arts.
P.   Language and literature. PA, classical languages; PC, romance languages; PD, Teutonic languages; PR, English literature; PS, American literature.
Q.   Science. QA, mathematics; QC, physics; QD, chemistry; QE, geology; QL, zoology; QP, physiology.
R.   Medicine. RB, pathology; RE, ophthalmology; RK, dentistry; RM, therapeutics; RT, nursing.
S.   Agriculture—plant and animal industry. SB, plant culture; SD, forestry; SF, animal culture; SK, hunting sports.
T.   Technology. TA, engineering; TH, building construction; TK, electrical engineering; TN, mineral industries; TR, photography.
U.   Military science.
V.   Naval science.
Z.   Bibliography and Library Science.

---

news that's fit to print," it is taken by most college and city libraries in the United States. Even if you should wish to search other newspapers, the index is still useful, for it serves to date events precisely enough for you to look them up in other newspapers and magazines.

Reference Books

Reference books have an important value, not only for digging out material for writing papers, but also for answering sundry problems that may interest you or turn up in connection with courses you take. They fall into several categories, and each one has a different use: encyclopedias, yearbooks, and dictionaries.

Encyclopedias. If you want to work up some specialized topic like imperialism or Greek mathematics, a general encyclopedia is a good place to start. The best-known American encyclopedia (despite its name) is the *Encyclopaedia Britannica*, but for many pur-

poses other works such as *Encyclopedia Americana,* are equally good, if not better. If your library is a large one, you will find an enormous number of encyclopedias from almost every country in every language. An article in a general encyclopedia can give you a good introduction to a topic and sometimes a lot of detail as well. Such articles have well-selected bibliographies, and these make good starters for further reading in a field.

In recent years, two good encyclopedias have appeared that are neither general nor highly specialized. One, covering the natural sciences, is the *McGraw-Hill Encyclopedia of Science and Technology.* This series of volumes has a comprehensive coverage of articles in engineering, physics, chemistry, biology, and experimental psychology. Another covering the social sciences is the *International Encyclopedia of the Social Sciences.* In its volumes, it has articles on psychology, sociology, social anthropology, political science, and economics. Between the two encyclopedias, they cover well all subjects in which you might write papers except in history and the humanities. They are therefore good places to start in the natural and social sciences.

Yearbooks. If you have occasion to refer to facts pertaining in a particular year, one of the yearbooks is a good reference. Two major encyclopedias publish such yearbooks: *The American Annual* (1923-   ) is the annual supplement to the *Encyclopedia Americana,* and the *Britannica Book of the Year* (1938-   ) is a similar supplement to the *Encyclopaedia Britannica.* Both of these contain articles concerning events or important new developments in the year or so preceding publication. These articles usually find their way into subsequent editions of the encyclopedia.

The other yearbooks mostly contain statistical information or brief summaries of events. Between them they give almost any conceivable sort of statistical fact you may be interested in.

World Almanac and Book of Facts, 1968-   , a compendium of facts, mostly about the United States.

Information Please Almanac, 1947-   , a similar compendium emphasizing topics of more general interest to lay readers.

Whitaker's Almanac, 1869-   , A British publication similar to the *World Almanac.*

The Statesman's Yearbook, 1864-   , information about world governments.

United States Statistical Abstracts, 1876-   , statistical information on industrial, social, political, and economic facets of the United States.

Dictionaries

We have already talked about the kind of dictionary you should have on your desk. Libraries have different kinds of dictionaries that you will occasionally need to use. They fall into two general categories: English dictionaries, and biographical dictionaries.

The English dictionaries found in libraries are the large ones, called unabridged, that are too expensive and unwieldy—also not necessary—to keep in one's place to study. The two most widely used unabridged dictionaries of this sort are *Webster's New International Dictionary* and the *Funk and Wagnalls New Standard Dictionary.* These contain about all the general terms in use in recent times. A newer partially abridged dictionary—it contains about half of the terms of the two unabridged volumes—is the *Random House Dictionary of the English Language.* It has a large, easily read format.

For technical terms not found in these dictionaries, you should use more specialized dictionaries. There is one or more of these, in various states of up-to-dateness, in most of the subjects you will study. You may find them useful. However, you will probably do just as well in technical fields to use the glossaries now often included in textbooks or to look up the term in the *McGraw-Hill Encyclopedia of Science and Technology* or the *International Encyclopedia of the Social Sciences.* Most terms in which you are interested will be found in one or the other of them, and if you look them up there, you will find not only a definition but also an informative article on the subject.

A biographical dictionary is the one to use when you are trying to find information about people. For American statesmen, writers, and other important people who are no longer living, there is the *Dictionary of American Biography.* For important Englishmen, there is a reference series called the *Dictionary of National Biography.* For living people, such as congressmen, judges, public officials, writers, etc., there are the various *Who's Whos. Who's Who* itself contains information mostly about Englishmen. *Who's Who in America* is the most general biographical reference for living Americans. Accompanying it in recent years is a volume of *Who Was Who* to cover deceased individuals formerly in *Who's Who in America.* Also, a new addition to the stable is *World Who's Who in Science*; this gives sketches of leading scientists, living or dead, from early times to the present. In addition, there are a lot of specialized books, such as *Who's Who in Education* or *American Men of Science,* which contain information about people in special fields, and there are now regional *Who's Whos* for different parts of the United States.

In General

This concludes our description of the resources you have in your college library for the preparation of papers and for studying outside of your assigned books. You can see now that it is not too difficult a job to hunt down the most obscure subject in the world if you know how to use a good library. The number of books and articles published each year is staggering, but by means of reference book, abstracts, indexes, and the like, you can pin point just one particular fact out of this whole mass of material. Learning to use these resources puts the whole world of printed matter at your disposal and enormously increases your abilities. Indeed, learning to use these sources is one of the most valuable things you can get from a college education.

Improving Writing Skills

Teachers and other people can teach you the rules of composition and show you in specific instances how to make your speech and writing better, but in the long run improving your ability to express yourself is something that only you can do. Like most skills, skill in writing comes only through practice. If you worry about your writing only when you must write a theme or report, you will not improve much. To acquire real skill, you must make your use of language a continuing project for improvement.

Aids to Writing

There are certain materials you ought to have on your desk at all times for ready reference. How far you go in building such a collection depends somewhat on your financial resources and what field of study you emphasize. Those in humanities and social sciences, where papers are written more often than in natural sciences, should have more. As an absolute minimum we recommend a good dictionary and a book on English style. In addition, some books dealing with the meaning and use of words are recommended. We shall explain these in turn.

The dictionary. You should have a dictionary that is up-to-date—dictionaries change—and complete enough to include the general, non-technical vocabulary used at the college level. There are several good desk dictionaries available: *Webster's New World Dictionary, The American College Dictionary* and *Webster's New Collegiate Dictionary.* If you are buying one and must choose, we recommend the last because it is the authority used frequently by major publishers.

Just having a dictionary isn't enough, though. Get into the habit of consulting it every chance you get. You'll be surprised at the amount of information you'll find in it. First of all, of course, dictionaries can tell you how to spell words, and most of us find it necessary to use a dictionary for this purpose fairly often. Secondly, dictionaries can tell you the meanings of words and how to use them. One of the best things you can do to improve your study habits is to become a definition hunter. Whenever you find a word that puzzles you or a strange use of a familiar word, look it up in the dictionary. You'll find that such regular use of a dictionary helps a lot to lighten the load of reading an obscure or difficult textbook.

You'll also find a lot of useful miscellaneous information in the dictionary. It usually contains a terse but adequate summary of grammar. In many dictionaries there is a gazetteer (look that word up in the dictionary—you will probably be surprised) and a list of the names and principal works of famous people. These things are all useful.

Style guides. Besides a dictionary, you also must have handy at all times a reference on grammar and punctuation. Your textbook in English composition may serve this purpose, but we especially recommend the little book called *Elements of Style* by William Strunk, Jr. and E.B. White (Macmillan Paperbacks, #107).

13485. **Wolff, Harold.** (Boston U. Coll. of Business Administration) **The impact of society on science.** *American Behavioral Scientist,* 1967, **10**(9), 2-7.—Criticizes social scientists, in general, for avoiding critical issues and oversimplification, and, in particular, for engaging in rabble rousing rather than investigating important social phenomenon such as the space research effort.

13486. **Zuckerman, Harriet.** (Columbia U.) **Nobel laureates in science: Patterns of productivity, collaboration, and authorship.** *American Sociological Review,* 1967, **32**(3), 391-403.—Nobel laureates in science publish more and are more apt to collaborate than a matched sample of scientists. Interviews with 41 to 55 laureates and comparison of their research output with the output of the matched sample indicate that these patterns hold at every stage of the life-work-cycle. As laureates report and as their publications corroborate, they exercise noblesse oblige in arranging coauthorship in collaborative publications. Receipt of the Nobel prize is followed by declining productivity and changed work practices, as a result of changed role obligations and activities. Reductions in productivity are more severe for laureates who experience comparatively large increments in prestige through the prize than for those who were already eminent. The prize generates strain in collaborative associations so that most of these terminate soon after the award. (45 ref.)—*Journal abstract.*

THE USE OF ABSTRACTS

Above are sample entries in Psychological Abstracts. Like the abstracts available in most special fields, they give a brief synopsis of the contents of articles and books. Below is part of a page from the index of Chemical Abstracts, illustrating the way you can find abstracts bearing on a particular topic.

Mass action, law of, app. for fitting data to, in enzyme reactions, 779*g.*
law of, cation-exchange equil. and, 7999*e.*
law of, condensation and, 7366*f.*
in metallic-system analysis, 11171*h.*
Mass defects. (See also *Packing.*)
history of, 5568*f.*
Massecuites. (See also *Jaggery.*)
calcn. schemes for, 2398*e.*
compn. of low-grade, 4237*a.*
reduction to polyhydric alcs., P 8820*a.*
viscosity of, detn. of, 4237*b.*
treatment of—see *Sugar manufacture.*
Massicot. See "PbO" under *Lead oxides.*
Massoia lactone*, identity with 5-hydroxy--2-decenoic acid δ lactone, 14126*g.*
Massoy oil. See *Oils.*
Mass spectra. *(For mass spectra of specific elements see the headings for the elements.)*
of alcs. (C_6 and C_7). 3849*f.*
of benzene monoderivs., 9806*b.*
of bibenzyl, ethylbenzene and toluene, 4307*e.*
of carbon dioxide isotopic mols., 8025*d.*
of coal-mine gases, 11757*c.*
of elementary particles, 8645*e.*
of ketene and its dimer, 5087*g.*
of methane mono- and dihalo derivs., 9806*d.*
of nitrites (aliphatic), 3796*h.*
of polyat. mols., high-energy ions in, 7425*c.*
theory of, 11906*c.*
of s-triazine, 12545*f.*
Mass spectrographs. See *Mass spectrometers.*
Mass spectrography. See *Mass spectroscopy.*
Mass spectrometers, Mass spectrographs. (See also *Omegatrons.*), P3148*de,* 6228*i,* P 9766*e,* P 11123*i,* 13401*d.*
for analysis of solids, 13463*g.*
with anastigmatic image, 8644*i.*
ion abundance ratios by, 6816*d.*

of ions from field emission microscope, 13405*e.*
in mineralogy, 3207*b.*
of nitrogen dioxide in gases, 1890*g.*
of org. compds. of large mass, 11912*f.*
of oxidation products of unsatd. hydrocarbons, 12672*g.*
of pentane pyrolysis, 8003*c.*
of petroleum fractions, 9660*f.*
in petroleum industry, 9661*d.*
of phenol adsorption by catalysts contg. Ni, 13340*c.*
photographic layer for use in, supported on elec. conductor, P 12562*f.*
reviews on, 3186*d,* 9762*c,* 13401*d.*
of solids, 9762*d.*
of solids, with high-frequency spark, 5015*f.*
of styrene polymer decompn., 5639*e.*
of sulfur dioxide, neg. ions formed in, 11183*d.*
trace-element detn. by, 1140*e.*
Mass transfer, in absorption in packed columns, film resistance and, 411*a.*
in absorption of gases, 5633*e.*
to air in flow over plate, 12473*c.*
by air jets in tubes, 9117*a.*
in ammonia absorption from air by water in rosette-packed column, 4265*e.*
in ammonia absorption, packing materials and, 6749*b.*
analogy with heat and momentum transfer, 2424*b.*
in atomization, 13282*d.*
book: Chem. Engineering.—Fluid Flow, Heat Transfer and, 12476*e.*
from bubbles, 1077*g.*
of carbon dioxide to aq. NaOH or H_2O in wetted-wall columns, 4292*c.*
in catalytic gaseous reactions, reactor design and, 2424*i.*
in convection at vertical plates, 1737*a.*

This book, in less than a hundred pages and for less than a dollar, summarizes the elementary rules of usage, the main principles of composition, some rules of form, and a guide to improved style. It will answer almost any question you may have about composition, and it certainly covers all of the mistakes we commonly see in the writing of college students.

There are other books that can help you master the use of your language. One is H. W. Fowler's *A Dictionary of Modern English Usage* or its American counterpart, *A Dictionary of American English Usage*. Also of great value is Roget's *Thesaurus*, which classifies and relates English words and phrases. This not only will help you find the word you want, but it also suggests ideas.

A PAGE FROM A DICTIONARY OF USAGE

From H. W. Fowler, A Dictionary of Modern English Usage, Oxford, New York, 1944. By permission of the publishers.

for *vicegerent*, & sometimes used pleonastically for *regent* (which word includes the notion of vice-), so that it seems to have no right to exist, & may be classed among SUPERFLUOUS WORDS.

vice-queen)(vicereine. The first is recorded from the 16th c., the second (in English) from the 19th only. *Vicereine* is now the regular word for viceroy's wife, & *vice-queen*, in much less frequent use, is now reserved for a woman ruling as a queen's representative—a useful DIFFERENTIATION.

viceregal)(viceroyal. There being no distinction of meaning, it would be better if there were one word only; *viceregal* is the better, & *viceroyal* may fairly be called a SUPERFLUOUS WORD.

vicinage is now, compared with *neighbourhood*, a FORMAL WORD, &, compared with *vicinity*, a dying one.

vicious circle. See under TECHNICAL TERMS. *There is a vicious circle in which starvation produces Bolshevism, & Bolshevism in its turn* feeds on *starvation*. What, then, produces starvation, & on what does starvation feed? The writer can no doubt retort with truth that nothing (i.e. no food) produces starvation, & that starvation feeds on nothing; but he will have proved his wit at the expense of his logic. Such blunders in stating the elements of a vicious circle are not uncommon.

victimize makes -*zable*; see MUT

victress. FEMININE DESIGNATIC

victual. The verb makes -*lle.*, -*lling*, see -LL-, -L-; pronounce vi'tl, vi'tler, vi'tling.

vide. Pronounce vi'di; literally 'see' (imperative). It is properly used in referring readers to a passage in which they will find a proof or illustration of what has been stated, & should be followed by something in the nature of chapter & verse, or at least by the name of a book or author. But it has, like RE, been taken over by the illiterate, & is daily

used by them in extended senses with an incongruity of which the following is a comparatively mild specimen: *Numbers count for nothing—vide the Coalition—it is the principles that tell.*

videlicet in its full form is now rare except in PEDANTIC HUMOUR, the abbreviation *viz* being used instead; see VIZ for meaning.

vidimus. Pl. *uses*; see -US. Pronounce vi'di-.

vie. For inflexions, see VERBS IN -IE &c., 3.

view forms part of three well established idioms each equivalent to a preposition, & each liable to be confused in meaning or in form with the others. These are *in v. of*, *with a v. to*, & *with the v. of. In view of* means taking into account, or not forgetting, or considering, & is followed by a noun expressing external circumstances that exist or must be expected: *In v. of these facts, we have no alternative; In v. of his having promised amendment; In v. of the Judgement to come. With a view to* means calculating upon or contemplating as a desired result, & is followed by a verbal noun or a gerund or less idiomatically an infinitive: *With a v. to diminution of waste*, or *to diminishing waste*, or (less well) *to diminish waste. With the view of* has the same meaning as *with a v. to*, but is both less usual & less flexible, being naturally followed only by a gerund: *With the v. of proving his sanity.* It will be observed that in the first phrase *v.* means sight, in the second eye, & in the third purpose. The forms of confusion are giving the first the meaning of the others or vice versa, & neglecting the correspondences *a & to, the & of*, in the second & third. After each of the following quotations a correction, or a statement that it is right, is bracketed:—*There was very little likelihood in the report of disaster to a Turkish destroyer in harbour at Preveza*, in view of *the fact that no Turkish destroyer was stationed there* (right)./

These aids to writing are those we recommend that you own personally and have handy on your desk. Other large and more specialized dictionaries are to be found in the library, and we have already covered their use in the section on using the library.

Good Writing

In this and the next three sections we shall give you some general pointers on good writing. They will be general because the details are to be found in books on composition, and this is not the place to go into them.

The main purpose of writing is to tell people something, to communicate. The basic difference between good writing and bad writing lies in how well it tells you what the writer had in his mind. Of course, some writing is literature, and literature has an aesthetic as well as an informative purpose. You may, as an exercise, occasionally be called upon to try your hand at literary writing, but your main job in college is to learn how to write clearly and effectively.

To do this, think of the paragraph as the unit of communication. Make sure that at the beginning, or near the beginning of it, you have a *topic sentence* that states clearly the substance of the paragraph. It should be expressed in language familiar to the reader at that point, taking off from the paragraph preceding it. If there is any need to bridge the gap between these two paragraphs, a *transitional sentence* may come before the topic sentence. Following the topic sentence, you elaborate and explain what you mean by the topic sentence, giving examples or important facts that justify the topic statement. Following that, you pull all that you have said together in a *summary sentence* at the end of the paragraph. The summary sentence is usually a different way of saying the topic sentence, built on the body of the paragraph and cast in a way that prepares the reader to go on to the next paragraph. Thus, in tying together the beginning and the end of a paragraph you make it a unit of communication.

The paragraph as a unit serves at various levels of your communication. The introductory paragraph in a paper may refer to the paper as a whole, giving its purpose and scope. The paragraph at the beginning of a section can summarize the section as a whole. In every case, the paragraph is the unit of thought, but it serves to express thoughts at different levels in your organization. This, incidentally, is why outlining is so helpful; it tells you at what level to construct each of your paragraphs.

We emphasize this point because people who have trouble writing usually have not mastered the paragraph. They either don't know or don't apply these principles of constructing a paragraph. If they could get their paragraphs straightened out, the biggest barrier to improving their writing would be removed. After that, they could concentrate on the details of grammar and on using the right words in the right places.

Grammar

Good writing is built on good grammar. And the rules of good grammar come from good writing. It's that simple! If something is clear, easy to understand, and not clumsy, it is grammatically correct. "Aha," you may say, "a statement like 'He sure ain't a real friendly dog' is clear and easy to understand, but it has several mistakes in grammar." As a matter of fact, such a statement is good grammar—good colloquial grammar. It is the kind of thing many people would say, and other people would understand them.

The important point, however, is that spoken language often doesn't look right in print because it is inappropriate to a diverse audience. Good grammatical writing is appropriate to the occasion. In written English people usually don't expect a word like "ain't" or an adjective like "sure" modifying a verb. Written English is more formal than spoken English mostly because formal writing is more exact and precise than informal writing. So when you write a theme or an essay, you try to be a little more formal. That's all. You don't try to be complicated or try to remember confusing and obscure rules of grammar. You learn a few simple rules, and you apply these in a sensible way. Above all, you continually ask yourself, "Is what I am writing clear, and does it say what I really mean?"

HOW'S YOUR GRAMMAR?

To assess a person's grammar and ability to punctuate requires a fairly lengthy and detailed test. You may take such a test when you enter college or take a course in English writing. If, however, you are unusually poor in grammar and punctuation, you will miss some of the items on the following brief test. See the correct answers below after you have taken the test. Underline the correct alternative.

1. Either history or economics (is, are) going to be my major.
2. The size of clothes (is, are) much too small for him.
3. Everybody wants to do (his, their) best.
4. The fellow asked me (who, whom) my teacher was.
5. She, like Jane and (I, me), is pretty tall.

6. Each of us (look, looks) forward to seeing her.
7. We have (began, begun) the college team.
8. He had (lain, laid) there for some time.
9. He called me "(The, the) smartest fellow of them all."
10. The title of the article was "(The, the) (Cool, cool) of the (Night, night)."

KEY FOR HOW'S YOUR GRAMMAR?

The following are the correct answers: (1) is, (2) is, (3) his, (4) who, (5) me, (6) looks, (7) begun, (8) lain, (9) the, (10) The, Cool, Night.

Punctuation

Punctuation is the backbone of good writing, and we can use it to show you how sensible good grammar can be. The surprising thing is that anybody can punctuate properly just by doing a little thinking. The purpose of periods and commas is to set apart separate ideas so that you can digest them without being confused by other ideas.

The period is the basic punctuation mark, and you use it any time you have an idea that is complete. For example, you can have a one-word sentence: "Stop." Here is a whole idea expressed by one word.

When do you know that you have a complete idea? For one thing, just talking out loud will help. Your intonation changes at the end of a sentence, and you pause. The change in intonation and the pause are a way of putting periods into what you say out loud. Thus you can just put periods where your intonation falls and you pause. This won't always work, but it makes the important point that punctuation in writing is just as easy as punctuation in talking. You punctuate in talking all the time without thinking about it. The trouble with many people is

that they do not have enough experience at punctuating in writing, and they are not sure of themselves.

Commas are used to separate ideas that are related. If one idea depends upon another, they should be separated by a comma (just as the ideas in this sentence are). Commas also separate out words for emphasis or in enumeration (when you are listing things), again in much the same way that you use emphasis and pauses in speaking.

Don't lose sight, though, of the purpose of punctuation. Punctuation is there to keep ideas apart and in this way to make things easy to read and understand. Sometimes it is very nice (and useful) to use elegant variations in punctuation. But if you tackle some of the more complicated rules, always keep the basic purpose of punctuation in mind.

The Use of Mistakes

Everybody makes mistakes in grammar. This is just another way of saying that the writing of most of us can stand some improvement.

Here is a page from the beginning of the section on punctuation in a dictionary. (By permission. From Webster's New Collegiate Dictionary, copyright, 1961; 1963, 1965, by G. & C. Merriam Company.)

PUNCTUATION

,	comma
;	semicolon
:	colon
.	period *or* full stop
—	dash *or* em dash
-	dash *or* en dash
~	swung dash
?	question mark *or* interrogation point
¿ ?	question marks, Spanish
!	exclamation point
()	parentheses *or* curves
[]	brackets, square
< >	brackets, angle
' or '	apostrophe
-	hyphen
= or ⸗	double hyphen
´	(é) acute accent
`	(è) grave accent
ʌ	(ô) *or* ⌢ *or* ~ circumflex
~	(ñ) tilde
—	(ō) macron
‿	(ŭ) breve

¨	(oö) diaeresis
¸	(ç) cedilla
∧	caret
" " *or* » «	quotation marks
≪ ≫	quotation marks, French
»« *or* „ "	quotation marks, German
' ' *or* ' '	quotation marks, single
" *or* " *or* "	ditto marks
/	virgule *or* slant
\	reversed virgule
{ *or* } *or* ⌣ brace	
. . . *or* * * * *or* — — ellipsis	
. . .	suspension points
*	asterisk
†	dagger
‡	double dagger
§	section *or* numbered clause
‖	parallels
¶ *or* ⁋	paragraph
☞	index *or* fist
. *or* .*.	asterism

0.1 Speech consists not merely of sounds but of organized sound sequences that follow various structural patterns and are uttered with significant modifications of pitch and stress and significant pauses. Besides representing the basic sounds of speech, the English writing system accordingly utilizes signs called punctuation marks to separate groups of words and to convey some indication of the varying pitch and volume and especially the pauses in the flow of speech sounds.

0.2 A pause in speech is accompanied by a significant adjustment in the pitch of the voice, which may rise, fall, or remain the same. There may also be an increase or decrease in stress with or without actual cessation of sound. Three principal types of pauses are readily perceptible in English speech: (1) The fading pause, a falling into silence with a full stop, is marked by a lowering of pitch and decrease of stress until the production of sound ceases. This pause signifies the termination of an utterance and in writing is usually indicated by the period or the semicolon. (2) The rising pause is characterized by an upturn in pitch often combined with a lengthening of word sounds just before the break. This pause is used to set off word groups within utterances, especially whenever there is anticipation of supplementary or explanatory matter to follow, and is usually indicated in writing by a comma or, at the end of a question, by a question mark. (3) The sustained pause occurs whenever there is a break without any change in the pitch of the voice or when the same pitch is continued across a break. This pause is often indicated in writing by a comma, particularly when a rising pause would also be appropriate. The sustained pause is indicated also by such marks as a dash or ellipsis where a person stops speaking without altering the pitch of his voice, as when he is interrupted.

0.3 Much written expression consists of discourse never actually spoken but formulated in the writer's mind and immediately expressed in writing. Somewhat more formal in its structural patterns than actual speech, such written expression is nevertheless a reflection of the spoken language, is itself capable of being spoken, and is therefore punctuated as the written expression of actual speech.

0.4 As will be indicated, punctuation marks are often used in an arbitrary or mechanical manner not directly related to language structure or to patterns of speech sounds. To a considerable extent, however, punctuation may be explained in terms of the structural divisions of speech—sentences, clauses, phrases, and other word groups—and some of the more obvious elements of pitch, stress, and pause that indicate their separation or their relationship.

1.1 Like a fading pause and full stop in speech, a **period** usually terminates a sentence that is neither interrogative nor exclamatory ⟨The mountain is 5000 feet high. If the climbers have a good day, they will reach the top in a few hours. At the summit they will eat the lunch which has been prepared, and then they will start down early enough to reach the bottom before dark.⟩

1.1.1 Utterances terminated by a fading pause do not always have a complete subject-predicate struc-

ture. In the context of consecutive speech, however, the meaning of such utterances is entirely clear, and in writing they are usually terminated with a period ⟨"Tell me when you came in." "Just now."⟩ ⟨"Please close the door." "Certainly."⟩

1.1.2 Structurally incomplete or fragmentary elements terminating in a period occur frequently in modern narrative writing and are usually

---

Some people make mistakes in rather elementary matters, however, and these are usually the people who run into trouble in writing themes and essays. If you ignore the really basic rules of grammar, you make your writing hard to read and leave the impression that you're ignorant and really not very bright. Frequently, however, students ignore basic rules because they are not in the habit of carefully examining what they write. Take, for example, the matter of agreement between subject and verb.

Nearly all of you can recognize that "He don't care" is not good written English. And most of you can put your finger on exactly what is wrong. If you can't, you probably have some very serious trouble with your writing and you ought to see someone who can help you. The correct form is "He does not [doesn't] care," and it is correct because a singular subject belongs with one form of the verb "does" and not another "do".

Little mistakes like this are not terribly important by themselves, but teachers of composition are concerned about them because students who make them are usually students who do not understand the English language as well as they ought to. Can you, for example, always identify the subject of a sentence? Or do you confuse the subject with any noun or with some part of the sentence that merely modifies the subject?

The real purpose of studying grammar is not to avoid trivial mistakes but to help you avoid writing things that are so unclear that they do not mean anything to anyone but you. Knowing something about grammar isn't the only thing that is important in good writing, but is one of the things that is most important.

That is the reason for the title of this section. We really didn't intend to give you a list of the "ten most common mistakes in grammar," but we mean to show you that you can make use of your mistakes and, by correcting them, improve your writing.

When someone corrects a mistake, always make sure you know what the correct form is and, even more important, make sure that you know why you made the mistake. This is the only good way you learn the proper use of your language. Get into the habit of carefully reading what you write in order to correct your own little mistakes. You will find that this is actually interesting. But, above all, if you don't understand why you made a mistake or why a correction was made, find out. If you don't, you will be handicapped all through college.

Incidentally, the little book by Strunk and White mentioned above contains a substantial list of common mistakes in grammar. Going over these, or referring to them when you are writing, can help you eliminate many of your mistakes.

The rules of grammar actually come from the way you and other people write and talk. Knowing them helps you to write and talk in the way other people do and to understand what they are saying. If you had your own unique way of writing and talking, that would be fine, except that nobody could understand you. Only by making your writing and speech conform to other people's can you make it possible for other people to understand you.

Spelling

A brief but emphatic word about spelling: As a college student, you're expected to spell correctly *all* the words you write. That includes not only the common words everybody uses but also the rarer and more technical words (and names) encountered in college training. To spell correctly all the time, you must do the following things: First of all, be careful. Students often misspell words they know how to spell simply because they're careless; they write hurriedly and don't look for their own spelling errors. Secondly, pay attention to the spelling of the new words and names you come across in studying. Make sure you can spell any of the names or important words in your textbooks or in the sources you use for writing papers. Thirdly, use the dictionary. Any time you are in the slightest doubt about spelling, look up the word in the dictionary. Finally, familiarize yourself with spelling rules, particularly for the special endings of words. You can find these rules in grammar books and also in dictionaries.

Misspelled words are serious offenses. They distract a reader's attention because they look odd, making him stop to see what's wrong when he should be concerned only with the meaning of what he reads. Spelling is also taken as a mark of the cultural training of an individual; if you don't spell well, you give the impression of being illiterate and poorly educated. Finally, a teacher takes the misspelling of special words and names as a sign that the student hasn't really mastered the material he is writing about. One student we know got an F on an otherwise good paper on Shakespeare's *Julius Caesar* because he repeatedly wrote Mark Anthony for the correct Mark Antony. Not every teacher would assess such a heavy penalty—though the error was inexcusable—but all are displeased and unfavorably impressed by misspelled words. A student who hopes to do well on his papers had therefore better be a good speller.

The spelling of words is partly a matter of principles, and partly rote. There are principles or rules governing spelling, and you can find them in books on the subject. Beyond that, the only way to spell correctly is to practice good spelling habits. If you have any reason to believe you are weak in spelling, you should find a book on the subject in your bookstore and study. There are some programmed textbooks on it that permit you to test and practice your spelling by yourself. One that we can suggest is Geneva L. Smith's *Spelling by Principles: A Programed Text* (Appleton-Century-Crofts, 1966).

Research Notes

We have separately gone over the ways you should take and keep notes on lectures and textbooks. We have, however, saved until now the topic of research notes because they should be taken and kept in a different way than other notes; they are the kinds of notes one takes in library research for the preparation of a paper.

Summary Notes
One of the main differences between research notes and other notes is that you do not need to outline them. These notes should be in the form of summaries. While you are reading you may jot down the rudiments of an outline; but when you are finished, you should take these rough notes as your guide and compose a summary of the principal points in the reading. How lengthy or detailed it is depends on the size of the reading, on what the instructor has suggested you do, and on your purpose in reading. Once you have your summary composed, you can usually throw away your rough reading notes.

Use of Cards
Another feature of research reading is that you don't know exactly how much of it you will eventually use until you have finished reading almost all your library-research materials. The topic you had in mind when you started may turn out to be too big, or some of the articles may prove to be too peripheral or unimportant for your purposes. Another feature of research reading is that you don't know either, as you read, just how you will organize your paper. This only begins to emerge when you are close to finishing your reading. And undoubtedly you will not use

the articles in your paper in the same order you read them in. Moreover, when you come to write your paper, some articles will be used many times and others hardly at all.

These two points have an important implication: They require that you be able later to organize and reorganize your notes in any sequence that suits your purpose. Consequently, they make it poor strategy to take notes on sheets of paper the way you take lecture or textbook notes. For this purpose, cards are much better materials to use. If you have one card for each article you read and keep all your notes for the article on this card, you can later shuffle and arrange these cards to have them in any sequence that fits the organization of your paper. People who write textbooks or scholarly articles have this problem on a large scale, often involving thousands of articles, and they almost invariably do all their note taking on cards.

In your bookstore, you can probably find all sizes of card for any purpose. The smallest cards are 3 by 5 inches, the next size 4 by 6 inches, and the largest size 6 by 9 inches. For most purposes, either the 3 by 5 or the 4 by 6 is best. You can't get many notes on a 3 by 5; and since it is best to get all notes on the two sides of a card, the 4 by 6 cards are usually the best bet. You'll want to decide, though, on the basis of the particular job you have to do. The main point is that if you are reading a number of articles, doing research on a topic, you should take your notes on cards, not on notebook paper.

It's a good idea, incidentally, to have a card box in which you can file your cards.

The first thing you put on a card is the *correct* reference. If your source is a book, your reference must consist of the name or names of the author(s), including all initials given on the title page, the title of the book, the place where it is published, the name of the publisher, and its copyright date (not the date of its last printing). Although you may not need it, you should also include the number of pages of front matter, which are indicated by Roman numerals, and the total of the regularly numbered pages. If your source is a magazine or journal, your correct reference must include author(s), title of the article, name of the journal, the year, the volume number, and the pages on which the article begins and ends. Be careful to take down these data without mistakes, for you or someone else may use the reference later and rely on its being correct.

The exact way in which you list the above information in a list of references varies from one field to another. Each professional group or sometimes a particular journal has its own customs governing citation. You should follow those accepted in the field you are working in, and the easiest way to determine the customs is to look at the references at the end of the chapters or articles you read. If these don't make the system clear, follow the form of the *World List of Periodicals,* a big book that can be found in the reading room of almost any library. Whatever you do, though, *be consistent* throughout any one assignment or paper.

chapter 8
STUDYING A FOREIGN LANGUAGE

The study of a foreign language presents some rather special problems. Your task isn't just to understand and remember what you read and hear; you must learn the skills of speaking and writing a new language. If you really want to learn a new language, you must work at it until it becomes as familiar to you as the habits of dressing or driving a car. In this chapter, we will suggest some of the ways of working at it that are especially likely to be fruitful. These will be discussed under three general headings: The General Approach, Learning to Read the Language, and Learning to Speak the Language.

The General Approach

Different students, of course, will have different problems in studying foreign languages. This is true of all subjects but particularly of languages. Some will find reading the language relatively easy but understanding the spoken language rather difficult, and vice versa. Some will experience their greatest trouble in composing thoughts in the language, others in translating it. You'll have to find out for yourself just what comes most easily to you and what gives you the greatest difficulty. And in reading the suggestions below, you'll find that some are much more applicable than others to your problems of studying foreign languages.

Keeping up with the Work
You can fall behind in economics, history, biology, or literature and later catch up on them, though we don't recommend it. You are really in hot water, however, if you fall behind in a foreign language. Consequently, regular, daily preparation of lessons and reading assignments is absolutely necessary, even if you are to do no more than pass in the course.

The reason is that learning a language proceeds in definite steps, just as a baby must stand before it can walk and walk before it can run. You must know the meaning of words before you can use them in simple phrases and sentences. You must know something about word order before you can use words or translate them in more complex sentences. You must know the various forms a word can take before you can get tenses straight and the relationship of words to each other in a clause or sentence. For these reasons, you must keep on schedule, taking the more elementary steps that are prerequisite to the more complicated ones. Otherwise, you'll find you just can't do the next assignment and won't know what is going on in class. Hence, in foreign languages, it is doubly important that you stick to a regular program of study.

Recitation
All the steps in the study techniques we have already outlined (Chapters Three and Five) are applicable to the study of language, but one, recitation, is especially important. You can't learn a language without it, and the easiest way to fail a course in foreign language is to neglect it. Indeed, 80 per cent or more of your time, particularly in the early stages of language study, should be spent in recitation.

You know, of course, that you cannot learn a special skill, like tennis, typewriting, or playing the trumpet, without practice. Like playing tennis or typewriting, using a language is a skill, and you can learn to use it only by practice. Therefore, when you tackle a foreign language for the first time, you might as well prepare yourself for some real work. If you approach the language in a half-hearted way, the chances are you're wasting your time. You can never get very far without practice—and practice means recitation.

Actually there are three skills you must master in learning a new language:

First of all, you must learn to read it and to translate it into your own language. Secondly, you should learn to understand the language when you hear it. Thirdly, you should learn to speak the language. Most American students are interested in the first skill, but with increased foreign commerce and American personnel in other countries, listening to, and speaking, a language are becoming more and more important. If you emphasize recitation in learning a language, you will be working at all three skills, since all are involved when you recite.

Learning Grammar

In American colleges, most courses in foreign languages place a lot of stress on grammar. Language teachers try to teach you the structure of a new language so that it becomes second nature to you. If you know the rules of grammar in a language, you can construct sentences of your own in that language as well as understand what other people say and write in the language.

There are several things that frequently get students into trouble with the grammar of a foreign language. The first is that many students either have forgotten or never knew the rudiments of English grammar. Consequently they are confused when their Spanish or French instructor talks about tenses, moods, possessives, declensions, gerunds, and participles. They find that the grammar of a foreign language is so much nonsense, a complete mystery. The reason is that they do not know the meaning of these grammatical terms in their own language whereas their instructor takes it for granted that they do. If you find yourself in this difficulty in a foreign language, you can make up your deficiencies as you go along with the aid of an ordinary English dictionary and a little work.

Very frequently students encounter grammatical terms for the first time in studying a foreign language. For example: few students of English grammar are likely to run across an expression like "a noun in the dative case" or, "a pronoun in the accusative case" and so on. This is because meanings in English are customarily given by word positions, English seldom employing special word endings (*case* endings) to show grammatical relations. Yet in many other languages such endings are frequent. Hence it is an advantage to be able to name and talk about the dative case, for instance, which may be indicated by a special ending on nouns and pronouns. There is nothing mysterious about the dative; it is just the indirect object of a verb. In the sentence "He gave me the book," "me" is in the dative case.

Whenever you run across new grammatical terms in a foreign language, make sure that you understand them. You usually can do that best by thinking about what kind of statement in English a particular grammatical term refers to.

Often students diligently memorize the special grammatical categories of a new language without attaching any real meaning to what they memorize. Thus they will learn the declension of a class of German nouns with the example "nominative, *das Haus;* genitive, *des Hauses;* dative, *dem Hause;* and accusative, *das Haus.*" Such students can rattle off lists like this for examinations, but when they come to using their understanding of what these different cases mean and how they are used in sentences, they are lost.

One problem with all languages is that they are full of irregularities. Grammarians try to make up rules describing the way all words are used in a language, but there are always exceptions to the rules. Therefore there are irregular nouns and irregular verbs, which do not follow the general rules for either case or conjugation endings. The only thing you can do with these is to memorize them. You must recite them—not only in lists but in phrases and sentences—until they become second nature to you. You'll then be able to employ them in sentences and consistently recognize them when you see them in print.

The teaching of grammar in a course in foreign languages is, however, merely a device for speeding your mastery of the language. We all learn to speak our native tongue fluently as children before we hear of grammar. With enough practice, a person learns to use a language in its proper form without knowing grammatical rules. The rules, then, are merely ways of helping the adult learn quickly the correct endings and word order without so much practice.

Thinking in a Language

The ultimate goal in studying a language is to learn to think in that language.

To think in a language means not only to be fluent in it and to know it well but something else even more fundamental. It means you don't have to "translate" any more. You come to know the meaning of foreign words and sentences without turning them back into English. After all, you don't read English by translating it; that is to say, you don't turn words into other words to understand them. Rather you have associated these words with objects, events, and qualities so that they have direct meaning for you. This is what you should work toward in studying another language. When you achieve it, you'll understand the foreign words and use them without thinking at all in English. As a consequence, you'll save yourself a lot of work going from the language to English and back again. You'll be master of the language, which is your real goal anyway; and that will give you satisfaction as well as a good grade in the course.

Learning to Read the Language

Because you must walk before you can run, you can't start right off thinking in a language, especially when you must proceed at the relatively slow pace of the typical college course in a foreign language. You must perforce begin thinking in English and translating foreign words into and from English. Only gradually can you abandon translation and come to think in the language. During your progress from one stage to the other, you may find some of the following suggestions helpful.

Studying by Phrases and Sentences

In the very first few weeks of a course in a foreign language, students nearly always translate word for word. This is all right for the kind of elementary sentences you get at this stage, but it won't do at all when the going gets rougher. Yet many students persist in this word-for-word translation throughout the entire study of a language. For a language like Spanish this is less likely to get you into trouble (because the grammar and word order are so much like English) than for languages like Latin and German, which have word orders quite different from English ones. A second-year student in German can easily get lost trying to find his way word for word through the seemingly impenetrable thicket of a German sentence, for the German word order is so different that it makes little sense translated literally. The student must learn to think in German word order and get the sense of the sentence as a whole before he looks up the specific words he does not know. And even when he is concentrating on specific words, he must keep in mind the relations between words, the over-all meaning, in order to translate them properly.

You will discover yourself that this is the only way you can translate complicated sentences. If you are doing no better than word-for-word translation, you are in trouble and you need help. We cannot tell you exactly what your difficulties are since they will be different for different people. One frequent difficulty, however, is that the student doesn't have the basic elements of a vocabulary, such as relative pronouns or irregular verbs, so well memorized that they are second nature to him. Other students don't know their syntax or word order well enough to be able to tell where they are in a sentence. This is a particular difficulty for students of German. Thus in a sentence like *Haben Sie den Bauer gesehen, der auf dem Wagen sass?* ("Have you seen the farmer who sat on the wagon?"), a badly confused student may try to translate *der* as a definite article rather than as a relative pronoun. An example of a parallel problem in French is the sentence *Elle a recu les fleurs que lui ont envoyees des amies* ("She received the flowers that friends sent her"), where the unobservant student may read the objective pronoun *que* as the nominative pronoun *qui*, thus making hash of the sense. By looking over the whole sentence and by relating the words to one another, you would not be able to make a mistake of this kind.

Looking up Words

Probably the most common mistake made by students attempting to translate a passage is to look up too many words. Each time the student comes to a word he does not know, he reaches for the dictionary and looks up its meaning. There are two things wrong with doing this.

One is that you may not have to look up the word if you read on and get the context in which the word is used. A dictionary is only one way of establishing the meaning, and it is both time consuming and relatively ineffective for it isolates the meaning from the surroundings in which it is used. Meaning can also be learned, and it is better if it can be, by knowing the context in which the word is used. In fact, most of us have learned most of our English vocabulary in this way. Context always limits the kinds of words that can appear in a particular place in a sentence. From this limitation, you can frequently guess quite accurately the meaning of such words.

The second thing wrong with looking up words as soon as you come to one you do not know is related to the first. When you look for the dictionary meaning of a word, you always find not one, but several meanings given. Which one is the "correct" one or the best one? The answer is given by the context in which the word is used. One meaning fits one context, another meaning another context.

The conclusion to draw from these two points is that when you read you should always read for context, and you should read the full context in which any unfamiliar word appears. This conclusion has two consequences: One is that you should never look up a word until you have fully explored its context. The second is that you should keep to a minimum the number of words you look up and try your hardest to infer the meaning of words from their context.

When applied to a strategy of study, these points lead to the following advice: When you are translating, go just as far as you can with intelligent guessing. From the context of a word, make an intelligent guess as to its meaning, and continue on. Do this until you get lost. If your guess is right, the sentences that follow will confirm your guess, and you have learned the meaning of a word in context, which is what you should be trying to do. If your guess is incorrect, the opposite will happen; before long, something in the succeeding sentences will tell you. Sometimes you will pick up clues as to what the word must have meant, and thus the later context will correct you, again permitting you to learn the meaning of the word.

If neither of these things happen, and you have lost the meaning of what you are reading, now is the time to look up the word that stopped you. At this point, underline the word so that you can find it again in subsequent study, and look it up in the dictionary. Then, having read its context, you probably can choose the meaning that is appropriate for the context. Now proceed again with your reading until you come upon another unknown word, and repeat the sequence over again. Make this your basic strategy in translating a reading assignment.

But there is more to it. You should continue on this tack for about half of your assignment. At this point, a rest is probably in order anyway. After your break, however, instead of plowing ahead, go back and reread from the beginning the first half of the assignment. This is a way of reciting while the material is still fresh in your mind. This time you will probably be able to read steadily ahead, remembering the words you have learned either from context or by looking them up, and your memory for these words will be much better by this immediate review.

But you will probably miss a few, in which case you can look them up again. This time put a dot or check mark in the margin to show that you had to look it up a second time. After you finish re-reading in this way the first part of the assignment, and perhaps taking another short break, go on to the second half using the same strategy.

There are two important points we are making here: Firstly, learn the meaning of words from context and in context, keeping to a minimum the number of words you look up during translation. Secondly, always reread a passage soon after translating it the first time. Later on, you can concentrate on learning the words that give you the most trouble while translating in this way (see below).

Dissecting Words

There is, of course, a time and place for paying attention to individual words. One is when you've read a sentence and can't get its meaning because you're not sure of one or more words in it. Another, naturally, is in the process of building your vocabulary. While learning a language, you're always adding to your store of usable words. You'll often find it necessary to look up a word in the dictionary and try to remember it. You'll be saved a lot of work, though, if you try to break words down into their elements and determine the meaning of the elements. We've already suggested that you do this in building an English vocabulary (see page 49),

and it is just as appropriate in the study of another language.

Languages are put together in different ways, but most of them, like English, have root words to which other words or parts of words have been attached. If you learn the general meanings of the affixes (prefixes and suffixes), you frequently can figure out a word you've never seen before merely by dissecting it into its root and affixes. Even if you don't get the precise meaning in this way, the process of dissecting the word will help you remember its meaning once you've learned what it is.

Cognate Words

Remember too that many of the words in European languages are similar to words in English. This is true because English has its historical roots in both the Germanic and Romance (French, Spanish, Italian) languages. Hence many words in these languages have carried over into English. The original forms have often been modified in the process, of course, but they are nevertheless similar in meaning and appearance to

THE USE OF COGNATES

Below are two passages, one in French (from C. T. Morgan, Psychologie physiologique, trans. by H. Lesage, Presses Universitaires de France, Paris, 1949, p. 1) and the other in German (from F. G. G. Schmidt, Beruhmte Deutsche neuerer Zeit, Knopf, New York, 1929, pp. 62, 63). For this exercise, select the passage in a language you have not yet studied. As you read it, have a pencil and paper handy. In one column, write any foreign words that look like English; in a second column, write the English words that are most similar to the foreign words; and in the third column, write your guess about the correct translation of each of the foreign words. When you have finished, turn to page 106 and compare your answers with the lists you find there.

La physiologie et la psychologie étudient, l'une et l'autre, l'organisme vivant mais chacune de ces deux sciences vise un but différent. La psychologie cherche à comprendre comment les stimuli physiques règlent le comportement de l'organisme. La physiologie, par contre, se propose de comprendre les processus qui se déroulent à l'intérieur de l'organisme.

Paul Ehrlich war geboren am 12 Marz 1854 in Strehlen (Schlesien). Er besuchte di Elementarschule seiner Vaterstadt, dann das Gymna-

sium zu Breslau, wo er besonders gut Latein lernte und ausgeprägte mathematische Begabung zeigte. Trotzdem empfand er die Schule stets als Zwang, und für gewisse Fächer besass er nicht das geringste Interesse. Die Prufüngen waren ihm fürchterlich. Wegen der guten Kenntnisse im Lateinischen war ihm schon der Wegfall der mündlichen Prüfung in Aussicht gestellt worden, als ihm "seine einseitige Begabung" einen Streich spielte. In der Schlussprufüng sollte er einen Aufsatz schreiben über das Thema: "Das Leben ein Traum."

THE USE OF COGNATES

The lists below contain most of the cognate words in the passages on page 105. Since similarity of words and their historical origins is to some extent a matter of judgment, your list may be somewhat different and still be a good one. Note how often guesses based on similarities are substantially correct. Also note some instances in which the similarities are misleading.

French word	Similar English word	English translation
physiologie	physiology	physiology
psychologie	psychology	psychology
une	one	one
autre	other	other
organisme	organism	organism
deux	deuce	two
sciences	sciences	sciences
différent	different	different
cherche	search	aim, search
comprendre	comprehend	understand, comprehend
comment	comment	how, in what manner
stimuli	stimuli	stimuli
physiques	physics	physical
règlent	regal	govern
contre	contrary	on the other hand (with par)
propose	propose	purpose, intend (with se)
processus	processes	processes
déroulement	roll	unroll, unfold
intérieur	interior	interior, the inside

German word	Similar English word	English translation
geboren	born	born
Elementarschule	elementary school	primary school
Vaterstadt	father state	native town
Gymnasium	gymnasium	high school
gut	good	good, well
Latein	Latin	Latin
lernte	learned	learned
mathematische	mathematical	mathematical
Schule	school	school
Interesse	interest	interest
Prüfung(en)	proof	examination, test
mündlichen	monthly	oral
über	over	concerning (with schreiben)
Thema	theme	subject, theme
Leben	live	life
Traum	dream	dream

their English descendants. If you look for such similar words, called *cognate* words, that have a common heritage, you will find translation much easier. To illustrate what we mean, take a pencil and piece of paper and study the sentences given in the accompanying exercise, The Use of Cognates. You'll find you can get pretty close to the meaning of many words in languages you've never studied.

You should be warned, however, that cognates can lead you astray and that you cannot rely blindly on the apparent similarities of foreign and English words. Sometimes a foreign word looks very much like an English word and yet has a rather different meaning. This can happen either by "accident" or because cognate words, words actually having a common beginning, have gradually changed their meaning through centuries of usage. Even when the meanings of cognate words are similar, there may be such fine shades of difference between them that you can't accurately translate them in the most obvious way. It's therefore a good rule to look up all words at least once to check their exact meaning, but only after you've attempted a guess about them based on their apparent similarity to English. In this way, you'll use their cognate relations for recitation and later as a device for remembering more easily their exact meanings.

Using Cards

As we've pointed out, there is a lot of memorizing in the study of languages, and students have always tried many techniques to make their memorizing easier and more efficient. A common one is to write a foreign word on one side of a card and its translation on the other side. (Indeed, you can buy such cards already printed.) You can test yourself by running through the foreign words while making translations of them. When you're stumped, you remind yourself of the correct translation by flipping the card over on its back. This can be a worthwhile practice if used judiciously.

First of all, you should make up your own cards. You learn by this, and your own cards will be much more useful to you than somebody else's set. Secondly, you should keep your working stack of cards small. Make sure you've thoroughly mastered one set of cards before you add other ones to the stack. When you're sure of a word, you can throw that card aside. This way you can keep the stack down to manageable size.

When you come to translating more difficult passages, it is a good idea to make up a card every time you must look up a word. If this is all you do, however, you'll soon have a bulging packet of cards. So periodically set aside time to study your cards. Run over them—perhaps once a day. Each time you know the word, put down a tally on the card; each time you don't, put down a zero. When you get up to five tallies in a row without any zeros, the chances are you won't forget the word again. You can then put this card aside.

There is one other way to use cards. As you acquire a reading knowledge of a language and are learning more complicated words and abstract words with many different meanings, it is a good idea to put down whole phrases, not just single words, on your cards. These help you to think in larger units and to use words in their proper context. Context is always the best support for meaning; things you can't remember at all when they are taken by themselves can easily be remembered when you have them associated with other things.

Students sometimes write English words between the lines or on the margins of passages they are translating. This is easier than using cards, but it isn't, as a rule, the best thing to do. It has two disadvantages: (1) It leaves the translation in full view when you are reading the foreign words and thus makes it virtually impossible for you to recite without prompting. It's much better to get the meaning yourself and look at the translation only when you fail—an argument for cards. (2) By focusing your attention on the translation, it tends to keep you thinking in English rather than in the foreign language. Since you eventually want to know the meanings of words without converting them to English, it is better not to refer to English any more than you have to.

Ponies and Trots

In advanced language classes, where you're reading books or lengthy passages from foreign literature, it is often possible to procure English translations of the material known informally as *ponies or trots*. In some cases, the trot supplies interlinear translation—English words between the lines of foreign material. In others, the trot consists of the foreign text on one page and the English translation on the facing page. Although in principle such trots should help you learn a language, as they are ordinarily used they are a detriment to progress in language study.

Interlinear translations have the disadvantage we mentioned above for English words written between or near the foreign lines you are reading. They also make life much too easy. The student doesn't have to figure out or look up a translation even once. Hence he deprives himself of the opportunity of recitation and of the precise knowledge of a word he gains by looking it up. This is also true of trots that give the translation on the facing page, though these permit you to read without looking at the translation if you really want to.

An even more serious objection to the trot is that it handicaps thinking in the language. When you get to the stage where you can use trots you should be making progress in thinking in the language and you should avoid as much as possible the step of translating the language into English. Trots obviously don't encourage you to think in another language; in fact, they do just the reverse.

A final objection to many trots is that they are such free and easy translations that the student never gets to know the exact meanings of the words and phrases he is reading. Free translation can be very desirable when the translator knows precisely what he is interpreting, but when offered to the person who isn't very skilled in the first place, it is a very poor teacher.

For these reasons, language instructors generally take a rather dim view of trots or similar aids to translation. Some instructors go so far as to fail a student who uses them. On the other hand, there are times when it might be profitable to read an English version of something you are going to translate. The best policy is to follow conscientiously the instructions of your teacher in this matter.

Learning to Speak the Language

The general pointers we have just given you for learning to read a language also apply to speaking it. In the early stages of training, the two usually go together, and speaking it helps one learn to read it. However, for students who are attempting to gain speaking fluency as rapidly as possible, there are techniques that especially need stressing.

Language as Habit

A baby starts out by learning the meaning of words as they are spoken by others around him and later uses them in sentences, copying from others and being corrected by them. By the time he goes to school and long before he has learned reading or writing, let alone grammar, he has a very good mastery of the language compared with that of the typical student who studies foreign language for a couple of years. All this without grammar and without reading or writing!

The child learns language this way simply because he practices and practices it until the language is merely a set of habits. Unfortunately, it is seldom possible to put college students in the position of the baby, where they are forced to rely exclusively on the language being learned. If language teachers had their way, they would do just this, for they know that living and thinking with a language every hour of the day is the one way to master it quickly and well. In special schools set up for language teachers, military personnel, and others whose chief goal is to master a language, the teaching usually stresses this way of learning.

Although the college student normally can't obtain this kind of training, he can take an important lesson from it. To make the most rapid progress in language study, he can do everything possible to practice it and to use it to think with. He can seek out foreigners who speak the language and converse with them in their tongue. He can secure foreign-language newspapers and read them regularly. He can try to take in foreign movies, which are often running somewhere in the larger cities. At the very least, he can arrange with other students taking his course to set aside periods when they can converse exclusively in the foreign language. In this way, using and understanding the language can gradually become second nature to him, and he won't have to stumble through it word by word.

But let us be more specific about the things you can do to learn language as a habit.

Imitating and Memorizing

Because language is a habit, not something you get the main ideas of, you must do those things that must be done in learning habits. In general, these boil down to practice, practice, practice. There are, however, two aspects of the practice. One is imitating, the other memorizing.

The only way you learn to speak a language is to have someone to imitate. Your teacher is there, among other things, for that purpose. If you can live with or spend time with a person speaking the language, that is very desirable. In recent years, with the aid of modern technology, a number of other devices provide material to imitate. One is the language-teaching phonograph record especially recorded for the purpose of helping you imitate the correct sounds, words, and sentences in the language. Another that is coming into use more and more in high schools and colleges is the language laboratory, in which a student can listen to tapes, himself record on the tapes and compare the two. If your college has such facilities, be sure to use them to the full. Without such a laboratory, you might combine language records with your own tape recording facilities to make your own language laboratory.

Secondly, you must memorize. Imitating is itself a sort of memorizing—at least of the ways to pronounce the sounds of the language—but beyond that you must memorize the meanings of words and phrases. Although knowing grammar will help speed such memorization, there is no alternative to rehearsing and reciting over and over again until you master the language as a habit.

Studying out Loud

When we discussed reading, we counseled you *not* to read aloud or move your lips because these habits slow down reading in a language you have already mastered. But quite the opposite kind of advice is in order for learning to speak (and also to read) a language. So long as you read silently, you are learning with only the visual sense. Language requires also an auditory memory, and it is at the same time a motor skill. Therefore, all three aspects of language, which reinforce one another, should be practiced together. You should, therefore, as much as possible do your language studying out loud. Try to find someplace to do this—a cubicle, a language lab, a balcony, or the lawn. If there is no such place outside you own room, try to schedule your language study periods at a time when no one else will be bothered by your talking to yourself in a foreign language.

Spacing of Study

Psychologists have learned through many experiments that learning, to be efficient, should be spaced rather than massed. Put another way, there is an optimum distribution of time for acquiring a habit. This is especially true of skills such as language. Your units of study should not be too large—or too small either. As we indicated in talking about translation assignments, it is best to break up any particular assignment into two parts and by re-reading and review to master each one separately.

At the same time, these units should be spaced with short rests or breaks. In language study, unlike other subjects involving more reading and thinking, you would do well, particularly when you are reciting out loud, to study for half an hour at a stretch, turning to some other subject in between. According to language experts, whose advice in this respect agrees with the results of psychological research, much more will be mastered over the long run in two hours distributed in this way than in two hours in one lump.

In General

Some courses emphasize reading the foreign language; others, speaking it. Some stress grammar while others don't. Some require a very precise understanding of words, and others permit rather free translation. Sometimes special courses are offered in scientific German or scientific French with the purpose of preparing science students only for reading the technical literature in their subject. Your instructor will stress those techniques best suited to the purposes of your particular course.

Some students get very discouraged in studying a foreign language and say they have no aptitude for it. Of course, aptitudes for something like the study of languages differ from individual to individual. Probably, however, a much larger amount of variation among college students, who tend to be rather alike in basic aptitudes, is due to work habits, techniques of study, and background information. Nowhere, except perhaps in mathematics, are things like work habits more important than they are in the study of a foreign language. After all, as Mark Twain remarked, even French babies learn to talk French. Your job is to learn a language, and the only way you can do it is to give yourself a lot of practice. If you think you have a low aptitude for language, you should allow more time for the study of it than almost anything else.

chapter 9

STUDYING MATHEMATICS AND THE SCIENCES

This chapter has two purposes. One is to instruct you in the best ways to approach the study of mathematics and the sciences—especially the natural sciences. The other is to help you improve the basic mathematical skills required to handle courses in these subjects. We include material on basic skills because surveys show that much of the trouble students have with courses in science and mathematics arises from deficiencies in elementary skills, the kinds of skill you are supposed to have learned in grammar school and high school. Many people never really master these, and others forget them because they don't use them. But first let us see what there is that is different about studying sciences and mathematics.

Studying Mathematics

Mathematics and languages are much alike in some respects, and different in others. From these similarities and differences, bearing in mind what we have already said about the study of languages, you will be able to see what needs to be done in studying mathematics.

The similarities begin with the fact that mathematics is a language. It is the special language of science. It is a language because it employs symbols to represent events in the world, and there are grammatical rules for manipulating these symbols. Hence both mathematics and languages have a grammar, and its rules need to be learned.

Another important similarity is that both proceed from the simple to the complex. Each step in learning either of them builds on the steps that have been taken before. If you miss one of these steps, you are in trouble with succeeding steps. This is rather unlike the social sciences and humanites, in which you can learn one segment quite well without having learned

other parts of the material. There are other similarities but these are the important ones for our purposes.

Now let us consider the differences. One is that mathematics is precise, while language is not. You can get the meaning of words from context, and word-meaning in most cases does not have precise boundaries. The meaning of mathematic symbols, on the other hand, can be and is assigned arbitrarily, and once assigned must be used in a precise way. Hence in mathematics one must be more careful than in using languages.

Another important difference is that in mathematics the rules are everything, whereas in language they are only aids to learning something that you would eventually learn anyway whether or not you could formalize the rules. Another way of saying this is that learning a language is, as we have said, a problem in memorization, while learning mathematics is a problem in understanding. In language, you don't think or reason your way to mastering it, but in mathematics this is exactly what you do. So when you approach mathematics you must be prepared to reason, and how well you do this will determine how much you learn.

Now from these similarities and differences you could deduce what is similar and different in the study of the two subjects. Let us run over these briefly.

Keeping up with the Work

In both cases, because they are cumulative subjects, you must keep up with the work. Although you can fall behind in other subjects and catch up without too much waste motion, you cannot do this in mathematics. You should plan your schedule to give priority to mathematics so that you do each assignment on time. In this way, you will not find yourself lost at some later point because there was something fundamental you missed earlier.

In both cases, too, practice makes perfect. In the case of languages, the practice is memorization of the words, phrases, and sentences. In mathematics, the practice is one of following rules in the solution of problems. It is essentially practice in rigorous reasoning. For this reason, in mathematics, your homework consists of practice problems to solve. By doing many of these, presented in different ways, you come eventually to see almost immediately how to solve any problem of a given type. When you do, you will know what is meant when the instructor uses that often-used phrase in mathematics, "It is obvious that. . . ."

Taking Notes in Class

You should, of course, take notes in mathematics courses just as you do in any other course, but there are some special points to keep in mind.

First, stick to main ideas and keep notes to a minimum. All you are trying to do is understand a rigorous train of thought expressed almost entirely in symbols. To do this, you record only the steps involved in solving problems or deriving an equation. This means you take down very little of what the instructor says, and record mostly what he puts on the black board. If you do more than this, it should be an example that helps you understand the steps involved.

Secondly, understanding what is taught at the time that it is taught is very important. In other subjects that are loaded with facts, you can take down things you don't understand and with later reflection and rereading understand them later. This may sometimes happen in mathematics, but you should try to keep such instances to a minimum. One way to do this is to be unusually alert in class, keeping your mind working all the time in the same path as the instructor's. Another is to ask the instructor for clarification at any point you need it. Mathematics is usually taught in small classes so that there can be just this sort of interaction between the teacher and the student.

Moreover, instructors frequently will skip points necessary to your understanding because they have learned their subject so well that what is obvious to them may not be obvious to you. Your important objective is to understand everything that transpires so that things become obvious to you, too.

Reviewing

We have said earlier that it is important to review lecture notes very soon after class. This is particularly true of notes taken in mathematics classes. In mathematics, it is easy to understand something at the time it is explained, and later to lose or miss the point. By going over your notes right after class, you can rehearse the steps presented in class while they are still fresh in mind and in this way imprint them on your memory.

Such reviews should always be done before you tackle problems in the same area. You will waste a lot of time trying to do assigned problems before you really understand how to do them. Doing homework problems is supposed to give you practice in applying quickly and accurately what you already understand. Hence the understanding must be there in the first place, and you should make sure you have it before you tackle problems. If you have much trouble figuring out how to do a problem, the chances are that you missed something in your understanding of how to solve it. In that case, stop working on the problem and go back to your class notes or your textbook to straighten out your understanding of the steps involved. Later on in this chapter, we shall give you some hints for doing problems, both in mathematics and in the natural sciences.

Preparing for Examinations

In mathematics, examinations tap your knowledge of formulas, the derivation of formulas, and the application of these formulas to specific problems. In this case, the formulas and principles for manipulating them are somewhat like vocabulary in language study. And a similar approach may be helpful. You can use 3 by 5 inch cards, recording one item on each card. On one side, put a cue word and on the other side record the answer. Carry these around in your pocket, and study them at odd moments, when otherwise you might be doing nothing.

Problem solving in mathematics is much like translation in language study. You need to practice it until it becomes a set of habits that are virtually automatic. So in preparing for an examination you should practice further on problems that you were given previously as assignments. Go back through these problems, sampling a few of each type, and do them over again. If you have acquired an understanding of the steps to take and have learned how to do them correctly in the first place, you will now find yourself setting them up with both the speed and accuracy required to perform well in the limited time allowed in an examination.

In reviewing the solution of problems, take advantage of any mistakes you may have made in previous work. If papers have been handed in and turned back "corrected," note particularly the kinds of mistakes you have made and practice more on such problems than on others. If you worked problems from a book and had difficulty getting the answer given, again give emphasis to those problems which gave you the most trouble.

Studying the Sciences

As most students know by now, the sciences are divided as a broad group into the natural sciences and the social sciences. The natural sciences study what nature has made (e.g., physics, astronomy, chemistry, geology, biology), and the social sciences study what man has made in his relations with man (e.g., sociology, economics, political science). Straddling the two main divisions of science are certain subjects that are both natural and social sciences. These include psychology, which in dealing with the nature of animal and human behavior is a natural science and in dealing with social relations of various sorts is a social science. Anthropology similarly has both its natural (physical anthropology) and its social (social anthropology) aspects.

All science is basically problem solving. It begins with collecting facts but it attempts to arrange these facts in an orderly way so that certain rules or principles can be formulated for understanding the facts and for solving practical problems in human societies. Collecting facts involves problem solving in devising methods for doing it. Arranging them in an orderly way is also a matter of problem solving—finding the simplest way of encompassing the greatest number of facts. And solving practical problems through science is, by definition, problem solving. So, in approaching the study of the sciences, bear in mind that the basic objectives of the sciences' are to solve various sorts of problems.

How well this has been accomplished varies enormously from one subject to another and from one area to another within a subject. And it varies from time to time with the state of our knowledge. In general, the sciences may be arranged in a continuum, from physics on one end to the social sciences on the other end, of problem-solving ability. More problems have been solved more precisely in physics than in the social sciences. But even within physics, for example, many problems are completely solved while others are in a rather confused state.

In general, you will find that the study of natural sciences is more like the study of mathematics than the social sciences. Indeed, they more frequently use the language of mathematics to express the solution to problems than the social sciences do. Many of the things, therefore, that we have said about the study of mathematics are also applicable to the study of the natural sciences. For example, *understanding* is relatively more important than learning facts because the understanding already achieved enables one to deduce most of the facts. Since problems can be stated precisely and have precise solutions, more of your homework is done, as it is in mathematics, by practicing the solving of problems. In addition, there are a few special points to keep in mind in studying sciences.

Scientific Language

The sciences, as they discover new phenomena and principles, continually invent terms to refer to their new concepts. Each science, therefore, has a vocabulary apart from that which you can find in the unabridged dictionary. You, therefore, have to be on the lookout for terms that are unfamiliar to you. In this respect, studying science is somewhat like studying a foreign language. You are building a vocabulary of words with special meanings that at first are about as unknown to you as the meaning of foreign words. There are certain differences, however, that should be pointed out.

One is that scientific language is more precise than ordinary languages, English or foreign. Terms have very specific meanings and very rigorous definitions. And these you must learn in one way or another. Unlike foreign words, you should *not* attempt to learn them from context. You can often make intelligent guesses from context, but you will be required to be more precise than that. Getting the general sense of a sentence is not enough, as it would be in translation. Rather you should be quite exact in your knowledge of the meaning of a term and in the way you use it.

To achieve such precision, you should make a special point of mastering the meaning of terms. You concentrate on learning exact definitions. Usually, in a scientific textbook, terms are carefully defined when they are introduced. If you should miss a definition at that point, you often can find it by looking in the index and noting the first page on which it appears. On the other hand, scientific textbooks are more and more providing glossaries of terms at the back of the books. If your textbook has such a glossary, use it frequently when you are trying to understand the exact meaning of something you are reading.

Beyond this, you may use devices such as you use in studying foreign languages. With 3 by 5 inch cards, you can collect terms on one side of the card with definitions on the other side. And you can study them from time to time, both at leisure moments and as part of a systematic review for examinations. You can also make a point of recording such terms in the "clue" column of your notebook, and when you review use these to recite meanings.

A special word about terminology in psychology and the social sciences. Many of the terms you will encounter in these subjects will seem familiar, because they are words you have been using and seeing in everyday parlance. But beware! As used by the social scientist, they have taken on more definite, more restricted, and sometimes a rather different meaning than they normally have. Hence, when you come upon any term that is familiar but is obviously used as a concept or important term in the subject, make sure you know the meaning of the word as used in this particular subject. (You may even have to learn that a word means one thing to a psychologist, another to the sociologist, and another to the physicist.) Note carefully the definition given by the author of the textbook, either in the text itself or in a glossary. Then make sure to use the term in your notes, in reading, and in taking examinations in the new meaning you have learned.

Visualization

Even though the natural sciences have more special terminology than the social sciences and humanities, they are much less wordy. Much of the material is presented in some visual form—the drawing of a model, a diagram of a cell, a graph of some physical change, a flow process chart, and so on. This fact will be evident in the profuse illustrations you typically find in textbooks of science. All this can be summarized by saying that the precise sciences present material that is more readily visualized, instead of verbalized, than other subjects.

Your reading and study should be geared to this difference. You should spend more time studying various visual materials, understanding them, and memorizing them. At the same time, your notes will contain many more diagrams or drawings of one sort or another. And your recitation should consist of drawing such visual materials. When you are reviewing, you will not merely think words, as you will mostly do in humanities and some of the social sciences. Instead, you keep a pencil and paper handy and check your mastery of material by drawing the appropriate charts, diagrams, or sketches.

Measurement

All sciences attempt to measure the phenomena they deal with, but the more exact sciences emphasize the measurements more. They use a system of measurement, the metric system, in which events are measured in physical units of time, weight, and length. There are literally hundreds of units of measurement in physics that unfold from the basic system. And these units are used to express many of the concepts and facts of the subject. In the natural sciences, therefore, you should pay particular attention to physical units, their definition, and the situations in which they apply.

Laboratory Work

It used to be that every college student was required in his first couple of years to take two natural sciences, each with a weekly laboratory. In recent years, this requirement has tended to be relaxed. In many schools, only one science course is required, and in some the courses that are required have no laboratory with them. The chances are, however, that in the liberal curriculum you will take at least one laboratory course. Here are some hints in case you do take such a course.

1. Most laboratory experiments are repetitions of classical experiments, that is, of experiments that established some important concept in the history of the science. Try to relate them to such concepts in your textbook and the course. Use them as means of practicing or reciting what you otherwise are learning. Don't just go through the motions.

2. Be careful and accurate in making your measurements and recording your data. Double check everything you do to make certain no major mistake creeps into your data or calculations. Painstaking care is the hallmark of any scientific experiment.

3. Keep a full record of everything you do in a special notebook kept for the purpose. Put everything in this notebook, not on loose pieces of paper, so that you will have a complete record of the work. Also make sure to label your records well with date, name of experiment, names of apparatus you use, and so on. In this way, you will be fully prepared with all the necessary information when you later write a laboratory report.

4. Write reports following the rules of report writing that we have given earlier. However, in writing reports of experiments, there is usually a set organization to the report. The instructor may give you some instructions for outlining the report. It will probably take some form of the following: (1) a statement of the problem, (2) the background and reasoning for stating the problem as a problem, (3) the apparatus and other materials used in the experiment, (4) the method and procedures followed, (5) the results obtained, (6) a discussion of the meaning of the results, and (7) the conclusions reached.

Doing Problems

It is typical of mathematics and of many textbooks in the natural sciences that problems and exercises are given in the text, usually at the end of a chapter. Moreover, all or part of an examination normally consists of problems. Hence, problems are both a means of learning and of examining you on your knowledge of the subject. In this section, therefore, we will give you some pointers on the use of problems in subjects that employ them.

Homework Problems

First and most important: *Do* all assigned problems. Some students don't because, they say, their instructors don't grade them on their daily problems. Even if no one checks you on your daily work, you will be graded on your examination problems, and the only way to prepare for these so that you solve them accurately in the time you are allowed is to do your daily assignments religiously. If you keep working problems as part of your daily routine, you will have no difficulty at examination time. Nor will you have to resort to the excuse that the instructor sprung some trick questions on you.

A problem is really a question. We've already seen how valuable questions are in learning. Problems are therefore important to learning too—not just hurdles to overcome. Problems are your opportunities to apply what you have learned and to test yourself about how much you know about what you have been studying. If you have problems assigned in a textbook or a laboratory manual, you should welcome the opportunity to use them in effective study.

Use of Models

When you have studied a particular assignment and are ready to tackle the problems in it, your first task is to make sure you understand the problem. For any particular problem, you must understand what information you are already supposed to know or be able to find quickly and what it is you are trying to find out. To do this, always keep in mind that there is a model for every problem. A model is like a mold; if you can fit your problem into the proper mold, you can easily solve it. To illustrate this, we will take a simple problem in elementary chemistry.

The problem is the following: If you are making carbon dioxide and start with 24 grams of carbon, how many grams of carbon dioxide can you make? If you know a little chemistry, the correct model, or mold, for this problem will immediately occur to you. The model is $C + O_2 = CO_2$. The next step is to put the correct numbers into the model to solve the problem. The person who would give you such a problem would assume you have learned what you need to solve it or at least that you know where to go to find this information. For this problem the information is the atomic weights of carbon and oxygen. These happen to be 12 and 16. You can now set up a proportion: $24/12 = ?/44$. The problem gives you 24 grams of carbon, and you supply the 12 and the 44 for the relative weights of carbon and carbon dioxide (the 44 comes from the combination of 12 for carbon and two times 16 for the oxygen). By solving the proportion, you get the answer, 88.

The problem illustrates the three steps essential in solving problems: First you must have the correct model, or mold, for solving the problem. This you should know from having mastered the relevant material. Then you put into the model the information given in the problem and the other information you may obtain from studying the book or your lecture notes. Finally you solve for some unknown.

To find the proper model for a problem and to check yourself when you think you have chosen the proper model, take advantage of the examples usually supplied in books. Some problems already worked out for you appear in practically all science and engineering books. These can provide models for first working assigned problems and later for solving problems on examinations.

When we say, however, that there is a model for every problem, we don't mean that you can or should always take one that is already made for you. Models are derived from laws and principles; you should always understand the principles underlying any model you use. Sometimes you'll have to make your own model by formulating the problem in terms of principles you've learned and by setting up your own formula or diagram for solving the problem. In elementary courses you'll usually be given examples or specific formulas that will serve as models for solving your problems, but in more advanced courses you may be asked to develop the proper model or formula for solving them. This you will be able to do if you understand the underlying principles. In any case, you are better off and can remember the model better if you make sure you understand the rationale of any model you use.

Using a Slide Rule

Once you have your model and understand how to go about the problem, we strongly recommend that you use a slide rule to make your calculations. Because you can do multiplication and division so easily and accurately enough for most problem solving, we believe no student should attempt to work problems without a slide rule.

There are all kinds of slide rules for different purposes. The simpler ones are relatively inexpensive; the more complicated ones can run up to $10 or $20. If you're not a science student and not likely to do a great many computations other than simple multiplication and division, one of the simpler ones will do. The more elaborate slide rules let you compute answers involving special functions, like the sines and tangents of angles. If you are a science or engineering student, you should get one of the special models designed for your particular field. The instructor in the course concerned can probably suggest the proper model to buy. You can learn how to use your particular slide rule by reading carefully the instructions that come with the rule. In some mathematics books, you'll find instructions for the many "tricks" you can do with the more complicated rules.

Checking Your Results

If you do a problem and do it incorrectly, making a mistake along the way, you will be penalized if the paper is handed in, and if not, you will have learned some bad habits. You must always strive for perfection and make sure in one way or another that you come out with the correct answer. Aside from answers given in the book, there are several aids to checking results.

Substituting simple numbers. If a problem involves the use of equations, and you are uncertain about whether an equation you have is true, you can check it by substituting simple quantities in place of the symbols in the equation. For example, by letting a equal 3 and b equal 1, you can quickly see that the equation $(a + b) / b = a + 1$ is false. Even fairly complicated equations may be quickly tested by such substitutions.

If a problem is presented to you in a very complicated form with large numbers or numbers with many decimals, you may have trouble getting a model for it because the numbers interfere with your understanding of the problem. In this case, too, first substituting some simple numbers that keep the same relations of size as those in the problem, and working the problem with

these, can let you check the model you are using. If this makes sense and checks out, you can then proceed with the real problem and the model you have chosen for it.

Reworking the problem. Another way of checking results is to rework the problem in a different way. Set the equation up differently, or proceed with your calculations in a different order. If by going a different route, you still get the same answer, you can feel rather confident that you are correct.

Substituting the answer. The most common method of checking a result in mathematics is to substitute your answer for the unknown and then see whether the model you have will balance or cancel out. Always use this method where it is applicable to the problem.

Guessing the answer. Another good practice is to make a guess at the answer before actually working the problem. You can frequently do this by rounding off the quantities given in the problem and doing some quick multiplication and division in your head. In this way, you can arrive at a "ball park" answer, one that is of the right order of magnitude. Having this in mind, you can see whether working the problem precisely agrees in general with the answer. Making such a guess will sometimes prevent you from coming up with an absurd answer—one that is wide of the mark—because you put a decimal point in the wrong place.

Examination Problems

If you work all the problems in daily assignments but still complain that those on examinations are "different" or trick problems, it means that you just aren't prepared for all the changes that can be made in a problem to make it look different.

For example, in the illustration we took from elementary chemistry, there are several ways of putting this same problem: Instead of asking how much carbon dioxide can be made from so much carbon, you can ask how much carbon dioxide can be made with so much oxygen or how much carbon or oxygen it would take to produce a given amount of carbon dioxide. These are all different ways of putting the same problem. You use the same model and the same information. The only difference is in where the unknown appears in the proportion.

To prepare yourself for problems that are different (to learn how to get around trick questions!), practice turning problems around. Take some sample problems and ask yourself how many different ways the same problem can be put. Write out the possible alternatives. If you do this frequently, you will find that you will not be surprised so often on examinations.

Of course, another way to pose similar problems is to switch the elements referred to. You might, for example, get an examination problem about sulfuric acid rather than carbon dioxide. If you are prepared for such possible switches, you will not be in difficulty. You can do that by making lists of the specific things that can be changed in any problem without changing the model.

By the time, for example, that you've encountered the carbon dioxide problem, you probably have already covered a series of reactions such as the making of sulfuric acid, sodium hydroxide, water, and so on. Jot down a list of these and then make sure that you know the models (in this case, reaction equations) and the numbers (atomic weights). If you do this, you should be prepared for all the instructor can fairly ask you.

One of the hazards of examinations consisting of problems is that they require you to work fast. Students taking such examinations are forever finding that they manage to complete only a third or half of the problems they are supposed to do. Or if they do manage to finish the whole examination, they make trivial mistakes in arithmetic. The consequences are often disastrous, for the instructor generally gives credit only for the problems completed correctly; and the difference between the slow student and the fast one or between the inaccurate and the acurrate one may be a difference between a failure and an A. Speed and speed with accuracy are more important in problem type examinations than in any other.

Time can be lost because the student doesn't have the basic skills to do his work correctly and quickly. It can be lost because *he* is lost trying to understand what the problem is about. If the student improves in these respects, he can manage to do more problems accurately in an examination. In addition, however, students are often too slow because they haven't practiced working fast.

The best way to meet this difficulty is to do homework assignments as if they were examinations. When you get ready to do a problem, time yourself as you work fast. Later, you can check yourself at a more leisurely pace. The important point, as in the case of reading faster, is to practice working faster. If you do, you'll find you don't lumber along so slowly and you will feel at home taking an examination.

This brings us to the matter of planning the time allotted to you for taking an examination. Always survey an examination before you start. If you have any choices, decide in advance which problems you will work. Estimate how much time you should spend on each, and keep track of the time to guard against spending too much time on any one problem. Work the easy problems first, leaving the hard ones for last.

In problem-type examinations it is especially important that you leave a little time to check your answers. If a lot of computation is involved, leave enough time to check it thoroughly. This can turn up trivial mistakes that could prevent you from making a good showing on the examination.

Significant Figures

Whenever you carry out any computations with numbers, you always have to decide how many numbers to use, both when you start solving your problem and as you proceed through its various steps. Where decimals are concerned, this is the question of whether you carry figures to the second, third, or nth decimal place. Also, in dealing with large quantities, like the distance of the sun from the earth or the speed of electricity, how many digits should you use and how should you round off your answer? To decide such a question you need to know how many digits in your number are significant, which is to say, how many are reasonably trustworthy and which ones are rather doubtful.

If you're making a measurement in an experiment or exercise, the rule is to record no more than one doubtful figure. If, for example, you're making a measurement with such a crude instrument as an ordinary meter stick, you would probably record your result to two places, for example, 4.2 meters, for you'd be quite sure it was nearer to 4 than to 3 or 5, but you wouldn't be so sure that it was nearer to 4.2 than to 4.1 or 4.3. By writing 4.2, you indicate that you are sure of 4 but somewhat doubtful about the .2 and consider any digits beyond .2 as meaningless. If you had a more accurate metric measure, graduated in centimeters as well as decimeters, you might express the same measure as 4.22 meters since you are now sure of 4.2 but doubtful about the digit representing centimeters.

There is a rule too for the additon, subtraction, multiplication, and division of significant numbers. You shouldn't write digits beyond the first column that contains a doubtful figure. Thus if you add 4.0 pounds of dirt to 3.4365 pounds of gold, the result would be 7.4 pounds of mixture. When your certainty about the weight of dirt doesn't go beyond 4 pounds, the accuracy of the weight of gold is of no use to you, for you can be no more certain about the total than you are about the component with the least certainty. (Remember "A chain is no stronger than its weakest link"?)

When you are multiplying or dividing numbers, you follow the same principle. In this case, it dictates that you carry out the operation to no more figures than are in the one that has the fewer significant figures. If, for example, you multiply 4.0 feet by 6.273 feet (assuming that 4.0 represents all the significant figures), your answer is 25, not 25.0920, for you had only two significant digits in 4.0 and you should have no more than this in your answer.

When you drop figures or round them off to the proper number of significant fig-

ures, you follow the rule of raising any digit by 1 when it is followed by more than 5, otherwise leaving it unchanged. For example, to round off 7.46639 to two significant figures, you end up with 7.5; if the number were 7.4499, you would have 7.4. (There's a special rule for rounding a digit followed by 5: If the digit is odd, raise it by 1; if it is even, drop the 5 without changing the digit.)

These rules have two important consequences: First, they keep you from fooling yourself about the precision of your measurements and calculations; dropping figures that aren't significant is merely a matter of getting rid of numbers you can't trust anyway. Secondly, they save you needless work and reduce the possibility of error involved in handling unnecessarily long strings of numbers.

Using Graphs and Table

To solve many problems you encounter, you'll need to use a graph or a table. In fact, you need to do this merely to read and understand many of your assignments in the natural and social sciences. Hence it is essential that you know how to use graphs and tables.

Graphs

The very simplest graphs are bar graphs that show, by the height of their columns, the number or amount of some particular quantity. One bar might give the government budget for 1950, another for 1951, and so on up to the present. Graphs of this kind convey information quickly and give you a more vivid impression of something than you can get by reading numbers. For that reason, they are used widely in nontechnical magazines and newspapers. They are usually not much use, though, in the solution of problems.

For this purpose, the graph you use is more likely to be a line representing a functional relationship between two variables. The graph, in other words, will say the same thing as an equation and will give the results of working out the equation for a number of different values of each variable. In the accompanying graph, for example, the straight line represents the equation $y = a + bx$, where $a = 2$ and $b = \frac{1}{2}$. If you have any calculations to do with such an equation, you can read the answers off merely by consulting the graph. If you want to know what y equals when $x = 2$, look on the graph and you'll see quickly that the answer is 3. You can do the same thing with any other value of x.

Notice how the graph is set up. The value of x is found along the horizontal axis, called the *abscissa*, and the value of y is found along the vertical axis, called the *ordinate*. To find an answer, you locate the value of x on the abscissa, then erect an imaginary line from that point upward until it intersects the line, which in this case is a straight line, and then finally run an imaginary line horizontally across to the ordinate. The corresponding value of y is your answer. Although the line in the graph may be any shape from straight to complexly curved, this simple operation is the same in reading all rectangular graphs.

Note that x is laid out on the abscissa and y on the ordinate. This is a custom among scientists, but it is an important one because there is usually a reason for it. Most of the time, when you wish to represent the relation between two variables, one of the variables is an *independent variable*, the other a *dependent variable*. The independent variable in an experiment or series of measurements is the one the experimenter varies or has control of—the variable whose value he can set—and the dependent variable is the one he measures or lets depend on the independent variable.

In the carbon dioxide problem above, the independent variable is the amount of carbon you start with—the amount you use—and the dependent variable is the amount of carbon dioxide you get out of the process. If you wanted to, you could set up a graph for this problem that would let you read off the amount of carbon dioxide you'd get by starting with any amount of carbon. The formula would be $y = a + bx$, where $a = 0$, $b = \frac{44}{12} = 3.67$, $x =$ amount of carbon, and $y =$ amount of carbon dioxide (see graph). You could work out the equation twice, once for 12 grams of carbon dioxide and again for some other amount like 36 grams, plot these two points on your graph, and then draw a line passing through the two points. Thereafter, by using the graph, you could solve the problem for any amount of carbon.

READING A GRAPH

Each line represents an equation. For any given equation, you can find the value of y that corresponds to any value of x. Note that the constant a determines where the line will intercept y when x = 0 and that b determines the slope of the line.

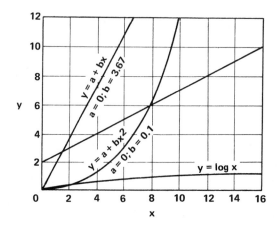

The important point is that we have a convention for plotting the independent variable on the x axis (abscissa) and the dependent variable on the y axis (ordinate). Of course, once a graph is set up, you may happen to know y and not x. In that case, you can read the graph backward, starting with y and finding the value of x that intersects with it on the line.

Some of the lines you encounter in graphs will be straight ones, but most of them will be curves representing formulas other than $y = a + bx$, the formula for a straight line. Any formula, however, no matter how complex it is, can be plotted on a graph as long as you know (or can assume) values of the constants (such as a or b). Changes in the constants merely alter the slope of the line or the point at which it intersects the ordinate. For example, in the equation $y = a + bx$, changing the value of b from ½ to 2 makes y grow four times as rapidly with respect to x as it did before; the line now moves upward at a steeper slope. Changing a, however, alters the point at which the line intercepts the y axis. When a is 1, this point is 1; when it is 2, it is 2, and so on.

A graph expresses a set of calculations from some particular formula. It is exceedingly handy because, once you have the graph, you don't need to make a new calculation for every change in one of the variables. All you have to do is read the answer off the graph. For this reason, many data and exact functions are presented to you in graphical form as well as in formulas. By using the graph, you can get around a lot of needless work. Graphs are therefore an aid in doing calculations. It will frequently pay you to make up your own graphs when you have a series of calculations to do based on one equation.

Tables

A table can be used to present the same kind of information a graph does but in different form. It gives the information to you in numbers rather than in lines. For that reason, it is more accurate than a graph. A graph usually can't be read to more than two

significant figures, but you can put as many significant figures as you wish (assuming you have them) in a table. That is one of the reasons why tables are sometimes used instead of graphs.

Notice another thing about a table. The lefthand column is usually a set of values for the independent variable x, the same variable plotted on the abscissa of a graph. Then each succeeding column, reading toward the right, represents the y values corresponding to x. From one column to another, only the constants in the equation may change; or the nature of the equation may be changed. In the sample table nearby, the first y column is a set of figures for $y = a + bx$, where $a = 2$ and $b = ½$, the same values of constants we used in illustrating graphs. In the second column, the constants have been changed to $a = 3$ and $b = 1/3$. In the third column, we have given values of y when $y = x^2$; and in the last column, we have given the logarithm of x, the value of y in $10^y = x$, or $y = \log x$. These are just examples, for we could put in the table any set of numbers for any formula representing the relation between y and x.

Notice that a table gives discrete, not continuous, numbers. It gives only certain values of y for certain values of x. A graph, on the other hand, may be continuous, for you can read any value of y from any value of x—any that fits on the graph. So the graph is much better for solving a set of calculations for any and all values of two variables. On the other hand, the table is more accurate; it will let you have any degree of precision you want. And when there are only a certain few values you may use the table for anyway, a table is better than a graph.

Tables also have a couple of other advantages. You can use them when the several lines they represent are so mixed up, overlapping, and intertwining that you couldn't read them in graphical form. Similarly, you can use them when the magnitudes of different sets of numbers are so different you couldn't show them conveniently on the same graph. Of course, you can also put in tables information you can't plot on graphs, such as a series of constants for different substances or other things that are not represented by equations.

To use tables and graphs effectively, you'll have to practice using the ones that you need for your particular purposes. If you have relatively little to do with numbers and mathematical problems, you may never need any more than a log table, a square-root table, an interest table (if you save or borrow money), a premium table (for insurance), and an annuity table (for your retirement plan). Textbooks in many subjects, however, employ tables and graphs to present principles and factual information. You must therefore be able to read them without difficulty. If you're a science or engineering student, you'll have a lot more use for tables and graphs. You'll probably want to purchase a book of mathematical tables and a handbook or two giving data, formulas, and constants important in your particular field.

Improving Basic Skills

As we said at the outset of this chapter, many students are handicapped in studying

mathematics and science because they are deficient in the basic skills of arithmetic and algebra that they were supposed to have learned before coming to college. For that reason, we will in this section run over some of the basic skills that are required in science courses and may be improved if you are weak in any of them. To help you check yourself, we have listed on an accompanying page a few examples of these elementary skills.

You will probably wonder what a discussion of addition, subtraction, multiplication, and division is doing in a book written for college students. If so, you might ask yourself whether you can, for example, add and subtract rapidly and without error. Some college students still add by counting to themselves or on their fingers; if you do this, you are in need of some serious drill. If you have a tendency to make mistakes at all, you must be on guard and double-check any simple computations you make.

If you have trouble with long division, addition and subtraction of fractions, multiplication of fractions, and so forth, you might glance at the rules on page 124. Here you will find succinct directions for a lot of

READING A TABLE

Value of y for different values of x in different equations.

x	$y = a + bx$		$y = x^2$	$y = \log x$
	$a = 2; b = 1/2$	$a = 3; b = 1/3$		
0.00	2.00	3.00	0.00	$-\infty$
1.00	2.50	3.33	1.00	0.000
2.00	3.00	3.67	4.00	0.301
3.00	3.50	4.00	9.00	0.477
4.00	4.00	4.33	16.00	0.602
5.00	4.50	4.67	25.00	0.699
6.00	5.00	5.00	36.00	0.778
7.00	5.50	5.33	49.00	0.845
8.00	6.00	5.67	64.00	0.903
9.00	6.50	6.00	81.00	0.954
10.00	7.00	6.33	100.00	1.000
11.00	7.50	6.67	121.00	1.041
12.00	8.00	7.00	144.00	1.079
13.00	8.50	7.33	169.00	1.114
14.00	9.00	7.67	196.00	1.146
15.00	9.50	8.00	225.00	1.176
16.00	10.00	8.33	256.00	1.204

these basic skills. If you don't know some of them, practice by working on some examples. If you have trouble with the examples, set up for yourself a program of drill, say, in multiplication and division of fractions. You can find help for such a program in books written specifically for the student who is weak in mathematical skills. You might also ask your science or mathematics teacher for some suggestions.

In subjects like physics and chemistry, you'll have to do over and over again the kinds of arithmetic we've been talking about. Also in such courses, you'll need other specialized skills; in this section we'll describe some of them.

Proportions

In chemistry, one of the most common computations is in the form of a proportion. A proportion is an equation in which one fraction equals another, but in which you don't know one of the numbers (numerator or denominator) of one of the fractions and must try to find out what it is. In other words, you must find a missing number in one of the fractions. For example, $4/7 = 5/?$. Sometimes the problem is written this way:

$$4 : 7 :: 5 : ?$$

Written in this form, it means "Four is to seven as five is to what?" In general, these names are given to the parts of a proportion:

$$\text{Extreme : mean : : mean : extreme}$$

The rules for solving the proportion and finding the unknown quantity are:
1. If both extremes and one mean are given, multiply the extremes and divide by the mean.
2. Or if only one extreme is given and two means are given, multiply the means and divide by the extreme.

If you look at the problem we gave you, rule two applies since only one extreme but two means are given. Therefore you would write the problem like this:

$$\frac{7 \times 5}{4} = ?$$

The answer is 8¾.

PRACTICE PROBLEMS

You should be able to perform the following problems rapidly without making any mistakes and without marking the paper except for the answers. If you make mistakes or resort to counting or scratch work, you need drill in the fundamentals of arithmetic (adapted from J. S. Orleans and Julie L. Sperling, "The Arithmetic Knowledge of Graduate Students," Journal of Educational Research, 48:177-186, 1954).

Add

3	18	10	18	48	37	11	310
8	6	8	12	5	11	15	22
6	10	4		11		21	25
		4				43	

Multiply

20 x 1¼	15 x 110	8 x 33
11 x 0.67	5 x 1.21	2 x 216

Divide

$\frac{120}{70}$	$\frac{1.2}{10}$	$\frac{13.6}{50}$
$\frac{183}{4}$	$\frac{400}{32}$	$\frac{276}{150}$

(*Hint.* $\frac{150}{3} = 50$; $\frac{276}{3} = 92$)

Subtract

48	100	54	163	3.28	110.08	111.10
15	46	21	93	0.05	15.71	34.21

SOME RULES FOR COMPUTING FRACTIONS

Definitions

1. A fraction is one or more of the equal parts into which something can be divided. Examples are:

$$\frac{1}{2} \quad \frac{1}{3} \quad \frac{3}{4}$$

2. Fractions are written $\frac{1}{2}$ or ½.

3. The lower number is the *denominator.*
4. The upper number is the *numerator.*
5. *Mixed numbers* are whole numbers and fractions. Examples are:

$$3\frac{1}{2} \quad 2\frac{2}{3}$$

Adding fractions

1. To add fractions, the denominators must all be the same. Thus $\frac{1}{2}$ and $\frac{1}{3}$ cannot be added until the 2 and 3 are changed.
2. To make the denominators the same, find the *smallest* number (the lowest common denominator) that can be divided evenly by all the denominators. Examples are:

> For 2 and 3, it is 6.
> For 7 and 13, it is 91 (7 x 13 = 91).
> For 2, 8, and 9, it is 72.

Note. For many cases, you will have difficulty finding the smallest number by inspection. Find the smallest number into which you can divide as many of the numbers as possible. Then multiply that number by the number you *cannot* divide into it. This will be the lowest common denominator. An example is:

2, 3, 6, 7, 8, 9: All but 7 can be evenly divided into 72. The lowest common denominator is therefore 72 x 7 = 504.

3. Multiply the numerator by the number of times the original denominator goes into the lowest common denominator. An example is:

$$\frac{1}{2} + \frac{1}{3} = \frac{1 \times 3}{6} + \frac{1 \times 2}{6} = \frac{3}{6} + \frac{2}{6}$$

4. Add the numerators and place the lowest common denominator as the denominator of the sum. An example is:

$$\frac{3}{7} + \frac{1}{13} = \frac{3 \times 13}{91} + \frac{1 \times 7}{91} = \frac{39}{91} + \frac{7}{91} = \frac{46}{91}$$

5. If the numerator is larger than the denominator, change to a mixed number. An example is:

$$\frac{23}{7} = 3\frac{2}{7}$$

Subtracting fractions

1. All the rules are the same as for addition except rule 4.
2. For rule 4, subtract instead of adding the numerators. An example is:

$$\frac{3}{7} - \frac{1}{13} = \frac{39}{91} - \frac{7}{91} = \frac{32}{91}$$

Multiplying fractions

1. To multiply fractions, multiply the numerators together and the denominators together. Write the result as a fraction. An example is:

$$\frac{3}{4} \times \frac{5}{7} = \frac{15}{28} \quad \text{or} \quad \frac{5}{6} \times \frac{2}{5} = \frac{10}{30} = \frac{1}{3}$$

2. To multiply a whole number and a fraction, multiply the whole number by the numerator and place the result over the denominator. An example is:

$$5 \times \frac{2}{3} = \frac{10}{3} = 3\frac{1}{3}$$

Dividing fractions

1. Turn the divisor upside down and multiply. An example is:

$$\frac{4}{9} \div \frac{1}{3} = \frac{4}{9} \times \frac{3}{1} = \frac{12}{9} = 1\frac{3}{9} = 1\frac{1}{3}$$

2. Whole numbers may be written in the form of a fraction with 1 as the denominator. An example is:

$$3 = \frac{3}{1}$$

3. Therefore, to divide a fraction by a whole number, write the whole number as a fraction and invert. An example is:

$$\frac{4}{9} \div 3 = \frac{4}{9} \div \frac{3}{1} = \frac{4}{9} \times \frac{1}{3} = \frac{4}{27}$$

Try working out some examples of both types of problem. If you feel that just a couple of examples let you understand the principles, don't stop there; keep practicing examples until the rules and the procedures become second nature to you.

Another thing you will want to make sure you can do is to translate problems into the correct form. Here is a typical problem in proportions: "A pulley 20 inches in diameter making 300 revolutions per minute is belted to a pulley 15 inches in diameter. What is the speed of the smaller pulley?"

$$15 : 20 :: 300 : ?$$

You set it up this way because the smaller pulley must make *more* revolutions than the larger pulley since it is smaller. Would you have set this problem up the right way?

Power and Roots

A power of a number is gotten by multiplying the number by itself one or more times. Thus 3 squared, or 3^2, means 3 x 3, which is 9. The number of times you multiply gives you the exponent of a number. The exponent in the problem we gave you is 2, and it is written to the right and a little above the number. Exponents can have any value, but the rule is always the same. Thus 3^3 means 3 x 3 x 3, or 27.

The root of a number is one of the equal numbers that will produce the number you started with when they're multiplied together. Thus the square root of 9 is 3. The sign for a square root is $\sqrt{9}$. (This can also be written $9^{1/2}$.) Just as the power of a number is indicated by an exponent, the number of the root can be shown. For example, the cube (second) root of a number is written $\sqrt[3]{27}$. The answer to this problem is 3.

Squaring numbers is easy, if you know multiplication, but many people have trouble with finding square roots. Fortunately, tables of square roots are readily available; so you usually don't have to do the work of computing (see sample page).

Sometimes you will find powers with negative signs in front of them, like 3^{-2}. Those of you who remember high-school al-gebra will recognize that this is the same thing as $(1/3)^2$, or $1/9$.

Another difficulty will sometimes face you when you see a problem like this: $3^{1.2}$. How do you multiply a number 1.2 times itself? The way to solve this problem is to resort to logarithms, which are the subject of the next subsection.

Logarithms

Logarithms are a boon to engineers and physicists, for they make it possible to do very involved computations quite easily. If, therefore, you're going to have anything to do with scientific subjects, from physics to statistics, you'd better be acquainted with logs. The logarithm of a given number is the power to which another number (called the *base*) must be raised to produce the given number. The base most commonly used is 10. In this case, the logarithm of 100 will be 2 since 10 raised to the second power (10^2) is 100. This is generally written

$$\log 100 = 2$$

If you multiply 10 by itself three times you raise it to the third power (10^3), and

$$\log 1,000 = 3$$

The logarithms of simple powers of 10 are easy, but what about, say, log 200? Here you have to resort to tables for part of the answer; another part is easy to obtain. The log of 100 is 2, and that of 1,000 is 3; 200 is between 100 and 1,000; so the log of 200 is going to be somewhere between 2 and 3. This is a general principle; the log of 2,000 is somewhere between 3 and 4 (make sure you can tell why).

But what is the exact value of log 200? It is 2.30103. How do you find this? The 2 part, or the easy part, is called the *characteristic*, and you can always recognize it as 1 less than the number of places to the left of the decimal in the number you start with. The other part, .30103, is called the *mantissa*, and you have to look it up in tables. We won't give you a complete log table; but you can find one very easily, and you will need

FINDING SQUARES AND SQUARE ROOTS

Here is a sample page from a table of squares and square roots. Note how easy it is to find the appropriate answer. For very large numbers whose roots are to be extracted, you work backward from the column of squares and, if necessary, interpolate between the numbers in the table (from Herbert Soren-sen, Statistics for Students of Psychology and Education, McGraw-Hill, New York, 1936, p. 348).

Number	Square	Square root	Number	Square	Square root
721	51 98 41	26.8514	761	57 91 21	27.5862
722	52 12 84	26.8701	762	58 06 44	27.6043
723	52 27 29	26.8887	763	58 21 69	27.6225
724	52 41 76	26.9072	764	58 36 96	27.6405
725	52 56 25	26.9258	765	58 52 25	27.6586
726	52 70 76	26.9444	766	58 67 56	27.6767
727	52 85 29	26.9629	767	58 82 89	27.6948
728	52 99 84	26.9815	768	58 98 24	27.7128
729	53 14 41	27.0000	769	59 13 61	27.7308
730	53 29 00	27.0185	770	59 29 00	27.7489
731	53 43 61	27.0370	771	59 44 41	27.7669
732	53 58 24	27.0555	772	59 59 84	27.7849
733	53 72 89	27.0740	773	59 75 29	27.8029
734	53 87 56	27.0924	774	59 90 76	27.8209
735	54 02 25	27.1109	775	60 06 25	27.8388
736	54 16 96	27.1293	776	60 21 76	27.8568
737	54 31 69	27.1477	777	60 37 29	27.8747
738	54 46 44	27.1662	778	60 52 84	27.8927
739	54 61 27	27.1846	779	60 68 41	27.9106
740	54 76 00	27.2029	780	60 84 00	27.9285
741	54 90 81	27.2213	781	60 99 61	27.9464
742	55 05 64	27.2397	782	61 15 24	27.9643
743	55 20 49	27.2580	783	61 30 89	27.9821
744	55 35 36	27.2764	784	61 46 56	28.0000
745	55 50 25	27.2947	785	61 62 25	28.0179
746	55 65 16	27.3130	786	61 77 96	28.0357
747	55 80 09	27.3313	787	61 93 69	28.0535
748	55 95 04	27.3496	788	62 09 44	28.0713
749	56 10 01	27.3679	789	62 25 21	28.0891
750	56 25 00	27.3861	790	62 41 00	28.1069
751	56 40 01	27.4044	791	62 56 81	28.1247
752	56 55 04	27.4226	792	62 72 64	28.1425
753	56 70 09	27.4408	793	62 88 49	28.1603
754	56 85 16	27.4591	794	63 04 36	28.1780
755	57 00 25	27.4773	795	63 20 25	28.1957
756	57 15 36	27.4955	796	63 36 16	28.2135
757	57 30 49	27.5136	797	63 52 09	28.2312
758	57 45 64	27.5318	798	63 68 04	28.2489
759	57 60 81	27.5500	799	63 84 01	28.2666
760	57 76 00	27.5681	800	64 00 00	28.2843

USING A TABLE OF LOGARITHMS

Find the first three digits of your number in the left-hand column, then move across the row to the column headed by the fourth digit of your number. The entry is your mantissa. You supply the characteristic by counting one less than the number of digits to the left of the decimal point. If your number has less than three digits, add zeros to bring it up to three and look up the mantissa in the zero column. Below is a sample section of a table of logarithms (from Myron F. Rosskopf, Harold D. Aten, and William D. Reeve, Mathematics: . . . , McGraw-Hill, New York, 1955, p. 411).

Table of Five-Place Mantissas

No.	0	1	2	3	4	5	6	7	8	9	Proportional parts	
250	39 794	811	829	846	863	881	898	915	933	950		18
251	967	985	*002	*019	*037	*054	*071	*088	*106	*123	1	1.8
252	40 140	157	175	192	209	226	243	261	278	295	2	3.6
253	312	329	346	364	381	398	415	432	449	466	3	5.4
254	483	500	518	535	552	569	586	603	620	637	4	7.2
255	654	671	688	705	722	739	756	773	790	807	5	9.0
256	824	841	858	875	892	909	926	943	960	976	6	10.8
257	993	*010	*027	*044	*061	*078	*095	*111	*128	*145	7	12.6
258	41 162	179	196	212	229	246	263	280	296	313	8	14.4
259	330	347	363	380	397	414	430	447	464	481	9	16.2
260	497	514	531	547	564	581	597	614	631	647		17
261	664	681	697	714	731	747	764	780	797	814	1	1.7
262	830	847	863	880	896	913	929	946	963	979	2	3.4
263	996	*012	*029	*045	*062	*078	*095	*111	*127	*144	3	5.1
264	42 160	177	193	210	226	243	259	275	292	308	4	6.8
265	325	341	357	374	390	406	423	439	455	472	5	8.5
266	488	504	521	537	553	570	586	602	619	635	6	10.2
267	651	667	684	700	716	732	749	765	781	797	7	11.9
268	813	830	846	862	878	894	911	927	943	959	8	13.6
269	975	991	*008	*024	*040	*056	*072	*088	*104	*120	9	15.3
270	43 136	152	169	185	201	217	233	249	265	281		16
271	297	313	329	345	361	377	393	409	425	441	1	1.6
272	457	473	489	505	521	537	553	569	584	600	2	3.2
273	616	632	648	664	680	696	712	727	743	759	3	4.8
274	775	791	807	823	838	854	870	886	902	917	4	6.4
275	993	949	965	981	996	*012	*028	*044	*059	*075	5	8.0
276	44 091	107	122	138	154	170	185	201	217	232	6	9.6
277	248	264	279	295	311	326	342	358	373	389	7	11.2
278	404	420	436	451	467	483	498	514	529	545	8	12.8
279	560	576	592	607	623	638	654	669	685	700	9	14.4
280	716	731	747	762	778	793	809	824	840	855		15
281	871	886	902	917	932	948	963	979	994	*010	1	1.5
282	45 025	040	056	071	086	102	117	133	148	163	2	3.0
283	179	194	209	225	240	255	271	286	301	317	3	4.5
284	332	347	362	378	393	408	423	439	454	469	4	6.0
285	484	500	515	530	545	561	576	591	606	621	5	7.5
286	637	652	667	682	697	712	728	743	758	773	6	9.0
287	788	802	818	834	849	864	879	894	909	924	7	10.5
288	939	954	969	984	*000	*015	*030	*045	*060	*075	8	12.0
289	46 090	105	120	135	150	165	180	195	210	225	9	13.5
290	240	255	270	285	300	315	330	345	359	374		14
291	389	404	419	434	449	464	479	494	509	523	1	1.4
292	538	553	568	583	598	613	627	642	657	672	2	2.8
293	687	702	716	731	746	761	776	790	805	820	3	4.2
294	835	850	864	879	894	909	923	938	953	967	4	5.6
295	982	997	*012	*026	*041	*056	*070	*085	*100	*114	5	7.0
296	47 129	144	159	173	188	202	217	232	246	261	6	8.4
297	276	290	305	319	334	349	363	378	392	407	7	9.8
298	422	436	451	465	480	494	509	524	538	553	8	11.2
299	567	582	596	611	625	640	654	669	683	698	9	12.6
300	712	727	741	756	770	784	799	813	828	842		
No.	0	1	2	3	4	5	6	7	8	9	Proportional parts	

one if you are going to do any complicated computing. A part of a log table is on page 127. What you do is look up the number given (200) and find the mantissa in the table. For other numbers in the 200s, say, 263, there will be a different mantissa, but the characteristic is the same. The log of 263 is 2.41996. Written in exponents, 263 would be $10^{2.41996}$

Suppose you want to find log 2.63. You know that the log of 10 is 1; so the characteristic of log 2.63 is going to be 0 (1 less than the number of digits to the left of the decimal in 2.63). The mantissa is exactly the same as in 263. This makes an important point about reading log tables: The mantissa is always the same if the specific digits are the same. Thus the mantissas of 2,630, 263, or 2.63 are all the same. The complete log for 2.63 is 0.41996.

What about log 0.263? The principle, of course, is exactly the same. But the log will be less than zero, and it makes some special problems because of negative numbers. The log of 0.263 is usually written 9.41996 − 10. If you are going to deal with problems involving logarithms of numbers less than 1, you should get a copy of a textbook in algebra and study the section on logarithms. If you have been able to understand this brief discussion of logarithms, you should have no trouble with a complete textbook account of logarithms.

You can do lots of computing with logs, and that is one of their values. For example, if you want to multiply two long numbers together, you can find it by adding their logs (this is what a slide rule does for you). Thus 200 x 263 can be given by finding the sum of the logs, which is 4.72099. By looking up (backward) in a log table the antilogarithm of 4.72099, you find the product of 200 and 263, or 52,600. The antilog is the number corresponding to a logarithm.

Now we are ready to show you how to find $3^{1.2}$. The rule is as follows: To find the power of any number, multiply the log of that number by the power and find the antilog of the result. Thus $3^{1.2}$ can be found by writing 1.2 x log 3. This gives 1.2 x 0.47712,

or 0.572544. Since some log tables go to five places only, you might have to round off the last number and look up the antilog of 0.57254. The answer will be 3.74 (rounding off). Thus $3^{1.2}$ = 3.74 (approximately).

The purpose of this section has not been merely to show you how to use logs but to show you that their principle is not hard to understand. If you have been avoiding logarithms all your life, you might get hold of a mathematics text and try learning about them.

Negative Numbers

In arithmetic, we use a minus sign to mean subtraction. Thus when you see

$$\begin{array}{r} 100 \\ -\ 25 \end{array}$$

you know that you are to subtract the 25 from the 100. In algebra, however, the minus sign is used to indicate numbers whose values are less than zero. These are negative numbers. Everyone is acquainted with negative numbers because they turn up in weather reports. When we read that the temperature was −8 in Chicago yesterday, this means that it was 8° below zero. The negative numbers increase in the opposite direction from positive numbers:

$$-5\ -4\ -3\ -2\ -1\ 0\ 1\ 2\ 3\ 4\ 5$$

There are lots of ways in which negative numbers can be used. For example, if I owe $15 more than I have, I might say that my assets are −$15.

Be careful when you add and subtract negative numbers, for it is very easy to add them when you're supposed to be subtracting them and vice versa. If you look at the series of numbers above, you'll see that the difference between −3 and 2 is 5, not 1. Not so obvious perhaps is the fact that −3 subtracted from 2 is 5, not −5, and 2 subtracted from −3 is −5, not (+)5.

Addition and Subtraction

The rules for the algebraic additon and subtraction of numbers, or the addition and subtraction of negative *and* positive numbers, are very simple, and they should cause you no trouble if you are careful. Here they are:

1. If all the numbers in a problem are entirely negative or entirely positive, the ordinary rules of arithmetic will do. You add their values for addition and find the difference for subtraction.

2. To add two numbers opposite in sign (one positive and the other negative), you find the difference between them and give the answer the sign of the larger number. Thus if you want to add 3 and −7, the answer is −4. Suppose you won $3 at the race track, but you had to pay $7 to get there and get in. You're out $4. Or to put it another way, the algebraic sum of your winnings and expenses at the race track is −$4.

3. To subtract numbers opposite in sign, change the sign of the number to be subtracted and then add. Thus the difference between 8 and −3 is 11. For example, it the temperature is 8° this morning in Chicago and −3° in Minneapolis, it is 11° colder in Minneapolis than in Chicago. This is algebraic subtraction. *Note.* If you want to find the difference between two positive numbers, the rule is the same: The difference between 13 and 8 is 5; you have changed the sign of 8 and added algebraically. Likewise, the difference between 12 and 16 is 4 (−12 and 16).

4. If you must add a series of numbers which have different signs, you separately find the simple sums of the positive numbers and the negative numbers and then find the *algebraic* sum of these two. Thus if you wish to add −5, 3, −1, 6, −2, −7, and 8, you would find the sum of −5, −1, −2, and −7, which is −15, and the sum of 3, 6, and 8, which is 17. The sum of −15 and 17 is 2.

The operations of algebraic addition and subtraction are very easy but students sometimes have difficulty realizing when these operations should be applied. Watch out for problems in which numbers can be both positive and negative; then make sure you are solving these problems the right way.

Multiplication and Division

If you are going to take elementary physics or statistics, you had better brush up on a few other fundamental operations in algebra. You should get a highschool textbook in algebra and assure yourself that you can add and subtract polynomials (expressions like $2x - y$, which have two or more terms), that you can do algebraic multiplication and division, and that you can solve equations for numerical values.

This last point is especially important, and most simple problems involve only two elementary rules: (1) You can move any term preceded by a plus or minus sign to the opposite side of an equation by changing its sign; and (2) when a term is to be divided into one side of an equation, it can be moved to the other side and used to multiply. Thus for rule 1,

$$30 - x = 5$$
$$-x = 5 - 30$$
$$-x = -25$$
$$x = 25$$

For rule 2,

$$\frac{x}{10} = 5$$
$$x = 5 \times 10$$
$$x = 50$$

You will have occasion in courses like elementary physics to solve simple simultaneous equations. You use such equations when you must solve for two unknowns. By reading over the section on simultaneous equations in a highschool algebra book, you can brush up on the rules for handling them.

Elementary trigonometry is something else that you will find useful for introductory physics and similar subjects. At the very least, you should make certain that you know and can use properly the ratios that exist among the sides of a right triangle, that is, the trigonometric functions. These ratios are quantities such as the sine and cosine.

None of these things are really difficult. If you have been able to understand the last few pages of this book, you will have no real problems with any kind of elementary mathematics, such as trigonometry or college algebra. Many students are so fearful of mathematics and numbers that they never give themselves a fair chance to find out how well they can do at them.

chapter 10

GETTING HELP AND BEING HELPFUL

This is a do-it-yourself book, intended to show you how you can help yourself become a better student. We have concentrated on classroom teaching and the use of textbooks, for these will constitute the bulk of your study in the first two years of college. There are, however, other resources sometimes used by your teachers, found in your library, or available in your bookstore that deserve some consideration. And there are some matters of student behavior that are related to becoming a better student. In this chapter, we will consider these important odds and ends of being a good student.

Beyond Textbooks

Workbooks and Outlines

In most college bookstores you will find some paperback books with titles such as *Outline of Chemistry, Outline of European History,* and so on. One or more outlines are published for each regular introductory course and some for more advanced courses. These outlines are just what their name implies; they give the bare essentials without extended explanations, illustrations, or details.

These outlines are useful, but they have limitations. They help a student see the fundamentals of a given subject, and they are likely to be of help in reviewing. On the other hand, some courses are not standardized, and the outlines are not likely to be a reliable guide to the subject matter of your particular course. Therefore, you can't follow them blindly.

Perhaps one of the best uses of outlines is for review of a more elementary subject. Suppose you are taking physics and you run into trouble with mathematics. An outline of highschool algebra will probably be quite useful to you.

Something more generally useful are the student workbooks, or manuals, written specifically to go along with some of your textbooks. These workbooks often accompany textbooks in introductory courses. They are designed to help you study your specific textbook. Content varies, but typically they include special projects and exercises to illustrate and explain the book, review questions, and sometimes self-test items that provide practice for examinations. In any case, the author who prepares the workbook strives to give you devices for becoming interested in and effectively studying the subject.

Sometimes your instructor will require the workbook; in other cases, he'll recommend it but not require it; or he may say little or nothing about it. No matter what he does, you will be wise to find out if there is a workbook that accompanies your textbook. (The preface will usually say whether a workbook or manual is available.) If you can, examine a copy of the workbook to determine whether it is likely to help you. Almost all workbooks are of some value and some will help you enormously.

Outside Readings

Textbooks and workbooks usually provide the core of reading for most courses. In many cases, however, instructors assign outside readings; and even if a particular instructor doesn't assign them, he is likely to recommend them; in any event, nearly every textbook will have lists of general references at the end of each chapter.

How valuable are these outside readings? Should you bother with them? Many, perhaps most, students don't unless they are required to do so. The fact is, though, that it is things like outside readings that give a genuine depth to your education.

In the first place, outside readings can and do help you better understand your basic textbook. They tell you about things that were missed in the textbook, and they sometimes give you a sufficiently different slant on some difficult topic so that you can understand it more easily. More than this, though, outside readings can add satisfaction to your study and arouse new curiosity in you.

In some subjects, particularly those in the humanities, outside readings provide the real meat of learning. The textbook is frequently just a skeleton on which the instructor hangs the body of the reading. To read about Plato in a textbook on the history of philosophy is only an introduction to reading Plato himself.

Finally, outside readings give you guidance in things you wish to study on your own. If you are undecided about whether you want to major in a particular subject or not, frequently a very little time spent skimming through some of the general references given in an introductory textbook will tell you whether you should go ahead with your plans or not.

Another kind of outside reading ought to be mentioned: journals and magazines in the general field of study. Many of these make interesting and educational reading. Sometimes they provide information and understanding of direct value in a course, but they are sure to make your formal studies more interesting and meaningful, in this way providing motivation and satisfaction in study. For example, if your major interests are in business and economics, there are the *Wall Street Journal, Barron's,* and *Business Week.* For the student of physics, there is *Physics Today;* for the general student of science, *Scientific Monthly,* or *Scientific American;* for the student of history, *American Heritage.* These are just a few examples that by no means exhaust the list. Some can be obtained on newsstands or in your bookstore. The rest are probably in your college library.

Text Films

Motion pictures are being used more and more as teaching aids in the classroom, and you'll probably find that some will be shown in courses you take. Motion pictures can be extremely effective aids in learning, for they not only combine the best features of a teacher's explanation with the visual materials of a textbook but also can present experiments, demonstrations, and real events that otherwise are not feasible to bring into the classroom. For that reason, more and better teaching films are being produced each year, and they are gradually assuming a more important role in classroom teaching.

Because you are accustomed to being more entertained than taught by motion pictures, you probably tend to sit back and relax when a film is shown in the classroom. At least, we've seen a lot of students do this. If you are to learn from films, though, you have to regard them as something to be studied as carefully as your textbook or your class notes. In fact, since it is frequently possible to pack much more information and explanation into a motion picture than can be done in a comparable amount of talking or reading, you must really be on your toes to get the most from a film.

Films, like other things, ought to be surveyed before they are watched. You, of course, can't do this yourself, but the instructor usually does. Before he shows the film, he'll usually tell you what it is about and why he is showing it. Take notes on his explanation as you would on the survey he gives of what he is going to say in a lecture. Furthermore, you'll find that most teaching films have their own survey at the beginning.

Ideally, you should take notes fast and furiously while a film is being shown. In practice, however, you can't always do that because you may not be able to see what you're writing. (This is the chief disadvantage of films.) If the lighting is such that you can take notes, by all means do so; if not, try to make notes in your head. Recite to yourself the important points during the course of the film. Then, as soon as the film is over, jot down rapidly all you can remember from it.

One word of warning. Because films are pictorial and make considerable use of every-day situations, you may have the impression that there isn't much that is technical or specific to take notes on. This is usually an illusion, however, for teaching films actually make definite points. You needn't remember every detail of each illustration, just as you don't take notes on all the illustrations an author uses in a textbook, but you should keep looking for main ideas and important details—as in reading textbooks—and write them down at the first opportunity. Because things move so fast in a film, it is even more important to review and recite what is covered as soon as it is over than it is to review lecture notes and textbook notes.

TV Teaching

With the invention of video tape after World War II, it became feasible and economical to use it, instead of film, for recording teaching material. Such tape is relatively cheap, it does not wear out, and it can be erased and edited with little trouble. To use it for this purpose, all you have to do is have the appropriate video camera equipment and facilities for playing the tapes on closed-circuit screens. Such facilities are by no means cheap, but many of the larger institutions are installing them so that segments of courses, and sometimes whole courses, can be put on TV tape.

If you encounter TV teaching, your first reaction may be that this is another step in making people part of a mechanized system. Certainly a TV screen is an impersonal "teacher," with which you have no direct personal interaction. However, the kinds of material taught with TV are the kinds that otherwise would be presented in lecture form where the student also has little interaction with the teacher. And as compared with the conventional lecture, TV teaching has certain advantages. One is that demonstrations can be seen better by the student. Another is that it is worthwhile to take considerable time to prepare carefully something to be presented only once and thereafter stored for mechanical reproduction rather than delivering the same material repeatedly. In this case, the preparation of the tape is costly, but once done saves

considerable teaching time. And if the original tape is done well, it usually is a much better teaching job than otherwise is done by the typical instructor. Also, there is frequently an instructor present in TV teaching, and it can be done in small classes, so that the student has more chance to ask questions and express himself than he would in the large lecture course.

So far as what you do is concerned, there is little difference between TV teaching and a course taught by conventional methods. You use the methods that are appropriate to the kind of course presented in this way. Perhaps only one warning is in order. TV courses, being carefully prepared, waste less time and are more packed with meaty material than conventional courses. Like a film, video tape can present a lot of material in a short period of time. You, therefore, need to be unusually alert, and prepared to take notes at a good clip. On the other hand, the organization of a TV film is usually so good that you will find it easier to understand the material presented and easier to put it in note form than you will in many other courses. Hence you should find that TV teaching, though it may seem strange at first, is effective teaching that makes your job of learning the material easier.

Programmed Learning

Another method for teaching and studying that has appeared on the educational scene in recent years is one in which the material is presented in a fixed program. When this method was first invented, it took the form of a teaching machine. The machine was constructed according to the subject being taught. In the case of arithmetic, problems were presented to children one at a time, and the child recorded his answer on a board resembling an adding machine. If correct, that is, if it matched the answer recorded in the machine, a bell rang; if incorrect, nothing happened and the student, knowing he was wrong, attempted to solve the problem again. In the case of a subject like physics or psychology, in which concepts as well as calculations were taught, both a question and its answer were recorded on a disk or tape with the answer remaining covered until the student had written his answer. At that point, he could then compare his answer with the one in the machine.

The chances are that you will not encounter a teaching machine in college. It is more likely that you will meet up with programmed learning in a different form, that is, in the form of a programmed textbook. These are more economical to produce and to employ with large numbers of students than teaching machines. Nowadays, one or more programmed textbooks are available for most of the basic subjects in college. So let us say a little about ways of using programmed textbooks.

There are many formats for programmed textbooks depending on the subject being taught and the resourcefulness of the textbook designer. All of them, however, are basically sets of questions and answers with varying amounts of illustrative material. In all cases, the format provides for some means of keeping the answer to a question out of sight until you have formed your own answer and can then refer to the textbook answer to see if you are correct. This is done in order to promote recitation on your part.

This format is designed to do certain things for you that otherwise are up to you. One is to motivate you. This is accomplished by the use of questions that generally arouse more motivation than simple statements. A second is that the programmed textbook allows you to proceed at your own pace for your temperament, intelligence, and level of preparation, whereas in classroom teaching the same time is required of everybody. Thirdly, the programmed textbook is designed to make the steps in learning reasonably small. Small steps are within almost everybody's grasp, when large ones may not be, and they insure that relatively few wrong responses—responses which may impede learning—will be made. Finally, programmed textbooks provide immediate knowledge of results. The student receives immediate information about the correctness of his responses, and this is an aid to learning.

Programmed textbooks can be, and have been, constructed to teach all sorts of subjects. They are best, though, at teaching facts and rules, rather than complicated relationships. For that reason, they are most often used to augment a conventional textbook and lectures. The programmed text provides drill in solving problems, in using rules, and in applying terms correctly, while the lectures and conventional text furnish understanding.

So in using programmed textbooks you should keep this in mind. If you need help in basic skills like spelling, arithmetic, composition, etc., you should look for a programmed book on the subject. By working through it, you will probably make more progress than by reading a textbook on it. After all, you had most of your previous training with such books, and if that did not take, you probably need help in correcting specific mistakes and establishing better habits. For this the programmed text is excellent.

If you are assigned a programmed text in a course, use it as an aid to recitation. Do not substitute it for the methods of study we have described. Continue to take notes in lectures and from readings as you would without the programmed text. However, much of the time you would spend in recitation with your notes can now be used with the programmed text. Having worked through the program, you should find that you have learned better with less recitation the material in your notes—assuming the two cover the ground.

Many students, particularly bright ones, find programmed textbooks boring and even frustrating. Because the format is a standard one with questions being asked over and over again in a similar form, the task seems repetitive. And the work is tiring because it calls on you to do memorizing work. To combat this reaction, if you have it, we suggest that you use a strategy appropriate to language study, namely, that you distribute your study time. Take a fair-sized segment of the program requiring twenty or thirty minutes, rest briefly, review the segment, take another rest, and turn to something else. Then, after studying another subject, come back to the program and tackle another segment in this way. Such a distribution of study time will reduce fatigue and boredom and be more efficient in learning.

Fraternity Files

To some fraternity members, the most frequented library and the most familiar outside reading is that wonderful collection known as the "fraternity files." Dormitories and student cooperatives have files too. As a matter of fact, the existence of these files is so widespread that many colleges and individual instructors have arranged for files of old exams to be deposited in the college library so that they are available to all students. Old examinations are probably the most treasured items in such collections, but old outlines and course notes, themes and term papers, and almost anything may be in them.

There are few things in this world that are either all good or all bad, and this is true of fraternity files. Some good things can be said about them. They may help you, when you are studying for an examination, to get a good idea about what the examination will be like and to look over the sorts of items that can be expected. It is often useful too to look at other people's course notes to see how they have organized the material and what they found important enough to write down. If a student has been absent from class, he needs to consult such notes to fill in what he's missed. And in getting ideas for papers and the way they should be written, you will find it helpful to see samples of what others have done in the past.

In so far as such files serve these purposes, they are of value to the student. In practice, though, they can't really do these things very well. For one thing, they're old. They have in them what happened last term, last year, or even some years back. Occasionally there's an instructor who hasn't changed his textbook, his lectures, or possibly his examinations for some time, but in most courses the outlines and lectures undergo some change, textbooks change periodically, and even if all these things are not too different, the examinations change. Al-

most any instructor using objective questions has a system for devising new questions and "rotating" old ones so that no two exams ever contain more than a small percentage of the same questions. Sometimes, in essay examinations, an instructor has some pet questions or old chestnuts that tend to pop up repeatedly, but he usually has some new ones too. Even his old ones may be rephrased enough to call for rather different answers even if, superficially, they seem to be the same as before.

What all this means is that you can waste your time with files of old examinations unless you know how to use them properly. One thing not to do with them is to use them to predict what you will get on an exam. Undoubtedly you will have a few lucky hits, but the chances are that for every such hit you will be misled into not studying something which didn't appear on one of the old exams.

The fact that fraternity files are old and that courses change also applies to using old course notes and outlines. Most instructors continually alter their courses in many little ways (even if the courses do not have new instructors). When you rely too much on old course notes, you don't know how much you are missing of what is current in the course. The only way in which old course notes and outlines are useful is when they are placed side by side with a good set of notes on the course as it is currently being given. Even here, they are apt to be rather dangerous if there has been a radical change in viewpoint or method in teaching a particular course.

Another thing wrong with unofficial course files is that they are of unknown quality. You don't really know how good the material is that you're studying. Furthermore, even if you have some idea of the quality, from marks on the examinations or term papers, you don't know how relevant the material will be for what you want. In the case of class notes, you really have no way at all of knowing how good the notes are.

Probably the worst thing about fraternity files is that they encourage poor study habits. They give you a false sense of security, and they encourage piecemeal and disorganized study. Files of old examinations can be somewhat useful to you if you approach them the right way. Don't rely blindly on your ability to memorize individual questions, but instead try using old examinations as self-testing devices. You can get a rough idea of how much you know about a particular subject by taking one of the old examinations yourself. Even this has to be done judiciously, for it can lead you to emphasize the wrong things.

To a lesser extent, old papers and notes are useful for the same purpose. If you look at old term papers, look especially at the kinds of corrections the instructor has made. You may be able to avoid mistakes in form and style this way. But above all, do not use old papers and lab reports for copying. This is the surest way to misunderstand the content of a course. Sooner or later the instructor is going to find out that you really don't understand and that you have been blindly copying somebody else's work, and then you will be in trouble.

All this adds up to a warning not to rely too heavily on files. They may be useful if you approach them with the idea of actually doing some work and not just using them as a crutch, but don't depend on them to take the place of good techniques of study.

Getting Help

There are times when every student needs help from other people. The good student is self-reliant, but in order to plan his program and to know what to study and what is expected of him, he needs help from other people. We'll discuss the matter of getting help very briefly in this section.

Other Students
Students help each other in a number of ways. You can pick up a good deal of information about particular courses from other students. Sometimes this information is valuable. You should take it, though, with a grain of salt. The judgment of students is

not infallible, and things change from time to time. Be prepared to make your own assessment of a course and your own decisions about handling the work in it.

Students who are taking a course together should also occasionally compare notes. In this way you can exchange ideas on class notes and check with one another on important and difficult points.

Studying with other students for an examination can be valuable if done properly. Don't rely on other students as your sole or principal preparation for examinations. Before you go into a session with other students, you should have studied the material thoroughly by yourself. A session with other students should serve only as a review and checkout for what you've already studied.

Group studying does one important thing: It provides a good opportunity for oral recitation. This is the most valuable aspect of group studying. But, in addition, it allows you to correct one another, and it gives you a better prediction of what an examination will be like.

To be effective, such groups should be run in an orderly fashion. When the group first meets, it ought to discuss its plan of action and set up an agenda much as any other conference would. Then you can take turns giving oral summaries of important points.

Don't get bogged down arguing about little points. And, above all, don't take on faith what another student says about something. He can be wrong. Make a habit of checking anything new that you hear from another student.

Aside from studying together for examinations, there are, of course, other times when students can help each other. If there is something in a course you don't understand and you know another student who clearly understands the particular point, you can ask him to explain it to you. It will pay you, in fact, to keep tabs both on your weak points and on the abilities of other students so that you know when and to whom to go for help. If, on the other hand, someone asks you for help on a point, you should be willing within limits to give him some time. Besides being the friendly thing to do, assisting other people can help you because it gives you a chance to recite what you know. Consequently you'll remember and understand better the points you've helped others with. (It's an axiom among teachers that there is no better way to learn a subject than to teach it to somebody else.)

Instructors

Instructors can help you in ways other than in classes. The most important thing about getting help from your instructor is not to ask him for help with anything you should have gotten yourself. If you've been cutting class or going to sleep, don't ask him to tell you what you should have heard if you had been listening. This will leave an unfavorable impression with the instructor, and it is impolite and unfair. If you miss something, try to recoup your loss by asking your fellow students about what you have missed.

Avoid asking your instructor for unreasonable or special favors. Don't, for example, ask to borrow his notes. This kind of request will merely annoy him. Incidentally, under the heading of unreasonable or special favors usually comes the request to take an examination late. There are few things which impress an instructor more unfavorably than such a request, and you will be wise to avoid it unless it is absolutely necessary.

As examination time draws near, students ask all sorts of questions about what will be on the examination. One of the silliest questions, often heard, is "How much are we supposed to know?" The answer, of course, is "As much as possible." It is more reasonable to ask specific questions about your responsibilities for an examination. You might, for example, ask, "Are we responsible for all the names of people mentioned in the textbook?" Or "How much stress will be placed on dates?" (Or derivations, formulas, experiments, and so on.) The instructor is usually willing to tell you his general policy on such matters. You will surely want to know what kind of examination to expect; if the instructor doesn't tell you, ask.

Instructors have a limited amount of time. Therefore you ought to try to get help from your instructors immediately before or after the regularly scheduled class hours. Be brief and businesslike.

Don't let this advice, however, discourage you from raising legitimate and interesting questions with your instructor. If there is an important point he hasn't made clear or something you just don't understand, don't hesitate to ask him to straighten you out. Don't shy away, either, from asking questions that interest you or questions about the implications of the things you learn in a course. Instructors like to have interested students, and they particularly like to see students with an inquisitive bent who learn more than is required and who want to understand the meaning of things they learn. If you choose a convenient time and avoid pestering your instructor with picayune questions, you can benefit immensely from discussions with him. He, on the other hand, is pretty sure to enjoy and to profit from your genuine expression of interest in his course.

Faculty Advisers

In many colleges, each student is assigned to a faculty adviser. His responsibilities vary from one college to another. In general, however, the adviser's duty is to help the student with decisions about course programs and with any special academic problems that come up. How well this relationship works out in practice depends both on the student and on the adviser.

First of all, do for yourself all that you can do. You must read your college catalogue to see what courses are offered, consult schedules to see which courses conflict with each other and hence cannot fit into your schedule, and do the arithmetic involved in determining how many "credits" you should take or are planning to take in any particular term. In so far as you are sure what you are going to do, you should make out yourself the forms required for the adviser's approval or action. In general, go to your adviser only after you have thoroughly studied your own problems, learned all you can about them, and have specific questions well formulated.

Remember, too, that an adviser's job is to advise and not to make your decisions for you. He'll give you information you can't get yourself as well as opinions based on what he knows about courses and their value for your objectives. In the end, though, the choices to be made among electives and different arrangements of courses are up to you. You shouldn't want to be told what to do, nor should you ask your adviser to decide matters of individual interest, taste, or preference.

Students often have personal problems that may, within reason, be taken to the adviser. If you are failing or doing poorly in any of your courses, if you have trouble studying (which you shouldn't after you've read this book), or even if personal worries or difficulties seriously hamper your work, you should be able to present these problems to your adviser for some help and guidance. Don't expect too much, though, or take too much of his time. If you state your problem clearly, he may be able to give you some helpful hints, but he can seldom solve your problem for you. That's something only you can do. Moreover, if you have serious personal and emotional problems, the typical faculty adviser has neither the time nor training to do much about them. About the most he can do is to send you to a counselor or someone else professionally trained to deal with such problems.

Help from Special Sources

Sometimes students need help from special sources. You may need some remedial work to make up serious deficiencies in basic skills like arithmetic or reading. Or you may need some personal counseling and advice. In these and other cases, you will usually find that there are people at your institution specifically designated to help you. It is a very good idea to find out what kinds of special service are available to you in the way of counseling, study clinics, and so on, and make use of them if you have the need. These services exist because college administrators are convinced that far more students

fall by the wayside than is necessary. We know that these special services help keep some students in good standing in college who would otherwise leave or flunk out. If you are in trouble, by all means find out what services are available to you.

When You're in Trouble

We are sure that much we've said in this book will help you stay out of trouble as far as your studies are concerned. You may have gotten the book too late to help you much with the troubles you already have. Or you may find yourself in some kind of difficulty despite all your best efforts. Certainly it is the exceptional and lucky student who can escape ever having any bad moments in college. So in addition to all the things we've said up to now, we have a few points of specific advice about what to do when you find yourself in any one of the troubles that are typical of college students.

Suppose you've been working hard at a course, doing all you know how to do, and yet you just can't seem to master it. You're doing poor work, falling behind, not understanding the subject, and find it over your head. What do you do?

If this is the case, you should, first of all, try to diagnose it as early as possible. Don't drift along hoping for the best any longer than it takes you to tell that something is wrong. Don't wait for a failing mark on an hour exam to demonstrate what you had good reason to suspect before the exam. When you've a good idea you're in trouble, try to do something about it.

To do anything, you'll have to figure out, at least roughly, what the trouble really is. Are you inadequately prepared for the course? Is there some one thing about the course that seems particularly wrong? Does its special vocabulary give you trouble? Do you have difficulty with calculations, problems, or laboratory work? Ask yourself questions like these to formulate as well as you can what may be wrong.

Your next problem is to decide whether you can do something to remedy your difficulties or whether you must consider dropping the course. At this point, your instructor may help you. If you go to him prepared to tell him what your particular problems are, he may be able to tell you the steps you should take to get straightened out. He may be able to spot something you're doing consistently wrong. He may discover a weakness in your preparation and prescribe some reading or special exercises that will help you. On the other hand, he may find that you've simply gotten into a course that is too difficult for you—this can easily happen, for example, when students continue a foreign language they've previously had in high school—and suggest some other course that is better for a student with your background.

If you realize your trouble and seek help early enough in a course, you usually can work out some wise course of action. If you can improve, you can find out how. If you aren't likely to, there is still time to drop the course and rearrange your program without undue hardship. It's usually not a good idea, though, to drop a course impulsively and without seeking competent advice, especially if the course is one that is required or recommended for your field of study. For this reason, many colleges require the approval of both the instructor and faculty adviser for the dropping of a course—not a matter of red tape but to encourage the student to seek their help in deciding whether it is a wise thing to do. In any case, it is a good idea to get the advice of your instructor and faculty adviser before dropping a course because you find it giving you trouble.

You don't have to be in serious trouble or on the verge of dropping a course to seek some substantial help in it. Even good students find there are often some aspects of a course they have trouble handling. If they make a list of the things that bother them and then arrange with the instructor for a few minutes of his time, they often can run down the list and get a few pointers to straighten themselves out.

Suppose now that you get pretty well along in a course with an hour exam or two behind you and find that you are doing unsatisfactory work. It's probably too late

to drop the course without some sort of penalty. What we've said throughout this book about learning from one's mistakes and poor grades is particularly appropriate here. Instead of quibbling about your grade and then putting aside the paper that received the grade, it's time to find out specifically what's wrong. If you can, you might go over your paper with another, better student to see if you can learn anything that way. If you're still not satisfied that you know where your shortcomings are, ask your instructor to go over it with you. If you are really interested in improving, instructors are almost always willing to take a little time to show you exactly what you did wrong and what you should have done to do it right.

Sometimes things get to such a point that you have little hope of pulling yourself out of a hole. You've done poor work all term and then, at the end, are still doing poorly. In this situation, it may be too late to raise your grade, but it's not too late to learn something that will help you avoid similar difficulties in the future. Far too many students who have received a final grade in a course don't bother to collect papers they could obtain from their instructor to see why they did badly. In many cases, they should ask to go over the paper with the instructor, not with any thought of getting their grade changed but with the idea of pinpointing their own weaknesses and mistakes. If they did this, they might get off to a good start in the next term and not get into trouble again.

Sometimes the trouble may lie not in mistakes or doing things that can be corrected but rather in something more deeply rooted. The student may be in personal difficulties with other people, worrying too much about nonacademic things, and generally not able to apply himself the way he knows he should. If that's the trouble, it's not one for the instructor to handle. Rather it's time to take advantage of some of the special services we mentioned above and particularly of the services of a psychological counselor. If you feel deeply depressed, terribly anxious, or are forever getting into social difficulties, you ought to go to such a counselor without delay or, if such a counselor isn't available, to a psychiatrist. There is no point in jeopardizing your academic work and your own happiness. If you're in emotional trouble, go immediately to someone professionally competent to help you.

We'll mention finally the possibility of trouble arising because you're a "round peg in a square hole." You may be attempting to take a course of study in which you aren't really interested. There may be another set of courses in which you will be more interested and more capable. You may, similarly, be shooting for a vocational objective for which you are not suited. As a consequence, you may be so poorly motivated that you simply can't muster the effort to do the sort of work you know you should. Again, this is a situation for professional help; seek out a psychologist, vocational counselor, or someone equipped to help you find the vocational objective and course of studies for which you are best suited.

Student Manners

We should say a few things, finally, about student manners. These have a bearing on your academic success as well as on the happiness of your relationship with instructors and fellow students.

Classroom Behavior

Get to class on time. In addition to the things that you miss by coming to class late, late arrivals disturb other students and the instructor. Once in class, carry your share of class activities and be a good listener. If the class is a discussion class it is to your advantage to take part in the discussion. This is the way you will learn, and in some cases instructors are apt to judge you by the degree to which you participate. If your class is a lecture class, be an attentive and a polite listener. Whether you realize it or not, the instructor is usually very sensitive to the demeanor of a class; a roomful of students sprawled out, half asleep, is not an inspiring sight and lowers the lecturer's morale.

Finally, don't jump the gun at the end of the hour. Wait until the instructor is through before snapping your notebook shut and gathering up your books.

A really basic point about your relationships with your instructors is to do your work on time. To be late with daily assignments, term papers, and similar kinds of work is a sign of bad management on your part. Some instructors justifiably penalize students for being late, but even if you aren't penalized, it is grossly unfair and a reflection on you not to be on time.

Conferences

As we've pointed out above, students have occasions for seeking conferences with instructors, and instructors consider consultation with students a part of their job as teachers. You should remember, though, that their time is valuable. Besides classroom teaching and preparation for classes, faculty members have hundreds of things to do: a lot of reading to stay on their toes as teachers, professional meeetings to go to, letters and recommendations to write, committee meetings to attend, and many miscellaneous chores connected with the running of the college. In some institutions, research is a substantial part of teachers' work.

What all this means is that you should try not to waste an instructor's time. If your question is a brief one, don't run him down in his office and interrupt him there; try to catch him just before or after class when he can handle it quickly. Don't ask him silly questions or questions you should figure out for yourself. Don't ask him to do what you, as a self-respecting young adult, should be able to do for yourself. Where papers or recommendations are concerned, make them out as fully in advance as possible. Even little things like writing in your name or addressing an envelope are time-consuming and annoying. If you can do them, don't ask him to.

If your problem really requires a conference lasting several minutes, don't just "drop in" on the instructor unless he has previously told you to or posts office hours.

Ask him for an appointment, stating your business when you ask for it. Once the appointment is made, by all means *keep it.* Later on in life, you'll have to keep your appointments punctually, and college is none too early to learn such considerate and businesslike habits.

When you get to a conference, be prepared to state your problem succinctly and clearly. Don't fumble and stumble, doing the thinking you should have done before you came. Stay on the subject of your business; when your business is finished, exchange an amenity or two and be on your way. If you can't tell when you're finished, be sensitive to the signals in the situation. If the instructor gets fidgety, leans forward in his chair, stands up, or provides some other hint that the end has come, close things up promptly.

If you manage your conferences with your instructor in a businesslike way, he'll have a much better impression of you, which may come in good stead when the time arrives to write a letter of recommendation for you. More important, he'll think more kindly of students in general and be more inclined to be helpful. And he'll have more time to do the things he needs to do to be an effective teacher and scholar.

Students seldom mean to be unmannerly in class or to impose on the instructor. They're often just thoughtless or impatient. These brief comments about student manners are intended simply as a reminder of some of the things you can do to help make studying and teaching a little easier—for both your fellow students and your teachers.

chapter 11
LIVING COLLEGE LIFE

This book is about *How to Study* because studying is the main job to be done in college. Your over-all purpose in college, however, is to prepare for the life you will live after college. This preparation will require making career plans and choosing courses of study to fit them. It will also involve the patterns of adjustment to your personal problems and to other people that you develop in college life. And finally, it involves your participation in campus life and activities other than going to classes and studying. In this chapter, we shall cover the major points to be made about these aspects of college life.

Forming Career Plans

If you are enrolled in a specialized school such as engineering, journalism, or education, you have already made, at least tentatively, a general decision about your career. Even so, because there are many areas of specialization within a given field, you will be deciding at some point on your particular area and later how you will work in that area in the job world. Students in arts and sciences, on the other hand, may have some vague ideas about what they want to be, but on the whole they are rather undecided. This uncertainty often has a lot to do with the lack of motivation to study one sees so frequently in college students.

Even among students who enter college thinking they know what they want to become, change seems to be the characteristic pattern. First, they are going to major in one field, a little later in another. Such changes in plans are natural, for the student is learning new facts about the world and finding that what he learns in some courses is much more interesting than what he learns in others. In any case, what we see in college students in their early years is a lot

of uncertainty in their occupational plans. This uncertainty could be reduced if they gave some thought to how far and in what direction their abilities and interests might permit them to go.

How Far Will You Go?

You undoubtedly know that some students who enter college drop out in the first year or two, others go on to a college degree, and still others go farther. What you may not realize is that students are stopping at various points along the line from the freshman year in college to a point several years beyond the doctorate. The point at which they stop either voluntarily or because they get stopped determines the kind of occupation they can enter.

Consider the casualties in the first two years. Approximately one third of all students enrolled in college are to be found in junior colleges. As these are being built and expanded throughout the country, the percentage will probably increase. About three out of four students in these colleges think that they will transfer later into a senior college. In actual fact, about one in four do. Of the students who begin college in a four-year school, there are also high casualty rates, depending on the kind of school. Losses are relatively small in the prestigeful private schools with very high admission requirements. But they are very high in state universities with relatively low entering requirements. Many schools, particularly in the Middle West, have long followed the practice, usually at the insistence of the legislature, of admitting all high school graduates. In schools like these, approximately one third of the students are flunked out or drop out in the first two years. Altogether, the losses in college, mostly in the early years, are such that only about one in two of the students who start will finish with a bachelor's degree.

This is something to ponder, for you may very well be one of these casualties. If so, your choice of occupations and your success in an occupation is going to be limited to that for which people without a college degree can be admitted. There are, fortunately, many careers for such people, but they are different than those available to college graduates. If, for any reason, you are going to be one who stops short of a degree, you ought to plan on it as early as possible and alter your program accordingly. If you really want to enter an occupation requiring a degree and you are in the danger zone grade-wise, perhaps the realization of possible failure will motivate you to develop better study habits.

Suppose you are shooting for an occupation-required advanced degree, that is, a degree such as the master's or doctor's, you ought to know early what is required. The basic requirement for admission to graduate school to study for advanced degrees is a much higher grade average than the typical student makes. Generally this is a minimum of a B average. What proportion of students make this throughout college varies from school to school. In some of the select colleges, it may run as high as one third. In other schools, it will be closer to 10 per cent. In any case, you will have to do superior work in college. (Students with less than B averages are sometimes admitted to graduate school if they improve a lot later in college and if their aptitudes are high, but one should not bank on this.)

Admission to graduate school, like admission to college, is no guarantee of success. There are casualties at this level, too. Again, figures vary from school to school and from one area to another, but the over-all average is that only one half of those who enter graduate school proceed to the doctorate. In many cases, the goal is only the master's degree, particularly in engineering and professional fields; in others, especially women who marry men heading for the doctorate, people may stop voluntarily after a year or so with or without a master's degree. You will undoubtedly be able to secure, later in college, better advice on graduate school than it is appropriate to give you here, but you should understand that there are different occupational goals and abilities

EXAMPLES OF OCCUPATIONS REQUIRING DIFFERENT LEVELS OF EDUCATION AND DIFFERENT INTEREST PATTERNS

Major interest	High school plus special training	Bachelor's degree or some college	Post-graduate degrees
Mechanical	Engineering technician	Engineer	Research & Development Engineer
Computational	Bookkeeper	Accountant	Mathematician
Scientific	Optician	Chemist	Psychologist
Persuasive	Salesman	Journalist	Lawyer
Artistic	Artist	Architect	—
Literary	Proofreader	Editor-Writer	—
Musical	Musician	Composer-Arranger	—
Social service	Nurse	Home economist	Social worker
Clerical	Clerk-typist	Executive Secretary	—

to attain them at the graduate level just as there are at the lower levels.

The point, then, of this section is that you ought to be thinking about how far you can go or want to go in higher education. And then you ought to think about preparing yourself in the program you follow for that goal. Much will depend on your abilities and interests. And you ought to know these in order to set realistic goals.

What Are Your Abilities?

You have undoubtedly been taking tests of "educational development" at intervals throughout your pre-college education. From these you have an idea of how you compared with fellow students, whether very high, high, or average. You probably did not score below average or you would not now be in college or headed for college. You probably also have taken such tests as the Scholastic Aptitude Test (SAT) administered by the College Entrance Examination Board, for this is generally required of entering college students. Of the tests you have taken recently, this is the one that should be most helpful in assessing your ability to do college work, for it is designed specifically for that purpose.

If you have taken such a test, you undoubtedly received with your test scores a booklet giving norms for various populations of testees. Of these various norms, the set to look at closely is the one consisting of those people who took the test and later went to college. Your percentile standing on this will be lower than it is on a norm for all people taking the test, but it is the most realistic one to use because it tells you how your abilities compare with the general college population.

When you find your percentile rank for this population, note particularly the difference in your standing on the two scores given by the test, the *verbal* and the *quantitative*. If there is substantial difference, such as 30 or 50 percentile points, this should tell where your chances lie of doing the best in college. If the verbal score is considerably higher than the other, you should find the verbal subjects in college easier than the

quantitative. The verbal subjects are the humanities and some of the social sciences such as history, psychology, and political science. If your quantitative score is much higher than your verbal score, you should do relatively better in those subjects that emphasize computation, mathematics, and statistics. Aside from mathematics itself, these include the natural sciences, especially physics, chemistry, and engineering, and some other subjects such as accounting and economics.

Even if there is a large discrepancy but both scores are on the high side, say, 95 and 60, you probably should not be swayed too much toward pursuing verbal versus non-verbal subjects. Even your poorest aptitude is good enough to get you by. On the other hand if the scores are low, say 5 and 40, you ought to avoid subjects emphasing the aptitude in which you are low, for otherwise you are bound to have considerable trouble, if not outright failure.

Abilities, as measured by an aptitude test such as the SAT, are far from perfect predictors of college success. In fact, there is no such perfect prediction. Through considerable research, however, we have found that the best prediction of grades in college can be obtained by combining high school grades with aptitude scores. Grades tell what you *have* done, while aptitude scores say what you are *able* to do.

Since the grades given for a particular level of performance vary a lot from high school to high school, college administrators who know the difference between high schools can improve the prediction by giving a handicap or bonus for the particular high school in which a student studied. You don't have the facts to do that, but you probably have some idea of the reputation of your high school for sending successful students to college. If this is high, you can form some estimate for yourself, knowing that your SAT scores and your high school grades indicate how likely you are to fare well in college.

Prediction of college success from SAT socres and grades is a statistical matter. Most of those with high ratings on these measures will be able to handle college work easily;

most of those with low ratings will not. In between are the middle students about which it is more difficult to make a prediction. When colleges use some combination of aptitude scores and grades to determine whom they will admit, they are simply "playing the odds." They are not putting up some artificial barrier to entrance. Rather they are admitting those with the best chances of success, and barring those with the poorest chances. (This must be borne in mind when a college lowers its requirements for disadvantaged students. Such students, on odds, are going to have more trouble in college unless special curricula or special remedial instruction is provided to compensate for their poorer readiness to do college work.)

Given your particular status in high school grades and SAT scores, your success in college will depend upon the college you go to, and, of course, on how well you work. Colleges differ enormously in their standards of admission, in the difficulty of the work required, and in grading practices. There are no statistics available for ranking colleges in this respect, but you can learn a lot by the grapevine and from your high school or college counselor. Then, you ought to choose a college that matches well your individual chances of performing well. If you are already in college and are in any difficulty, you might consider transferring to a college with lower standards. It may not be so prestigeful, but you will have a better chance of completing a college education.

The other point, that college success depends on you, is what this book is about. We have tried to show you ways to do best, so we will not belabor that point here.

One other point can be made about prediction from abilities and previous performance. Even at the freshman level, one can make some guesses about who is able to continue beyond college for advanced degrees. Scores below average on the SAT do not favor such a prediction. Those in the 80s and 90s definitely do. So, you can at the outset of college make a guess about whether or not you should shoot for an occupation requiring postgraduate work. Later

on, you can get a better prediction after the results of your college work are known and you take aptitude tests specifically designed to predict success in graduate school.

What Are Your Interests?

Predictions of relative success in certain college subjects and of occupational success can also be made from "measurements" of a person's interests. There are two general methods of doing this. One is to use a test known as the Strong Vocational Interest Test. This can be scored for forty-seven occupations in which men are employed and twenty-eight occupations open to women. This test can be used with both college and noncollege populations, but for those going to college it is probably most useful during the time in college in which a student is deciding on a major and choosing rather specific occupational goals.

The other method of measuring interests is the Kuder Performance Record. The scoring of this test gives a more general picture of a person's interests and is most useful in guiding the general direction of a person's preparation. It divides interests into nine general categories: mechanical, computational, scientific, persuasive, artistic, literary, musical, social, and clerical. Knowing a person's profile of interests in these terms, a counselor can select occupations at several levels having a corresponding pattern.

Perhaps you have already taken the Kuder interest test in high school, for it is frequently given by high school counselors to help them advise students. If not, it would be a good idea at some point to take such a test and obtain the profile of your interests. Do not rush to your counseling center with a request to take the test, but some time when you are in a position to discuss your vocational interests you might visit your counseling center and arrange, among other things, to include this test in whatever program of interviews and tests your counselor may think appropriate.

To summarize this section, we suggest that you start thinking seriously about your occupational goals. In so doing, you should make tentative decisions about how far you can go or want to go up the educational ladder. To help you with this decision, you need to know both your abilities and interests. You can make a rough assessment of the limits of your abilities from scores on aptitude tests and from a knowledge of previous grades. (There are other aptitude tests that a counselor can give you to help you assess your aptitudes.) To make the best over-all prediction you need to put these facts together with a knowledge of your interests.

Making a Good Personal Adjustment

College is often a tumultuous period in a young person's life, fraught with all sorts of anxieties and frustrations. A few people may take it in their stride, but most suffer somewhat in one way or another. We have already noted that college presents much stiffer competition, and this can be a source of worry, especially if the student early finds himself in trouble. Registration is often a complicating and harrowing process. There are more decisions to be made about courses, and because many schools are operating at top capacity, students frequently will be frustrated by not making the schedule they want. Books may be late in arriving at the bookstore. In any case, the student has to learn his way around a large, strange campus alive with people he doesn't know.

If a student goes away to school, his newly found independence may be a scary thing. He has previously been dependent on a particular environment provided by his family and community. Somebody fed him, looked after his laundry, and furnished a place to live. Now he has to start coping with these problems on his own. He must find a place to live, do his own shopping, and start handling money so it will cover his various living and academic expenses. Many students simply are not prepared yet for this sort of independence, though they may have thought they were.

Even if one goes to school in his home town and lives at home, he has new personal relationships to cope with. Some of his high-school friends will not have accompanied him to college. And in college he greets a sea of strange faces. He now has new people to deal with and new friends to make. All this can make a person insecure and anxious.

On top of the new academic and personal adjustments they must make at this time, students are beginning to see, and take seriously, the many ills that beset the world. The cold war between East and West goes on and on. Little hot wars are in the news. Hovering over college men in the United States is the draft that can take them into military service, and perhaps into a hot war, if they do not make out in college. There is racial unrest throughout the country, and perhaps there is even violence on their own campus. All this is happening without their knowing why, because they did not live through the history that produced these conditions.

The world you enter, then, as a freshman is likely to be an anxious one. The period may be the most difficult you will ever have in your life. And you will be attempting to cope with your problems without the experience that adults have had. There is no simple recipe for guiding you through the adjustment problems you may have. However, psychologists have come to understand fairly well the means by which people attempt to adjust, and they have some advice that might help you. If you later take a college course in adjustment, you will learn much more about the subject, but in the meantime, we will outline briefly some points that may be helpful.

Understanding Defenses

The basic problem of adjustment is this. Problems you cannot cope with make you anxious, and you consciously or unconsciously strive to reduce or eliminate your anxiety. To a large extent, most people reduce their anxieties in realistic ways. If you are anxious about an examination, you study for it. Knowing you are prepared, you feel less anxious. And if you do well on it, you learn not to be so anxious next time.

But suppose you do badly. Then you are still anxious, and for the present have no realistic way of doing anything about it. What do you do when you have an anxiety you feel you can do nothing about?

In this dilemma, we are all inclined to fool ourselves in some way. We can say the exam was not a fair one, and that will make us feel better, for it takes some of the blame of doing badly off our own shoulders. Or we can say that we had a poor background in high school for this particular course. With this, we blame the high school rather than ourselves for our poor showing. This reduces our anxiety, and thus makes us feel better.

Devices of this sort are called *defenses* for they defend us against anxiety. Let us see what kinds of defenses may be used for this purpose.

Rationalization. Probably the most common defense employed is rationalization. This is assigning an incorrect reason for what we did or feel. Suppose that a student's real reason for failing an examination is that he did not study enough, or perhaps did not know how to study for it. The blame for failure actually falls on him. But accepting this blame makes him anxious and uncomfortable, so he tries to find some other reason that removes the blame from him. In picking his reason, he finds one that is socially acceptable or can be believed and understood by others he tells it to. The whole process is largely unconscious.

Projection. Another common defense is to project to someone else the motives or faults that lie within the person. If, for example, a student has a strong desire to cheat on an examination but is unwilling to admit it to himself because he knows it is wrong, he may be unduly suspicious of others and accuse them of cheating when they are innocent. Or, if he feels like being nasty to other people and yet knows that this is not right, he may accuse other people of being nasty to him when in fact they have not been.

Displacement. This is a defense we use, particularly when we are angry, to substitute some person or object in place of the real one. A man may get angry at his boss but knows he shouldn't blow off at him, so he comes home and bawls out his wife. A little girl, finding her newborn brother the center of attention, would like to attack the brother, but knows she will be punished for this. So she tears up her doll. A student who is mad at the instructor may come back to the dorm and get in an argument with his roommate. These are all examples of displacement that can take place quite unconsciously.

Fantasy. Another defense against anxiety is to resort to fantasy or daydreaming. This is particularly prominent in adolescence, and happens to come in handy in connection with studying. By daydreaming, one can, in his mind, think of all sorts of satisfactions he does not have in the real world. It has been estimated that about 95 per cent of college students spend some appreciable time daydreaming. In this way, they avoid studying or find a substitute for inadequacies in personal relations.

Identification. Psychologists have distinguished quite a list of defenses sometimes employed by people, but the last one we think worth mentioning here is identification. In using it, we imagine that we are like some other person or that we belong to a group. It is used particularly to build up our self-esteem. For instance, when we identify with a successful individual or a victorious football team, we feel more worthwhile. Conversely, it is difficult to enhance self-esteem by identifying with a losing team. Perhaps this is one of the reasons for the great stress on winning in college, and other, athletics.

Use of defense mechanisms. In reading this list of defenses, you have probably recognized instances in which you and others you know have used them. Almost everybody uses them some of the time. Indeed, moderate use of defenses is a harmless and convenient way of disposing of minor problems. If they make us feel better and make others more comfortable, as they often do, their value in reducing tension and letting us get on with important problems more than offsets the trivial self-deceptions they entail.

Not all defenses, however, are so harmless. If used excessively to sidestep really persistent and severe problems, they can get us into a great deal of trouble. Defenses, when used to excess, have two major weaknesses.

First they fail to solve the problem that made us use them. Defenses are directed at the symptom—anxiety—rather than at the problem which gave rise to it. Hence, if a problem is serious and persistent, using a defense merely postpones its solution; the problem is still there, and it will probably rise again to plague the person.

Secondly, defenses may not protect the person in new and unusual situations, when the problem arises in a more severe form. Under these conditions, the defenses may break down and cause the person to experience a "flood" of anxiety. These breakdowns are called *anxiety attacks* and can be mighty uncomfortable. To give an example from student life, a student may rationalize his poor performance in the hour examinations of a course by giving excuses about poor lectures, a difficult textbook, unfair examinations, or the like, and in this way feel fairly comfortable. But when he comes up to the final examination and knows the chips are down, his defenses will no longer work. He may then become so anxious that he cannot study, and he may go into the final examination in such a state of anxiety that he can't think clearly in the examination. Hence, the defenses that aided him in the little problems of the hour examinations failed to stem the anxiety arising when he faced the big problem.

Ways to Adjust

If you should have severe and persistent emotional problems, you will not solve them by reading this or any other book. In that case, seek professional aid through your college counseling center, a psychological clinic, your family physician, or whatever facilities of this sort may be available to you. There are, however, certain pointers we can give

you to help you if you are experiencing the usual run of problems encountered by college students.

Be realistic. The most general characteristic of a well adjusted person is that he is realistic about himself. He does not fool himself much about his motives, he sets goals for himself that are reasonably attainable, and he avoids unnecessary trouble. This means that he tries to find out what he can realistically expect to achieve and adjusts his efforts and goals accordingly. He faces his personal problems objectively, much as one would go about solving a problem in arithmetic. He acquaints himself with the relevant facts, makes sure he understands what the problem is, then proceeds toward its solution.

These, of course, are very general statements. Let us see more specifically how you can deal with personal problems realistically to achieve a better adjustment.

Accept anxiety. To make a healthy personal adjustment, you must learn to accept, rather than to avoid, anxiety. Anxiety, being the natural outcome of experience with fear-provoking situations, can never be completely eliminated, but by facing up to it you can accept it and in the end experience less of it. Your attitude here should be like a good attitude toward dentist chairs. You probably don't like to have your teeth drilled any more than the next fellow, but if you decide to grin and bear it, you will find it is not so bad after all. Those who don't, find it ten times worse than it actually is. The same thing can be said of other anxiety-provoking situations. It has often been observed that the difference between the courageous soldier and the coward is that the courageous one accepts fear, whereas the coward lets himself be overcome by it. President Roosevelt's famous statement, "We have nothing to fear but fear itself," makes much the same point.

Abandon defenses. If you learn to accept a certain amount of anxiety, you can then stop fooling yourself with defenses. In fact, you can come to recognize, often with humor, your tendency to use defenses. If you are inclined to blame your instructor for a poor grade, you can recognize that you are rationalizing for your failure to attend classes, keep good notes, or study. If you are tempted to feel that a good friend has turned against you, you may suspect that you are projecting your fears and dislikes to your friend. Of course, the practice of looking for defenses can be carried to the point of seeing them "under every bush," but recognizing them in yourself and others can put you on guard against using them excessively.

Understand motives. Defenses are ways of fooling oneself about his own motives; if you learn to recognize them you are in a better position to unmask and accept your motives. Motives are not always easy to identify, but the well-adjusted person is better at it than the maladjusted one. If you are inclined to blame the instructor for a poor grade, as in our example above, you may ask yourself, "What do I really want? What are my motives and goals"? An honest answer, at least a very human one, may be that you want a good grade without doing any work. Admitting this to yourself, you can see that such a combination of goals is usually unattainable. You can decide "Better get to work" or "I'll settle for a lower grade and less work" without experiencing the hostility and anxiety of blaming someone else.

Alter goals. If you are well adjusted, you can alter some goals without disguising them with defenses. Merely recognizing a motive or goal may permit you to discard it. For example, a person who continually rebels against authority, refusing to take directions from superiors and evading the rules of living may quickly change his attitude if he realizes that his rebellion is really a reaction to an overbearing parent and that he is treating other people as though they were his father. Another person, made aware of his strong prestige-seeking motives, may find this strong interest in prestige dissipating.

Others may change their goals quite abruptly when they discover that they have taken over motives intact from other people. This may be true, for example, of vocational goals, which are often set for a young person by his parents. A boy may come to college with his heart set on being a doctor, only to be frustrated by lack of interest and ability in premedical work. When anxiety has mounted to an acute stage, he may re-examine his goals and recognize that being a doctor is not his own goal at all. He is then in a position to choose another vocational goal better suited to his own interests and abilities.

Not all changes in goals need to be radical ones. Some are matters of degree. You may settle for a B average, which you can attain, rather than to be so frustrated and anxious striving for As that you make Cs. Or you may choose a less prestigeful profession, or a less remunerative job, that is less frustrating because it better suits your abilities and interests.

Postpone satisfactions. When two motives conflict, such as wanting to have fun and also to make good grades, one way to resolve the conflict, eventually, is to postpone the satisfaction of one of the two competing motives. If you are both hungry and sleepy, to take a simple example, you can eat first, then sleep. If you want excellent grades as well as some fun, you can study tonight and go out tomorrow night. The principle is simple enough. It means having a plan that postpones, but nevertheless provides for the satisfaction of, one motive until some foreseeable time. This kind of scheduling reduces the conflict between motives and limits it to relatively short periods of time.

Build up frustration tolerance. Postponing a satisfaction for a time, of course, leaves the person temporarily frustrated. Hence, he must be able to tolerate some frustration. Indeed, frustration tolerance, like the acceptance of anxiety, is the mark of a mature, well-adjusted person. The healthy person accepts frustration as a normal reality of life. He learns that he cannot always have what he wants when he wants it. He stops fretting about what he cannot have and lets some of his less essential motives go unsatisfied. Once accepted for what it is, frustration is not nearly so frustrating.

Frustration tolerance, like habits and attitudes, can be acquired with practice. You start with little things—the frustration of waiting for an overdue bus, of failure to find a parking place, or being turned down for a date. When you can accept such little frustrations with grace, you are ready to tackle bigger ones. The aim, of course, is not to duck problems that can be solved, but rather to tolerate the frustrations that are inevitable.

Express emotions. Some personal problems arise because emotions, particularly hostile, have been repressed. Through previous training, a person may have become unduly fearful of acting aggressively. The well-adjusted person, on the other hand, can express feelings somewhat openly without fear of losing friends and alienating people. He realizes that other people expect occasional displays of impatience or anger and can take them in stride. He may even knowingly make others angry, but feel better releasing his pent-up emotions. He manages to achieve some balance between the excessive and inconsiderate display of emotions, on the one hand, and complete restraint or repression of them, on the other.

The best way of doing this is to develop socially acceptable ways of expressing one's feelings. Without losing your temper you can, if you are skillful, act sternly and state clearly what displeases you. By a joking retort, you can indicate displeasure and at the same time be good humored about it. By expressing emotions in a mature way you can manage not to lose the friendship and respect of others. This requires skill and skill takes practice, but you usually can learn to do this if you try.

Keep busy. Keeping occupied with useful work or other activities is another mark of the well-adjusted person. Most of the work one does, other than very repetitive activities, is directed toward some goal. It therefore provides the satisfaction of ac-complishing something. It also takes one's mind off other things, pushing into the background thoughts that may be anxiety-arousing. Hence useful work is a double-barreled remedy: It satisfies certain motives while weakening others. By itself, of course, work is not a sure cure for any emotional problem, but coupled with other measures it helps a healthy person stay healthy.

This concludes our list of dos and don'ts for making good adjustments to the emotional problems of life. If you think about the advice we have given, and try to apply it to yourself when emotional problems arise, you should find better ways of adjusting to them.

Extracurricular Activities

Assuming that you are average in your sleep requirements, taking eight hours a night, there are 122 hours in a week available for study and other activites. That is more than twice the time that the average student needs to spend in class and outside study. Hence, there is a lot of time left for extracurricular activities of one sort or another. Such activities, moreover, provide both fun and opportunities for learning things, particularly ways of working with and interacting with other people, not part of your formal studies. We shall point out briefly some of the ways to make use of your extracurricular time.

Our advice at the outset, however, is, "Take it easy." Do not get involved early in too many nonacademic activities. There is a lot of waste motion in getting started in the college program. You may have to work harder at first in learning new study habits and getting the hang of college work. And you will have to find out just how hard college is for you with your particular abilities and work habits. You should take most of the first semester getting academic matters under your belt, learning what you will have to do to cope, before committing yourself to any sizable amount of extracurricular activity.

Working Your Way

Many students must work part of their way through college. Some must secure all of their financing through some combination of work and loans. For them, the question is how much work can they do and still succeed in college.

Again, the advice, "Take it easy," is in order. We have occasionally known students who can hold down a full-time job and still do well in college, but these are unusually gifted individuals. Usually, however, a student can work no more than twenty hours a week, even after he is well adjusted to college life, without it impairing his academic performance. What is involved is not merely the twenty hours taken from study but rather the fatigue that goes with work. Most of the jobs students will obtain will be physically tired, and take additional time spent in one way or another recuperating to the point of being ready to study effectively.

For the entering college student, ten or twelve hours a week on a job is all that is safe. If after a semester he is doing academic work at a level suiting his vocational goals, then he can take on more work. In the meantime, it would be better to borrow money—and financial aid is generally available—than to endanger his chances of succeeding in college during the critical first year.

Recreation

In the early chapters of this book where we recommended ways of budgeting time, we emphasized the need for a reasonable amount of recreation. No one can work all the time, even unusual people who after years of experience have really learned the most efficient ways to work. A person must find ways of relaxing and of exercising that keep him in good mental and physical shape. Extensive research on fatigue and productivity indicate that above fifty-five to sixty hours a week of work, a person's productivity goes down—not just by the hour, but in the over-all. So you should plan on doing something else besides work over this limit.

What kind of recreation you choose is largely up to you. Somewhere in your schedule should be some exercise. At the minimum, according to medical experts, it should be the equivalent of a half-hour a day of walking. And walking is good exercise. If you have some sport you particularly enjoy, make plans to play it on some regular schedule. On the other hand, if you are getting sufficient exercise just walking to and from classes—and this is easily possible on some large campuses—do something else you find enjoyable such as playing bridge, going to the movies, watching TV, etc. Whatever it is, there should be periods set aside for some sort of recreation.

Clubs and Organizations

One of the things you should learn about your college is the extracurricular activities available through various clubs and organizations. Does it have a drama club? a radio or TV station? a student newspaper? a debating club? If so, consider one that interests you, then investigate what it does and where you might play a role in it. Then when you are sure you have mastered your academic problems, join it and participate in its affairs.

There are two different reasons for chosing a particular club. One is to do something you enjoy; the other is to gain experience at something related to your vocational objectives. A person who plans on becoming a physician might join the drama club as a recreational hobby. On the other hand, one who wants to be a journalist might work on the student newspaper to learn something about that kind of work. Club activities can, incidentally, be a testing ground for finding out whether you would like certain occupations. They also provide opportunities for leadership, and help you train in the art of working with other people.

One of the things to be careful about in participating in such extracurricular activities is the amount of work involved. Putting out a newspaper or putting on a play is no small job. You may find yourself putting in so much time that your academic performance suffers. Try to foresee in advance what the demands will be, and find some way of keeping them in reason.

Sororities and Fraternities

Sororities and fraternities offer a way of life that is attractive to some students. They provide opportunities for social interaction and leadership, in a living group in which friendships are made, and various social activities are planned and enjoyed. Whether they are for you or not depends on how much you thrive on this kind of activity. If you think you do, investigate the Greek letter societies on your campus, find out what their requirements are, and join. For some people, the experience will be enjoyable and contribute much to their informal education. You should, however, be careful not to get so embroiled in the social life of the fraternity or sorority that it gets in the way of academic studies. It certainly can, unless you take care to find a balance between your academic and extracurricular affairs.

Student Government

Nearly every college has some sort of student government. In some cases, it may be an active, even vociferous affair. For those who are politically oriented, who would like to have some say in how things are run, and who would like to gain experience in leadership for one reason or another, this is something to get into. It provides training in interpersonal relationships, in law making, campaigning, and a variety of things that will prove useful later on in business and professional life. Again, however, we must post the warning about time. Participation in student government can easily become too time consuming. Ration yourself to the amount of responsibility and time you can safely afford without sacrificing your academic goals.

OTHER BOOKS ON STUDY, READING, AND WRITING

Armstrong, W. H. *Study is Hard Work* (2nd ed). New York: Harper, 1967.

Bennett, M. E. *College and Life* (4th ed). New York: McGraw-Hill, 1952.

Ehrlich, E., and D. Murphy. *Writing and Researching Term Papers and Reports: A New Guide for Students.* New York: Bantom Books, 1964.

Harris, A. J. *How to Increase Reading Ability* (4th ed). New York: Longmans, 1961.

Herrick, M. W. *Reading For Speed and Better Grades.* New York: Dell Publishing, 1963.

Kalish, R. A. *Making the Most of College: A Guide to Effective Study.* Belmont, Cal.: Brooks-Cole, 1959.

Laird, D. A., and E. C. Laird. *Techniques for Efficient Remembering.* New York: McGraw-Hill, 1960.

Lewis, N. *How to Read Better and Faster* (3rd ed) New York: Crowell, 1958.

Libaw, F. L., and W. D. Martinson. *Success in College* (2nd ed). Glenview, Ill.: Scott, Foresman, 1967.

Miles, O. S., Bracken, D. K., Dougherty, M. A., and R. F. Kinder. *Tactics in Reading. II.* Glenview, Ill.: Scott, Foresman, 1965.

Miller, L. L. *Increasing Reading Efficiency* (rev. ed.). New York: Holt, Rinehart, and Winston, 1964.

Orchard, N. E. *Study Successfully: 18 Keys to Better Work.* New York: McGraw-Hill, 1953.

Pauk, W. *How to Study in College.* Boston: Houghton Mifflin, 1962.

Preston, R. C. *Teaching Study Habits and Skills.* New York: Holt, Rinehart, and Winston, 1959.

Robinson, F. P. *Effective Study* (rev. ed.). New York: Harper, 1961.

Shefter, H. *Shefter's Guide to Better Compositions.* New York: Washington Square, 1960.

Shefter, H. *How to Prepare Talks and Oral Reports.* New York: Pocket Books, 1963.

Smith, G. L. *Spelling By Principles: A Programmed Text.* New York: Appleton-Century-Crofts, 1966.

INDEX

PROVISIONAL WORKING SCHEDULE

Time	Monday	Tuesday	Wednesday	Thursday	Friday	Saturday	Sunday
8:00							
8:30							
9:00							
9:30							
10:00							
10:30							
11:00							
11:30							
12:00							
12:30							
1:00							
1:30							
2:00							
2:30							
3:00							
3:30							
4:00							
4.30							
5:00							
5:30							
6:00							
6:30							
7:00							
7:30							
8:00							
8:30							
9:00							
9:30							
10:00							

PROVISIONAL WORKING SCHEDULE

Time	Monday	Tuesday	Wednesday	Thursday	Friday	Saturday	Sunday
8:00							
8:30							
9:00							
9:30							
10:00							
10:30							
11:00							
11:30							
12:00							
12:30							
1:00							
1:30							
2:00							
2:30							
3:00							
3:30							
4:00							
4.30							
5:00							
5:30							
6:00							
6:30							
7:00							
7:30							
8:00							
8:30							
9:00							
9:30							
10:00							

PROVISIONAL WORKING SCHEDULE

Time	Monday	Tuesday	Wednesday	Thursday	Friday	Saturday	Sunday
8:00							
8:30							
9:00							
9:30							
10:00							
10:30							
11:00							
11:30							
12:00							
12:30							
1:00							
1:30							
2:00							
2:30							
3:00							
3:30							
4:00							
4.30							
5:00							
5:30							
6:00							
6:30							
7:00							
7:30							
8:00							
8:30							
9:00							
9:30							
10:00							

PROVISIONAL WORKING SCHEDULE

Time	Monday	Tuesday	Wednesday	Thursday	Friday	Saturday	Sunday
8:00							
8:30							
9:00							
9:30							
10:00							
10:30							
11:00							
11:30							
12:00							
12:30							
1:00							
1:30							
2:00							
2:30							
3:00							
3:30							
4:00							
4.30							
5:00							
5:30							
6:00							
6:30							
7:00							
7:30							
8:00							
8:30							
9:00							
9:30							
10:00							

FINAL WORKING SCHEDULE

Time	Monday	Tuesday	Wednesday	Thursday	Friday	Saturday	Sunday
8:00							
8:30							
9:00							
9:30							
10:00							
10:30							
11:00							
11:30							
12:00							
12:30							
1:00							
1:30							
2:00							
2:30							
3:00							
3:30							
4:00							
4:30							
5:00							
5:30							
6:00							
6:30							
7:00							
7:30							
8:00							
8:30							
9:00							
9:30							
10:00							

FINAL WORKING SCHEDULE

Time	Monday	Tuesday	Wednesday	Thursday	Friday	Saturday	Sunday
8:00							
8:30							
9:00							
9:30							
10:00							
10:30							
11:00							
11:30							
12:00							
12:30							
1:00							
1:30							
2:00							
2:30							
3:00							
3:30							
4:00							
4:30							
5:00							
5:30							
6:00							
6:30							
7:00							
7:30							
8:00							
8:30							
9:00							
9:30							
10:00							

FINAL WORKING SCHEDULE

Time	Monday	Tuesday	Wednesday	Thursday	Friday	Saturday	Sunday
8:00							
8:30							
9:00							
9:30							
10:00							
10:30							
11:00							
11:30							
12:00							
12:30							
1:00							
1:30							
2:00							
2:30							
3:00							
3:30							
4:00							
4:30							
5:00							
5:30							
6:00							
6:30							
7:00							
7:30							
8:00							
8:30							
9:00							
9:30							
10:00							

DATE DUE

FEB 13 '73			
FEB 26 '73			
MAR 12 '73			
SEP 13 '73			
SEP 27 '73			
GAYLORD			PRINTED IN U.S.A.